D0169224

The Last Gaiter Button

Recent Titles in
Contributions in Military Studies
Series Advisor: Colin Gray

THE LAST GAITER BUTTON

A Study of the Mobilization and Concentration
of the French Army in the War of 1870

Thomas J. Adriance

CONTRIBUTIONS IN MILITARY STUDIES,
NUMBER 73

Greenwood Press
New York • Westport, Connecticut • London

Library of Congress Cataloging-in-Publication Data

Adriance, Thomas J., 1937-
  The last gaiter button.

  (Contributions in military studies, ISSN 0883-6884 ;
no. 73)
  Bibliography: p.
  Includes index.
    1. France. Armée—History—Franco-German War,
1870-1871. 2. France. Armée—Mobilization—History—
19th century. 3. France-German War, 1870-1871—Manpower
—France. 4. France—History, Military—19th century.
5. Franco-German War, 1870-1871—Logistics. I. Title.
II. Series.
DC293.1.A37 1987   943.08'2   87-25220
ISBN 0-313-25469-9 (lib. bdg. : alk. paper)

British Library Cataloguing in Publication Data is available.

Library of Congress Catalog Card Number: 87-25220
ISBN: 0-313-25469-9
ISSN: 0883-6884

First published in 1987

Greenwood Press, Inc.
88 Post Road West, Westport, Connecticut 06881

Printed in the United States of America

The paper used in this book complies with the
Permanent Paper Standard issued by the National
Information Standards Organization (Z39.48-1984).

10 9 8 7 6 5 4 3 2 1

Contents

List of Maps

Preface

As an author I have incurred many debts along the way. It gives me great pleasure to acknowledge those who have assisted my efforts. I do so with two caveats. One is a familiar one, though no less sincere for that. What others have done for this monograph has contributed immeasurably to its quality; I remain solely responsible for its errors and faults. The other derives from the fact that this project, though small, has had a long life. I have often pulled it out, dusted it off, and worked on it, only to be diverted into other efforts. I am deeply grateful to those friends and colleagues who encouraged me to get back to it and see it through to the end. Alas time has erased some memories; consequently I shall probably omit some of the people who have given me assistance. To them I offer my thanks and apologies.

My research has benefited from varying forms of institutional support. A James B. Reynolds Foreign Scholarship from Dartmouth College funded a year's research in Paris and made possible the first draft of this work. Richard J. Dundas, formerly president of Castleton State College, put the college's business machinery at my disposal, which permitted me efficiently to generate the statistics cited in Chapter 4 and tabulated in Appendix III. The Virginia Tech Educational Foundation and the History Department at Virginia Polytechnic Institute and State University funded additional research in France and elsewhere. Furthermore, through the university's work-study program I obtained the services of Philip E. Culpepper, who drew the maps for this volume. Would that all undergraduates produce such work!

This subject was recommended to me by Shepard B. Clough; the manuscript has been improved through his helpful criticism. The keenest, most incisive and probing critic of this work was Joan Karle. She long ago rid the manuscript of its nonsense, muddled thinking, and jargon. Later versions have been read by Robert G. Landen, Jerry Cooper, Charles Burdick, and Robert Doughty. I have tried where possible to alter this work in the light of their commentaries. A pleasant afternoon's conversation with Michael Howard many years ago provided me with several useful suggestions, not to speak of his assurances that he had not intended for his own masterful and authoritative volume on the Franco-Prussian War to be the last word on the subject.

I am indebted to the staffs of the *Bibliothèque Nationale*, the library of the *Ministère de la Guerre*, the *Archives Nationales* and the archives of the *Ministère des Affaires Etrangères* in Paris. Likewise the curators and staff of the *Service Historique de l'Armée de Terre* in Vincennes provided invaluable assistance. In the United States I have benefited from the collections of the Library of Congress, the New York Public Library, the Baker Library at Dartmouth College, the Butler Library at Columbia University, and the Newman Library at Virginia Polytechnic Institute and State University. To the staffs of all these institutions, particularly the reference personnel who skillfully translated my awkward questions into meaningful--and fruitful--inquiries, I owe my thanks. Les Wright helped me locate some German sources and saved me a lot of time in the process. Donna Evleth provided invaluable research assistance in Paris.

Friends and colleagues from Vermont to Virginia supplied the moral support I needed over time to get this job done. I would particularly like to thank Harold Livesay, Gustavus Williamson, Lowell Dyson, Dean O'Donnell, William Ochsenwald, Michael Lanza, Donald Miller, Robert L. Patterson, Holman D. Jordan, Theodore C. Shelton III, and Bruce Davis. Members of the 1981 R.O.T.C. Military History Workshop at the United States Military Academy with whom I discussed this project encouraged me to complete the manuscript; Brig. Gen. (Ret.) Thomas E. Griess, then retiring head of the History Department at the Academy, suggested that I submit it to Greenwood Press. Finally I am greatly appreciative of the secretarial services of Rennie Givens, Debbie Rhea, Pat Cooper, Betsey Campbell, Teresa Phipps, and above all Patty Mills. Patiently and methodically they have put this study onto a word processor and transformed it into a book. Without their skill and assistance this text would still be messy and unreadable typescript.

I dedicate this book to the memory of my mother and father. Unfortunately they never got to see the finished product.

Blacksburg, Virginia
24 June 1987

Abbreviations

AN, Paris   Archives nationales, Paris

D.T.   France. Assemblée Nationale. *Enquête parlementaire sur*
                   les actes du Gouvernement de la Défense Nationale:
                   dépositions   des   témoins.   5   vols.   (Paris:
                   Germer-Baillière, 1872-75).

G.G.S.   Germany.   Army.   Generalstab.   Kriegsgeschichtliche
                   Abteilung. *The Franco-German War.* 5 vols. (London:
                   Her Majesty's Stationery Office, 1874-84).   Translated
                   from *Der deutsch-französische Krieg 1870-71* (Berlin:
                   Mittler, 1872-81).

Guerre   France. Armée.   Service Historique.   *La Guerre de*
                   1870-71. 35 vols. (Paris: Chapelot, 1901-1913).

J.O.   *Journal Officiel de l'Empire Français*

MAE, Paris   Archives du Ministère des affaires étrangères

SHAT, Vincennes   Service historique de l'armée de terre, Vincennes

Introduction

In the writing of military history the process of mobilization has not received much attention. The reasons are understandable. Although mobilization is partly a wartime operation, it has neither the fascination, the drama, nor the decisive impact of combat. The outcome of wars seems more the result of armies' performance on the battlefields than a consequence of complicated procedures required to get those armies into the field at all. With few exceptions military historians of both the more traditional campaign and battle narratives and authors of the newer analyses of the "face of battle" have glossed over the mobilization of armies, if they have treated the subject at all. Similarly, historians concerned with the broader issues of military history--the evolution of military institutions, the impact of technology, the elaboration of doctrine, the intersection of military developments and social history, all those, that is, who have studied the military in its peacetime as well as wartime context--have also paid little attention to mobilization procedures. Yet the mobilization and concentration of armies are also measures taken in peacetime because that is when they are prepared, and ideally such planning is conducted in the light of a nation's military policy, the structure of its armed forces, and its capacity and will to wage war.

Military officials, on the other hand, have not overlooked these matters. Since the time of the Franco-Prussian War of 1870, they have come to perceive mobilization and concentration as the bridge that connects an army's peacetime status with its state of combat readiness after the outbreak of war. They knew that because of developments in technology, notably the expansion of railroad networks in Europe in the nineteenth century, this bridge could be more and more rapidly traversed. Woe betide that army that did not cross at least as rapidly and completely as its opponent! The Franco-Prussian War showed them why.

This book contributes to the study of mobilization and concentration procedures through the analysis, in its historical context, of a notable failure: the dismal performance of the French army in the first few weeks of the War of 1870. Although participants in and observers of that conflict noted severe deficiencies in both the French mobilization and the subsequent and inadequate concentration of the Army of the Rhine, nobody has ever produced a monograph analyzing these processes. Studies that have addressed the topic have been insufficient. The major German one, published in 1905, treats the German, not the French, mobilization and then investigates only the means by which reservists were recalled and reincorporated into the armed forces of the German states.[1] A 1912 French study merely tabulates French muster rolls regiment by regiment. It does not account for shortages of manpower, nor does it describe the state of combat readiness of the men under arms, or trace the movements of troops from their homes and bases to the battlefield.[2]

Focused on the mobilization and concentration of the French army in 1870 this monograph attempts partially to explain France's defeat in terms of its inadequate preparations for and faulty execution of these operations. At the same time, it examines a military campaign in the changing circumstances of warfare. It asserts that insofar as mid-nineteenth century French strategists failed to grasp the imperatives of mass warfare and the opportunities afforded by expanding railroad systems, they risked defeat by a better informed opponent and suffered such in 1870 thanks to superior Prussian planning and organization. The consequences the French experienced could not safely be ignored thereafter.

This study begins by assessing those factors most significantly affecting the conduct of war in the nineteenth century, particularly those that induced Prussian strategists to elaborate the clearly defined and carefully worked-out mobilization and concentration of their army. It shows that the Prussians perceived mobilization and concentration as more than measures that came into play after the outbreak of war. They saw advance preparations as equally essential components of the process.

An examination of the structure of the French army on the eve of the war then demonstrates the inability of the French command to match Prussian perception and execution of these functions and exposes the inadequacy of the first few steps the French had taken. A description of the circumstances confronting the French command illustrates how urgently they needed to adopt adequate mobilization measures. It shows, however, that they overlooked certain key elements: an honest assessment of their foreign policy goals; the realistic management of relations with friendly powers; and a meaningful adjustment of military objectives in the light of these factors.

A significant part of this work consists of an analysis of the factors influencing the French mobilization of July 1870. First it examines the methods by which both the regular French army and the auxiliary *Garde Nationale Mobile* tried to mobilize reserve manpower. It seeks to explain why, despite the urgent need to place as many trained men under arms as possible, the French military failed to do so. Then follows an analysis of logistical shortcomings and the effects these exerted upon the army, stressing the inadequate preparation of support services and demonstrating that the French army was as immobilized by logistical problems as it was by the slow and insufficient methods incorporating reserve manpower.

The last two parts of this monograph examine the consequences of these events, analyzing deployment of French forces along the northeastern frontier, stressing the army's use of railroad lines and the results they obtained, and explaining why the measures taken more effectively to concentrate the army came to little. The book concludes by analyzing the French defeat in terms of mobilization and concentration procedures. It should be clear that just as mobilization and concentration flowed logically from the state of pre-war preparations, so too did subsequent military operations reflect the conditions within which the army deployed into combat. For the French the bridge carrying their army from peace to war proved a narrow, rickety, and poorly engineered structure, and France paid in consequence a costly, humiliating, and painful price.

NOTES

1. Gustav Lehmann. *Die Mobilmachung von 1870-71* (Berlin: E. S. Mittler, 1905).
2. Aristide Martinien. *La Guerre de 1870-71. La Mobilisation de l'armée: mouvements des dépôts (armée active) du 15 juillet au 1er mars, 1871* (Paris: L. Fournier, 1912).

The Last Gaiter Button

Mobilization, Concentration and the War of 1870

"We are ready, very ready!" So claimed General Edmond Leboeuf, War Minister of France, when on 14 July 1870 he was asked if France were prepared for war against Prussia. "Down to the last gaiter button," he is also said to have remarked, and if he did, he must soon have regretted saying so.[1] Events proved that France was not ready for the Franco-Prussian War of 1870, and critics have implied since then that this was so because the French military were so cavalier, so nonchalant, so out of touch with recent military developments as to be concerned with gaiter buttons rather than the matters that counted.

The charge is exaggerated and unfair, but the caricature has its use. Gaiter buttons are functional and thus are as necessary, if non lethal, a component of a soldier's equipment as bullets. But gaiter buttons suggest the shiny and showy images of ceremony, not the realities of combat. To accuse military officials of preoccupation with the accoutrements of display rather than the sinews of war is to imply that they have been distracted by things out of date. In this sense gaiter buttons have become symbolic. They stand for the kind of military system which the more efficient, conscientious, and professional Prussians made obsolete in the War of 1870. Leboeuf's last gaiter button is not merely an item French quartermasters failed to deliver in sufficient quantities in 1870; it is the French military system and the attitudes which supported it which collapsed before the invading armies from the east.

What happened in 1870 in simplest terms is that the French were unable--and the Prussians were able--to do what the Confederate cavalry general Nathan Bedford Forrest once said was the secret of a successful military campaign. "Git thar fustest with the mostest men," he remarked, and his advice was as sound as his grammar was weak. He understood clearly that one of the greatest advantages an army can possess is superiority of manpower, weapons, and equipment against an opponent's weakest points. "Gittin' thar" sooner and with more of everything is, however, one of the most difficult of military problems, especially in an age of large conscript armies, mass transportation systems, and the bewildering variety of supplies and equipment made available through modern industry. All of these resources have to be rationally assembled in the field if they are to produce the advantages they afford. In the past century and a quarter military experts have come to distinguish the operations which are intended to provide generals with exactly this rational assembly. The first of these is called mobilization; the other, concentration.

The importance of mobilization and concentration as two distinct phases of war that require careful preparation was first brought out in the Franco-Prussian War of 1870. The two armed forces engaged in that conflict were unevenly matched in these respects. When France declared war on Prussia and its South German allies, Baden, Bavaria, and Württemberg on 19 July 1870, the French had 492,585 trained men available for service.[2] The French began to mobilize this force on 16 July, but, when the Prussians attacked them on 6 August, they had succeeded in scattering at best 304,208 incompletely equipped, ill-fed, and irregularly supplied soldiers along about 200 miles of frontier. In the same time the Prussians had concentrated 426,000 troops around less than fifty miles of frontier, and these men were fully equipped, far better fed, and more regularly supplied than their opponents. By 1 September this German army had besieged five French army corps in Metz, crushed four others at Sedan, and left France nearly defenseless.

The consequences of this military reversal were considerable. The War of 1870 both created and destroyed. Out of it was born the united German Empire under the domination of Prussia. In France the war brought down the government of Emperor Napoleon III whose rule under a modified constitutional system had been overwhelmingly ratified by a plebiscite only a few months before. The war cost France the larger part of two provinces, Alsace and Lorraine, and an indemnity of five billion francs. The war furthermore constituted a significant shift in military relationships in Europe. Prior to 1870 France was still considered the leading military power in Europe, but after 1870 the German army became the standard by which military institutions were measured, and with its military strength Germany came to be regarded as the leading land power on the continent.

What had the French done, or rather failed to do, to suffer so humiliating a reversal? They had, first of all, neglected to raise and train enough soldiers. They had also failed to develop their artillery and, as a result, had to fight with guns of a quantity and quality inferior to those of their enemy. Furthermore, adequate training in the command of large military units, such as an army corps or field army, had never been made available to their officers, and the French staff system was inferior to the Prussian. Worst of all, the French were deficient in making best use of the military resources accessible to them, and these resources were not negligible.   Many of their troops were well-trained, long service veterans with combat experience.   Their rifle, the *chassepot*, was superior in range and accuracy to the Prussian needle-gun, and the French had acquired enough matériel to support the army in the field.   These resources, however, were so chaotically assembled on the Franco-German frontier that the army could neither maneuver against its opponent nor recover from the blows it was repeatedly to receive in August, 1870.   A significant shortcoming was its failure to execute a properly directed mobilization of its forces and then to concentrate these effectively against the Germans.

A TRANSFORMATION IN WARFARE

There is irony to this situation.   France had played a significant role in the round of wars which broke out in Europe in the mid nineteenth century, and French observers were witnesses to those in which France did not participate. Twice during the 1850's the forty year post-Napoleonic peace of Europe was shattered by war, and France participated in both.   The Crimean War (1853-1856) was the first engagement by a French army against a major European opponent since Waterloo, and French troops appeared to be the most competently led and best prepared of all the participants.   In 1859 France allied with the Kingdom of Sardinia and in a brief campaign drove Austria from Lombardy, thus setting in motion the events that resulted in the formation of the united Kingdom of Italy the following year.   Because of both of these conflicts the French army enhanced the reputation it had retained even after the fall of Napoleon I: that it was the finest in Europe.[3]

During the ensuing decade France continued to resort to arms, but in colonial rather than continental ventures.   One of these was becoming a long standing affair for French arms: the conquest and pacification of Algeria.   The other was the occupation of Mexico.   In neither of these did the French army suffer any setbacks, but the significant military developments of the 1860's were happening in central Europe where France was playing no role at all.   Here the Prussian army, by defeating the Danes in 1864 and the Austrians in 1866, gave the Prussian state hegemony in the area, particularly through the formation in 1867 of the North German Confederation, a state which was dominated by Prussia and which also denied Austria any further role in the affairs of Germany.   This was a surprising reversal, for in the previous decade the Prussian military had proven to be weak, especially when opposed to Austrian power.   In 1866, however, a reformed and efficient Prussian army, tested in the 1864 Danish conflict and ably directed by the army chief of staff Helmuth von Moltke mounted a six week campaign which culminated in the Battle of Königgrätz (3

July 1866), where the Prussians destroyed the main Austrian force commanded by *Feldzeugmeister* Ludwig von Benedek.[4]

For the government of Napoleon III this result was a disagreeable alteration of the balance of power in Germany. The French had been a Rhineland power since the age of Cardinal Richelieu and from that time had taken an active interest in German internal politics. Napoleon III's particular interest in German affairs was derived from his notion that French power and prestige could be enhanced by his becoming a patron of the nationalist aspirations of European peoples; thus he could "sponsor" German as he had Italian unity. As such Napoleon was not opposed to a form of German unity under Prussian leadership, as long as France received just compensation, and he anticipated a struggle for German leadership between Prussia and Austria. But he patronizingly thought the war would result in a stalemate into which France could step as an arbitrator who would both advance the cause of German unity and the interests of France at the same time. For Napoleon III the Battle of Königgrätz was a stunning surprise and a significant military reversal. It wrecked his policy, revealed its contradictions, and pointed out serious defects in the French military system in spite of France's official role as a neutral bystander in the war.[5]

The Battle of Königgrätz provoked considerable discussion of military subjects in France. This included several well-informed French officers whose knowledge of contemporary military affairs gave them a clear understanding of the new threat posed by the Prussians. One of the most notable of these was General Auguste Alexandre Ducrot. Assigned to the 6th Military Division, a peacetime command unrelated to any potential wartime combat "division," Ducrot took an active interest in military affairs across the Rhine. He sent subordinates to the South German states and traveled there on his own. He reconnoitered strategic locations, took notes on fortifications, and drafted recommendations for future operations in Germany.[6] He also collected information about Prussian military policies and activities, especially in the South German states where Prussian influence and alliances were quietly integrating the military systems of these three independent states into the Prussian one.[7] Ducrot warned the French government of the Prussian threat, particularly the speed with which Prussia could mobilize a force and invade France, but his messages had a tone of the frantic to them. In 1866 he claimed that a Prussian strike against France was imminent, when in fact no such situation was true. Two years later he prescribed a preemptive French invasion into South Germany; it would put a stop to Prussian meddling there at a time when South German sympathies still lay with the French, he thought.[8]

A far more acute observer was Colonel Eugène Stoffel, who served from 1866 to 1870 as the French military attaché at the embassy in Berlin. In these years he composed a series of reports on the organization and operations of the

Prussian army. Covering subjects from the concentration of the armies in 1866 to their medical services, his reports left the impression that France's armed forces needed substantial reform. Stoffel's attitude toward the Prussian army was reserved. He did not think it was superior to the French, but he was quick to appreciate its efficiency and its strength. On matters in which he believed the Prussians held an advantage over the French, he was very explicit. Nothing was clearer than his warning in 1869 that their organization permitted them "to concentrate several armies of 100,000 men each on our frontiers within twenty to twenty-five days."[9] This estimate was, as events proved, exaggerated, but its purpose was to impress upon the French the need for the careful preparation he knew was deficient.

As his warning suggests, Stoffel's reports often touched on a number of matters regarding mobilization and concentration. A sizeable portion of his dispatch of 24 June 1868 analyzed the Prussian system of "passage from peacetime to wartime footing." It informed his superiors that the North German Confederation would have 483,000 combat troops and 57,000 noncombatants in line for a campaign and yet have 400,000 more in reserve. Other reports commented on how the Prussians profitted from past mistakes and busily sought to rectify them. They noted how the Prussian military regularly kept abreast of improvements to German railroad systems with a view as to how these could best be exploited by the army. His report of 23 April 1868 compared the Prussian general staff very favorably to the French staff and counseled the French to beware of the Prussian staff system. An appendix to a report of 15 July 1869 analyzed the time required in 1866 to mobilize several sample units. It showed that most of them had completed the process within two weeks' time.[10] Together the information Stoffel was imparting conveyed a stern warning to the French. Prussia, he was saying, had more trained men available than did France; it could mobilize them in a short time; its staff was studying mistakes made in earlier wars; and it was implementing means of assembling and concentrating armies more efficiently than had been done in 1866.

Of the remaining commentators one other voice was particularly outstanding. It was that of General Louis Jules Trochu whose book, L'Armée française en 1867, ran through sixteen editions in three weeks in 1868. Through this volume Trochu made himself unpopular with his colleagues, for the book criticized some of the French army's oldest traditions and included the contents of a confidential report prepared for the Emperor by a military commission in 1867. Trochu's outlook was essentially conservative. He hoped to restore the old values of the army which he thought had been lost in the course of the nineteenth century, and he was opposed to universal conscription, the adoption of which was being advocated by Napoleon III. He did, nonetheless, demonstrate serious weaknesses in the French army. Army administration, he indicated, was cumbersome because administrators had to submit everything to the Minister of War for approval. Preparation for war, he said, requires profound study and takes a long time. But in the French army "we think that every effort can and must be made with the speed of electricity; it is admitted that a few weeks will suffice to prepare military operations--even for the least known countries, which are studied summarily and which are several thousand leagues from us."[11] Such criticism did little to win him the support of the army; rather it made him popular with the opposition to Napoleon III's rule. This popularity and his open Orleanist sympathies meant he was not in favor at court, and even potential friends were often offended by Trochu when they discovered that he was a long-winded bore. As a result, his ideas were not taken seriously.

Although these observers made the public aware of most of the faults of the French military system, their voices were not united. Consequently the solutions they recommended were contradictory. Many indeed were conservative critics who advocated modifications within the existing structure of the French army. Even so each one sensed that warfare was being profoundly transformed and that France was failing to respond to these changes. Their instincts were correct, even if events were happening too rapidly for them fully to absorb their meaning. It has taken a later generation of military experts and historians to put these changes into perspective. Here is how the eminent twentieth century British military historian B. H. Liddell Hart put the matter:

> The forty years from 1830 to 1870 saw a greater change in the means of warfare, both on land and sea, than during the whole previous span of modern history--or of all previous history. Most of the change was concentrated, at least in the sense of being demonstrated, within the last decade of the period. The technical, tactical, and strategical developments during the wars of this decade foreshadowed the operational trend, and social form, of warfare in the next century.[12]

In brief, what Ducrot, Stoffel, and Trochu were observing was the birth of the kinds of armies and the warfare they waged which predominated in Europe and eventually the rest of the world until at least the end of the Second World War.

The armies involved were armed forces recruited on the principle of universal military service, led by a corps of trained professional experts, equipped with the products of modern industry, and served by the most up-to-date means of communication and transportation. The warfare they waged has assumed proportions hardly known by Europeans prior to the middle of the nineteenth century. The number of men engaged came to number in the millions, and the vastly improved range and accuracy of their new weapons greatly increased the destructiveness of warfare. Huge as these new "modern" armies became and deadly as their weapons proved to be, perhaps the most outstanding feature of the new warfare was the mobility which modern armed forces acquired. With the construction of the railroad networks in Europe and America in the nineteenth century, commanders were able to transport men and matériel in a few day's time over distances which formerly required several weeks if not months. Since the mid nineteenth century, some commanders have been able to exploit these facilities so effectively as to inflict overwhelming defeats on a less well-prepared enemy in a few weeks time--a kind of war which we have learned since 1939 to call *Blitzkrieg*. The Franco-Prussian War of 1870 may certainly be understood as one of the first conflicts of this type.

This new "modern" warfare has been the result of two significant historical developments of the nineteenth century: the growth of the large nation-state and the industrial revolution.   The nation-state was nothing new to nineteenth century Europe, but a Europe divided politically according to the principle of nationality was. A century before the Franco-Prussian War, the map of Europe was dotted with hundreds of tiny, sovereign states and semiautonomous provinces; large states like France or Prussia were the exception rather than the rule. By 1870 most of these small territories had disappeared: Italy had become a unified country in 1860, and instead of the over three hundred sovereign states that made up Germany one hundred years before, there were only four--the North German Confederation, of which Prussia was the predominating member, and the three South German states of Baden, Bavaria and Württemberg.

A nation-state possessed obvious military advantages over the principalities it had replaced. Able to tap greater sources of wealth and manpower, it could afford to maintain huge armies.   Its leaders could appeal to the patriotic sentiments of the population and require its able-bodied male citizens to defend the fatherland in wartime. As a result, an armed force of over one million men became a possibility. In 1870 France and Prussia each eventually raised over one million men.[13]

Because of the industrial revolution vast new sources of power were available to the armies. Through the use of the steam driven machine in the manufacture of goods, the establishment of standardized production in factories, and the application of new science and technology to the development of products, Europe was witnessing a profound change in the ways men produce goods and perform services, and this change soon exercised an effect upon military establishments. If governments wished to expand their armies, they could be sure national industries had the capacity to feed, clothe, and arm the recruits.   Advances in metallurgy, ballistics, and precision engineering made possible the introduction of the breech-loading, rifled weapons, that in the 1850's and 1860's finally drove inaccurate and slow firing muskets as well as smoothbore cannon from the field. In 1841, the Prussians were the first to adopt a breech-loading rifle, the Dreyse needle-gun, and in 1866 the French followed suit with the breech-loading *chassepot* rifle. In the 1860's the firm of Alfred

Krupp developed a steel breech-loading cannon, the performance of which overcame the objections of conservative exponents of bronze guns.   The Prussians adopted Krupp guns in 1867, and in the 1,170 pieces they mobilized against the French in 1870, they had weapons of a range of about 4000 yards, a distance far superior to the range of the French guns.[14]

Of all the developments of the industrial revolution, the railroad exercised the most profound effect on armies.   Ever since 1833 when in two hours a battalion of infantrymen traveled by rail from Manchester to Liverpool, a trip that on foot required two days, professional soldiers were quick to appreciate the military utility of the railroad.[15]   Speed, however, was not the only factor that impressed them.   They could now get men to the theater of operations in excellent physical condition.   In the past, even long service veterans, hardened to the rigors of a campaign, dropped out of column during long marches.   Now armies could transport short service conscripts to the front and expect them to be in good health.   The railroad, furthermore, was capable of bringing up almost unlimited reserves of manpower and supplies so that, with a good rail network, a nation possessed a greater capacity to maintain an army in the field than it had ever had before.   Finally, the railroad gave armies the ability to keep their columns widely separated and yet to concentrate them when need be.   These advantages allowed armies to advance more quickly and to be more easily supplied when they were dispersed.   In short, the nation which developed the largest railroad system acquired an enormous military advantage over its potential opponent.

In 1870 both France and Prussia and its allies possessed adequate resources to conduct war along modern lines.   With populations of 36 million and 40 million respectively, they had ample numbers of able-bodied men to maintain huge armies, and, in fact, laws in both countries imposed some form of military obligation on their male citizens.   In the manufacture of pig iron, France produced 1.2 million tons a year, Germany, 1.3 million tons--enough in both states to be fashioned into sufficient reserves of weapons.[16]   Each nation had built lengthy networks of railroads, and these lines contained large rail yards in the zones where they were most likely to carry on military operations against one another.   In fact, since France and Prussia were roughly equal in all these respects, it is possible to state that the nation which made better military use of these resources had an advantage over its opponent at the outbreak of hostilities.

To gain such advantages, responsible military officials soon learned that they had to spend years readying their armed force for the test it would undergo on the battlefield.   Adequate training, powerful weapons, and competent commanders were three important components that required careful attention, but some military experts, especially in Prussia, soon learned that no general officer could made a mass of men and matériel respond appropriately to his commands unless that mass had somehow become a cohesive and articulate force. The key to this problem lay in organization, and this, experts believed, could be best attained at the beginning of a campaign when an army, by incorporating the reserve manpower it did not keep under arms during peacetime and by distributing the equipment the field army was expected to use, moved from peacetime status to wartime status. This process the Prussians soon identified as mobilization.

MOBILIZATION

The word "mobilization" was first coined by the Prussians, just as they were the first to identify the operation. The way they said it reveals the intent. *Die Mobilmachung* literally means "the process of making mobile," and obviously what they were thinking of was the formation of an efficient and articulate field army capable of moving rapidly to the places where it can be used to best advantage.   They also identified a related operation to follow upon *Mobilmachung*. It involved the assembly or disposition of the army prior to the beginning of the campaign, and this they called *der Aufmarsch*, a term translated as concentration because it allowed commanders to concentrate their forces wherever they deemed it necessary.[17]

"Making mobile, assembling, and concentrating," these were the identifiable components of what appeared to be a continuous movement. The Prussians perceived and labeled them; the French did not. Until the Franco-Prussian War they called mobilization *"passage sur le pied de guerre,"* and by this they meant creating a field army from the resources available to the military at the outbreak of war and getting it ready for a campaign. The definition is cumbersome; so too was the process. The French tried to make mobile, assemble, and concentrate all at the same time. Marshal MacMahon later noted that they had already so proceeded in the 1859 war, and in 1870 they repeated the process.[18] As shall be shown they failed either to mobilize, assemble, or concentrate their forces sufficiently to oppose the threat posed by the Prussians.

Mobilization is a more comprehensive term than many people have assumed. To the civilian it is what happens at the outbreak of war when trained reservists, released from active duty but still obliged to serve in wartime, are called back into service. This view evokes those World War I images of young Europeans abandoning civilian life and going off to war amidst crowds of enthusiastic citizens who cheered them in the streets and at the railroad stations. This picture, stripped of its romantic trappings, is not so wrong as it is incomplete. The recall of reservists is only one phase, albeit a very public, vividly dramatic, and intensely personal one, of the execution of the mobilization process.

A broader definition of mobilization--a more contemporary American one is useful here--reveals that the operation entails far more than what the popular view has included. Besides the calling up of reservists it comprises "conscription, major expansion of training facilities, the readying of weapons from storage, the issuance of equipment, and the preparation of all the measures necessary within the military establishment for support of a serious war effort."[19]

Since the time of the Franco-Prussian War military experts have realized that mobilization begins long before the outbreak of war.[20]   In the 1870 war it was initiated when army administrators started to elaborate the plans that governed the army's passage from peacetime to wartime status.   They realized that peacetime status generally differed so greatly from that of wartime that elaborate preparations became necessary to translate the one into the other.   In 1870 neither the French nor the Prussians kept all of their trained soldiers under arms at all times, and neither had distributed all their weapons, equipment, and supplies until the outbreak of war. These circumstances required both to prepare exhaustively for the embodiment of reserve manpower and the distribution of matériel as soon as war began.

Preparations for a properly executed mobilization, such as that accomplished by the Prussians in 1870, covered every conceivable problem an army could face at the beginning of a war.   In order to accelerate the recall of reservists to the colors, planners of mobilization filled out individual recall slips ahead of time and made arrangements for the rapid delivery of these documents. In order to ensure the army that the reservists would be ready to fight as soon as they returned to active service, the planners regularly supervised the supply and maintenance of bases. They also determined which units were to be sent off to war and which to be held back for service as garrison troops or as cadres for units which the army was to raise and train during the war.   It was also necessary for planners to assure an army that all auxiliary services, such as military convoys, medical teams, and communication corps, were ready to serve when war broke out.   They were responsible for preparing the rapid assembly of all weapons, munitions, supplies, and transport vehicles. Finally, they drew up a mobilization calendar, which, if it was carefully worked out, advised the army command of the time required for the army to be fully ready to begin military operations.[21]

If an armed force had fully prepared before war was declared, the actual execution of mobilization was very smooth.   With all orders written and all equipment ready, only a formal order for mobilization was necessary, which, when issued, set the entire machinery in motion.   Last minute frenzy was unnecessary, and a commander could feel assured that his army was ready to undertake subsequent military operations at the end of the mobilization period. Such assuredness was exhibited in 1870 by the Prussian Chief of Staff Helmuth von Moltke whose staff had prepared mobilization.   Two days before the

Prussians began to mobilize their army, a fellow officer paid Moltke a visit. Finding the general calmly resting on a couch reading a volume of Sir Walter Scott, the friend asked him why he was not concerned. "Why not?" asked Moltke. "Everything's ready. We've only got to press the button."[22] Moltke's calmness was fully justified. Prussian mobilization began on 16 July; by 23 July the first units completed their mobilization, and the transport of units to the zone of concentration began the following day.[23]

CONCENTRATION

Concentration, a more comprehensive term than the *Aufmarsch* the Prussians identified, was the process to flow from mobilization. It can be defined as the bringing together of mobilized forces within supporting distance of one another.[24] In 1870 it posed as complex a set of problems as mobilization. Both the French and the Prussians opened hostilities with armies numbering in the hundreds of thousands of men. Armed forces of this size were of little value to commanders on either side unless they could be formed into units large enough to counter the threat of an enemy and articulate enough to permit rapid movement. The creation of large units was relatively simple; long before 1870, commanders had taken an eighteenth century invention, the infantry division (by 1870, a force of roughly 10,000 men) and combined them into army corps of two or more divisions or into armies of two or more corps. Articulation, however, was another matter. An army corps was a complete fighting unit; besides the infantry it contained cavalry, artillery, and all auxiliary services, a combined force of approximately 30,000 men. On foot the army corps was an awkward and unwieldy force. At best it could cover ten or twelve miles a day, and it needed one day to deploy from column into battle formation. Clearly careful planning was necessary to turn this mass into an articulate and efficient force.

In 1870 the railroad was the chief solution to this problem, for it permitted both armies to travel rapidly from their bases to the zones of concentration. To make adequate use of the railroad, military planners, already burdened with the details of mobilization, had to assume further responsibilities: they were required to become experts in the details of railroad management. They had, first of all, to take into consideration the capacity of railroad equipment in order to determine the number of trains required to transport a given unit. Secondly, the direction and capacity of each line as well as the location of the major freight yards had to be ascertained. Without this information they could decide neither where concentration could take place nor the time it would require. Next, the planners had to determine how many troops, horses, supplies, and transport vehicles each train would haul. Finally, they had to draw up special military railroad schedules and make arrangements with railway officials to assure the army top priority in the use of the railroads throughout the war.

Even this work was not sufficient to complete the concentration of an army. In 1870 commanders protected their lines of communication by keeping their railheads well to the rear of the theatre of operations. Planners thus had to work out the details of marching dispersed columns through the countryside. This proved to be an enormously complex task. They needed to know where commanders intended to complete the concentration of their forces, but because the army, as it drew closer to the enemy, was in greater danger of surprise attack, commanders were never absolutely sure of the army's destination. Furthermore, planners had to be well-acquainted with all the roads in the zone of operations, for without use of all available routes, concentration was likely to be retarded. To ensure regular supply of food and equipment to the army in the field, they needed to establish convoys, which, to make the problem even more difficult, were required to make their way along the same roads used by the advanced guard and all the follow-up units. As the distance between the army and the railheads increased, planners had to determine where they could establish intermediate supply depots. If this problem had not been taken into consideration, the heads of columns of combat troops were in danger of marching beyond the range of the convoys. Finally, because the army, as it converged upon the final point of concentration, became more compact, planners had to be ready to deal with the problem of maintaining an ever-growing force over progressively fewer roads. Unless they could assure this dense force its daily requirements of food and equipment, the army was in danger of becoming a confused mass less able to take the offensive or defend itself against an enterprising and more mobile enemy.

As in mobilization, if the details of concentration were worked out before war began, there would be fewer unforeseen problems to solve at the last moment. The army could move quickly and efficiently from its scattered home bases and could gather strength as its units advanced on the enemy. When it became engaged in battle it would be at its fullest possible strength and capable as well of altering its positions to meet whatever new conditions it would encounter.

* * * * *

Careful planning of mobilization and concentration provided an army with unquestionable advantages over an enemy force deficient in this respect. In the first place, it promoted orderliness and thoroughness in the execution of both processes. Step by step the army took shape. The men received their orders to return to their bases where they obtained their uniforms, weapons, and equipment and joined the ranks of the men in active service. Then, at the preappointed moment, they marched to the railroad station to catch the train already scheduled to transport them to the zone of concentration where, as more units arrived, they assembled into divisions, army corps, and armies. According to prearranged schedules the quartermaster corps loaded trains with matériel, and the transport services prepared the vehicles to carry these supplies to the army in the field. In the meantime, the army high command put its staffs and equipment into readiness for the task of directing the army in its campaign.

The army which conducted methodical mobilization and concentration thus avoided much error and confusion. Since military officials had already worked out every move the army was to make, they had taken almost all last minute decision making out of human hands and eliminated most mistakes which men, who are overwhelmed with pressing duties, are likely to make. During the mobilization and concentration of an army, officers had fewer emergencies to face. All they had to do was carry out the orders they received, and ideally all the pieces of the army would fall into place as if they were directed by some complex and intricate machine.

A third advantage was speed. An army more quickly concentrated than the opponent could take the offensive, fall on the enemy's scattered units, disrupt his mobilization, and inflict defeats from which he could never recover. If both sides were mobilized and concentrated with the same rapidity, each at least would have the advantage of not being caught unprepared.

Probably the greatest advantage an army derived from systematic mobilization and concentration was greater mobility and flexibility. And an army capable of moving about with ease possessed a better chance to achieve the objective selected for it by its commanders. It could, for example, drive deep into hostile territory and yet maintain itself without having to rely on enemy resources. The army was also better able to respond effectively to all unforeseen events of war. A well-prepared army could generally continue to operate despite the highly disruptive conditions of war. It may have had to regroup its forces and change its objective, but it became neither the dispersed force nor the dense, incoherent mass that was the likely fate of an unprepared, poorly mobilized armed force.

These were advantages that merited serious attention. Because, as we shall see, the Prussians had recognized them, the French needed to as well. They did not. Instead they undertook hostilities with an army fashioned to the needs of the early nineteenth century, and against a modernized Prussian army they used an armed force which in structure was woefully out of date. The result is perhaps most succinctly summarized in an often quoted telegram sent by General Michel to the Ministry of War on 21 July 1870: "Am in Belfort; can't find brigade; can't find commanding general; what must I do; don't know where my regiments are."[25]   The general's message vividly illustrates what predicaments the French method of mobilizing and concentrating its forces could cause. Any discussion of these procedures, however, must first take into account the nature of France's military institutions.

NOTES

1. This boast is referred to in Dennis W. Brogan, *The Development of Modern France 1870-1939*, revised ed., 2 vols. (New York: Harper and Row, 1966), I, p. 22. Other sources quote Leboeuf as follows: "We are ready, very ready. If the war should last a year, we will not be lacking as much as a gaiter button." Michel Mourre, *Dictionnaire d'histoire universelle*, 4 vols. (Geneva: Cercle du Bibliophile, 1970), II, p. 1180.

2. France, Assemblée Nationale, *Enquête parlementaire sur les actes du Gouvernement de la Défense Nationale: dépositions des témoins*, 5 vols. (Paris: Germer-Baillière, 1872-1875), I, p. 67.

3. There is little written recently on the role of the French army in either of these conflicts. For the Crimean War the reader is advised to consult Brison D. Gooch, *The New Bonapartist Generals in the Crimean War; Distrust and Decision Making in the Anglo-French Alliance* (The Hague: M. Nijhoff, 1959). The best recent source covering the wars of the Italian Risorgimento devotes only 35 pages to the 1859 war: Piero Pieri, *Storia militare del Risorgimento: Guerre e insurrezioni* (Turin: Giulio Einaudi, 1962), pp. 589-623.

4. Although the literature of the nineteenth century Prussian army is voluminous, there is little of recent vintage on the 1866 war. See the fine but all too brief study by Gordon A. Craig, *The Battle of Königgrätz: Prussia's Victory over Austria* (Philadelphia: Lippincott, 1964).

5. The French referred to the result of the battle as "the *coup* of Sadowa," Sadowa being the alternate name for the battle.

6. "Reconnaissance des places de Landau, Mayence, Heidelberg, Darmstadt," 22 April 1868, SHAT, Vincennes, Papiers Ducrot, 1 K 189, carton 1.

7. See "Renseignements sur l'état militaire du Grand Duché de Bade," 25 January 1868 and "Rapport du General Ducrot sur son excursion en Allemagne avec le capitaine Schenck," 1868, SHAT, Vincennes, Papiers Ducrot, 1 K 189, carton 1.

8. Auguste-Alexandre Ducrot, *La Vie militaire du Général Ducrot d'après sa correspondance*, 2 vols. (Paris: Plon-Nourrit, 1895), see esp. II, pp. 144-146, 182-183, 242-251.

9. These reports have been published in Eugène Stoffel, *Rapports militaires écrits de Berlin., 1866-1870*, (Paris: Garnier, 1871). His 1869 warning is printed on p. 315.

10. Ibid., pp. 111-131, 173-184, 191-193, 263-270, 457-463.

11. See esp. Louis Jules Trochu, *L'Armée française en 1867* (Paris: Amyot, 1868), pp. 43-44, 88. See also Louis Jules Trochu, *Oeuvres posthumes*, 2 vols. (Tours: A. Mame et fils, 1896), I, p. 75.

12. B.H. Liddell Hart, "Armed Forces and the Art of War," *The Zenith of European Power*, by J.P.T. Bury, ed., Vol. X: *The New Cambridge Modern History*, 14 vols. (Cambridge: Cambridge University Press, 1957-1970), p. 302.

13. Germany, Army, Generalstab, Kriegsgeschichtliche Abteilung, *The Franco-German War*, Translated by F.C.H. Clarke, 5 vols. (London: Her Majesty's Stationery Office, 1874-1884), I, i, p. 46, (cited hereafter as G.G.S.); Michael Howard, *The Franco-Prussian War* (London: Rupert Hart-Davis, 1961), p. 244.

14. Barthélemy Edmond Palat, *Histoire de la guerre de 1870-1871*, Part I: *La Guerre de 1870*, 6 vols. (Paris: Berger-Levrault, 1903-1908), II, p. 230; Charles Antoine Thoumas, *Les Transformations de l'armée française*, 2 vols. (Paris: Berger-Levrault, 1887), I, p. 232 and II, p. 99; Frank Comparato, *Age of Great Guns* (Harrisburg, Pa.: Stackpole, 1965), pp. 25-28.

15. Edwin A. Pratt, *The Rise of Rail Power in War and Conquest*, 1833-1914 (Philadelphia: Lippincott, 1916), p. 1.

16. A.J.P. Taylor, *The Struggle for Mastery in Europe, 1948-1918* (Oxford: Oxford University Press, 1954), p. xxx.

17. These concepts are discussed by Jean Colin in *Les Transformations de la guerre* (Paris: Flammarion, 1911).   This work has been translated by L.H.R. Pope-Hennessy as *The Transformations of War* (London: Hugh-Rees, 1912). See esp. pp. 317-321 of the English language edition.

18. Manuscript memoirs of Marshal MacMahon, SHAT, Vincennes, Lr 1.

19. This definition is derived from George Lincoln, *et al.*, *Economics of National Security: Managing America's Resources for Defense*, 2nd. ed. rev. (Englewood Cliffs, N.J.: Prentice-Hall, 1954), p. 13.

20. See Victor Dérrécagaix, *La Guerre moderne*, 2 vols. (Paris: Baudoin, 1885), I, p. 376.

21. Ibid., I, pp. 374-376; Thoumas, *Les Transformations de l'armée française*, I, p. 554.

22.   Norman Rich and M.H. Fisher, eds., *The Holstein Papers*, 4 vols.   (Cambridge: Cambridge University Press, 1955), I, p. 41.

23.   G.G.S., I, i, pp. 40-41.   See also Gustav Lehmann, *Die Mobilmachung von 1870-71* (Berlin: E.S. Mittler, 1905), pp. 40-41.

24. This definition is derived from R. Ernest Dupuy and Trevor N. Dupuy, *Military Heritage of America* (New York: McGraw-Hill, 1959), p. 17. Strictly speaking *Aufmarsch* means the transporting and assembling of troops in such a way that they may be rapidly concentrated on the battlefield where they may then be deployed to best advantage.

25. Telegram, General Michel to Ministry of War, 21 July 1870, AN, Paris AB XIX 1711.

2
The French Army in 1870

The Franco-Prussian War was a contest between armies whose practices and institutions belonged to two different eras. The French army, characterized by many historians as an *armée de métier*, was manned by long-term soldiers, led by ill-prepared officers, given a rudimentary organization, and administered by cumbersome machinery. It was rooted in the political and diplomatic system of the post-Napoleonic era. The Prussian army, very different in all these respects, pointed to the military institutions of the twentieth century.

Although during its revolution France had been the first European state to create a citizen army and to cope with all the problems of articulating such a force, it established a more traditional type of armed force in the "restoration era" after 1815. French military institutions were fashioned to assure France its reduced but still prominent position among the great powers of Europe, provide her with an effective but inexpensive armed force adequate to the defense needs of the state, and make the army politically reliable. Although changes were introduced into the army over the ensuing five decades, none altered its basic structures and practices, and by 1870 these had become increasingly obsolete. Ultimately failure to keep up with military developments exacted a high price; in the Franco-Prussian War the French had to mobilize and concentrate their forces rapidly but with military institutions unequal to the task.[1]

RECRUITMENT, THE REGIMENTAL SYSTEM, AND ARMY ORGANIZATION, 1818-1866

In 1870, military experts, including Helmuth von Moltke, thought the French would be the first to take the offensive. Many also held, although Moltke was not one of these, that the French ought to possess one overwhelming advantage over the Prussians. French forces, although numerically inferior, were long-service regulars who presumably were under arms at all times and had their war matériel readily available to them. The speed and mobility which this situation afforded them gave them the opportunity to disrupt Prussian mobilization and, through skillful maneuver, destroy dispersed and unsupported Prussian columns.[2] The experts were mistaken, however. The French possessed no such advantage. They were not organized on a wartime basis, nor were they really an army fully made up of full-time soldiers. The basic reasons for this are rooted, first of all, in the system by which the French recruited and organized their army in the years after 1815.

The structure of the nineteenth century French army was as much a product of the government of Louis XVIII and the "restoration era" as its *esprit* was derived from the revolutionary and Napoleonic epochs. In post-Napoleonic France the purpose of the army was the protection of a society which wanted no more military demands upon its sons and no more wars. Facing no danger of invasion by hostile neighbors and concerned with political stability at home, restoration era politicians called for an inexpensive, politically conservative army and thus were wary of raising a citizen army.

Military experts agreed. A small army of 250,000 to 300,000 long-term soldiers, they thought, was sufficient to defend France and uphold her status; it cost little; and, best of all, it was a better army. In their opinion a man became a soldier only after several years of training. Conscripts, because they served only two or three years, did not have time to acquire the habits, master the skills, or adopt the *esprit de corps* of the regular long service men. Officers furthermore believed conscripts were of no military value after they were released from service: they would readjust to the comforts of civilian life and thus become incapable of returning to the army as reserves and enduring the rigors of a military campaign.[3] Others feared the reserve because they thought reservists were politically unreliable, potentially a discontented "republican" force, and they were able to translate this fear into policy. In 1824 the government repealed a requirement that veterans perform reserve duty; the Soult Law of 1832 embodied the same measure.[4] Although, as we shall see, the French eventually did create a sort of reserve force, the army's recruitment and financing practices continued to reflect the other points of view summarized here.

The basic recruitment practices of nineteenth century France were defined by the Saint-Cyr Law of 1818 and the Soult Law of 1832. In the Charter of

1814, Louis XVIII abolished the obligation of universal service. He intended to create an army based on volunteer soldiers, but the army soon learned it was unable to recruit enough volunteers to fill its ranks. Then, in 1818, after a long and heated debate which touched on the very constitutionality of the measure, the French Chambers passed the Saint-Cyr Law which restored the principle of universal military obligation and authorized the government to conscript men for military service.[5] The government, intending to enforce this principle as mildly as possible, devised the means by which, from then on, it made up the difference between the volunteers, whose service it highly valued and the manpower requirements of the army.

Their practice was the lottery. Each year the army selected a class of conscripts by lot from among all French male citizens twenty-one years of age. It then divided this group into two sections. One, called the "first portion", underwent full training for a term of service finally fixed in 1832 at seven years. The size of the "first portion" varied from year to year, depending on the difference between the number of volunteers and the size of the army as authorized by the legislature, but rarely did it exceed 20,000 in any year. The "second portion" received no training at all until 1860; it served rather as an untrained "reserve", subject for seven years to call if the army so required.[6]

So execrable a burden did military service appear even in this guise that in ensuing years the state modified its recruitment practices so that citizens could avoid service while at the same time the state could still maintain an adequate military establishment. One method was simple. The authorities placed a man's "number" in the lottery only once. If it were not drawn, he was forever free and never had to worry about the draft again. For those who had a *mauvais numéro*, there were still ways to escape the military. Their obligation was merely to *furnish*, not necessarily *do*, service, and the law provided the draftee the way out. It gave him the right to hire a substitute, and the 1832 law carefully set the requirements for the substitute. He had to be French, between twenty and thirty years of age, clear of all military obligations, unmarried, free of parental obligations if previously married, one meter fifty-six tall, and of unsullied reputation.[7] There was no set price for a substitute. The amount men paid fluctuated according to region, the international situation, whether or not young men thought the number they drew was bad, and even what the substitute himself thought he was worth.[8] Even so, the cost, whatever it was, was high, and the privilege of obtaining a substitute provided enterprising Frenchmen with some curious opportunities. Agencies did a thriving business providing substitutes, and insurance companies regularly advertised protection against military service.[9] An item in the records of the Compagnie de l'Est suggests how importantly citizens took the right to obtain exemption from military service and what burdens they were willing to bear to do so for themselves or their families. In 1869 a M. Lachaux, *chef de train*, borrowed 1,200 francs from his employers and promised to reimburse them out of his pay at a rate of fifty francs a month. Since his salary was close to 3,000 francs a year, he was willing to take a 20% reduction in pay for two years, and his reason for doing so was to obtain exoneration from military service for his son.[10]

By the 1850's the practice of allowing conscripts to hire substitutes no longer appeared to be acceptable. To some the practice of trafficking in bodies was shameful, but to the army leadership the problem was otherwise. Generals, especially the "African" pretorian guard who had supported Louis-Napoleon Bonaparte's *coup* which overthrew the Second Republic, favored a highly "professional" as opposed to citizen army, and such a force consisted of volunteers and trained soldiers who re-enlisted for another tour of duty upon discharge. This point of view came to be reinforced when the army dispatched reputedly poor quality recruits to the Crimea in 1854. The way to avoid a repetition of this predicament, they thought, was to retain skilled veterans in service.[11] But how? The answer was provided by the law of 26 April 1855. This legislation authorized the establishment of a public fund to which a conscript who had drawn a *mauvais numéro* had a right to contribute. From the fund came bonuses to soldiers who re-enlisted at the expiration of their term of service, and the re-enlistee was considered to be a replacement for the conscript, whose contribution, so implied the law, exonerated him from military service. The law also sought to induce reenlistments through the added benefits of higher pay and a more attractive pension for soldiers who completed twenty-five years of service.[12]

It should be noted, however that the cost of these exemptions, whether they be "substitutions" or "exonerations," was very high, and the result was that the burden of defending France fell on the shoulders of its poorest classes.[13] In spite of the cost the practice of hiring substitutes was very popular. Historian Joseph Monteilhet has pointed out that nearly 200,000 of the soldiers in the French Army in 1870 were paid substitutes.[14]

Clearly all these practices were aimed at producing an army of thoroughly trained veterans who had become so attached to army life that they would want to make a career out of military service.[15] They were to be so imbued with a military spirit as to be uncomfortable with civilian life and so "professional" as to offset any potential military disadvantage with matchless skill. Until 1870 this army lived up to the expectations of those who created it. To the officer corps which demanded men long practiced in the trade of soldiering, the resourcefulness, bravery, and patience displayed by troops in North Africa, the Crimea, and Northern Italy justified their point of view. To the ruling classes who demanded an army divorced from politics, the army could show both that it had no part in originating the upheavals which brought down three regimes between 1830 and 1851 and that it appeared both submissive and loyal to whatever regime held power.[16]

To be sure obedience and loyalty masked both pockets of disobedience and the pretences of political indifference. Republican activity frequently surfaced among soldiers during the Restoration era and the early years of the July Monarchy. It was more likely to be occasioned by conditions of army life than genuine adherence to ideology, but for a time it was a source of trouble for the regime in power. Officers feigned political neutrality, but historian William Serman has asserted that in fact they nurtured a genuinely conservative point of view throughout the nineteenth century.[17] But none of this brought about a military *coup*, so those who wanted an apolitical army had reason to be satisfied. So too could those who wanted an inexpensive army The nineteenth century army was maintained even though French legislators allocated only small funds to it. Rarely did the standing army ever rise above 500,000 men. On the eve of the Franco-Prussian War the army totaled only 16,869 officers and 350,981 men in active service.[18]

In one major respect, however, the army fell short of the ideal held by its creators. By 1870 it was no longer a trained force ready at all times to fight upon a moment's notice. By then it was in fact maintaining a system of reservists, whose services it required in wartime. Events had shown that trained reservists were desirable. During the Crimean War the French hoped to maintain an army of 200,000 in the field but could not do so and retain enough veterans on home bases to train recruits. Some sort of reserve could have made up the difference, and Napoleon III responded by increasing the size of the "first portion" of the annual contingent and creating a reserve by furloughing men before their seven-year term of service was completed. Even these steps were insufficient. During the Italian War of 1859, the Prussians, although not directly involved, mobilized their army. The Prussians were so inefficiently organized as to be incapable of undertaking a campaign, but the French felt threatened because there were not enough men left on bases in France to counter even this meager show of force.

The result of these experiences was the decision in 1860 to give a six months training course to the "second portion" of the annual contingent, so that it too became a kind of reserve. By 1870 these practices yielded 173,507 "reservists" upon whom the army depended: 61,382 regulars and 112,125 poorly trained men of the "second portion". In July 1870 the army mobilized both of these categories at the same time and sent men of both to the front.[19]

Army organization, however, made it difficult to effect a rapid reincorporation and deployment of these troops, and this predicament was derived from what we may call the "regimental system". Throughout the nineteenth century the French army divided France into territorial or regional divisions, misnamed corps in 1859, each commanded by a general officer destined for an equivalent level of command during wartime. They were administrative units only. The largest peacetime organized, manned, trained unit in the French army was the regiment, and it was this the recruit joined upon enlistment. If the recruit became the kind of soldier officials wanted, the regiment became his home, his career, and his whole life.

Each regiment in the French army was assigned a permanent base called a depot. Here recruits were taken into the army and given their training; here too they returned as "reservists" in wartime. Frequently, however, the army stationed its infantry and cavalry regiments away from the depot, some abroad on duty in Algeria or Rome, some at other locations in metropolitan France. This situation resulted from the army's deliberate policy of moving regiments from garrison to garrison in order, so ran the theory, to divorce soldiers from civilian surroundings and prevent them from getting used to staying for long in any one location.[20] In 1870 fifty-seven of the one hundred line infantry regiments and twenty-one of the fifty-seven cavalry regiments were garrisoned apart from their depots.

This practice prevented efficient incorporation of reserves in wartime. The French army recruited its men on a national basis and allocated them according to the needs of each regiment. Men were frequently attached to regiments whose depots were located far from the men's domiciles. During mobilization, reservists had to go first to their regimental depot to obtain their uniforms, weapons, and equipment, then be transported to some other place to join the active units of the regiment. Under these circumstances it ought to have been no surprise when detachments of reservists were scattered throughout the country on their way to depots, then criss-crossed France on their way to war. One detachment, often cited in the accounts of the War of 1870, departed from Strasbourg to join the colors at the regimental depot at Bordeaux whence it was sent on to its combat battalions--in Strasbourg.[21]

Nor were the effects limited merely to this sort of confusion. Because there were few peacetime units above the regimental level, the brigades, divisions, and army corps were created on an *ad hoc* basis, existing for the first time only when they were assembled in the zones of concentration.[22] Officer corps and staffs met for the first time at the beginning of a campaign. Only then were they able to learn about and adjust to the capabilities, habits, attitudes, and shortcomings of one another. Only then too could they become acquainted with the cadres they were to lead, troops whose training they had not supervised. General officers had become unused to directing and maneuvering large units in the field. Many subordinates got their first practice in learning how to receive and interpret instructions in the field in 1870. Worse yet, with no large units to serve, men of the transport companies (*Train des Equipages Militaires*) and the commissariat (*Intendance*) completed their service in central depots under the supervision of Ministry of War. Thus, no commander of a force in the field had any opportunity during peacetime to supervise the organization and training of these services, and he had no assurance that they were ready to serve the needs of the army.

All of these practices condemned the French army to immobility in 1870. By adopting a recruitment system that created a significant number of reserves upon whom it depended, the army required an organizational system which would allow for rapid mobilization and deployment of these men. It never created one. In the first instances, then, the faults of the mobilization and concentration of the French army in 1870 lay in the very structure of the army. It would have taken an unusually competent and dedicated leadership to overcome these structural difficulties. This too the army lacked.

LEADERSHIP AND ADMINISTRATION

There was little in the training or experience of French officers in 1870 to prepare them to cope with the overwhelming difficulties confronting them at the beginning of the war. Perhaps it is even fair to say that there was little in their past even to encourage them to think about these problems. The officer's education did not stress intellectual growth or thoughtful analysis of military problems; his promotion depended little on military skills; and he never gained the experience of commanding large bodies of men. In few ways was he competent to lead the army in the conditions of 1870.

The training of officers, their experience, and the attitudes this engendered are all central to the problem. If an officer received any formal military education at all, he obtained it in the military academies at the beginning of his career. The level of teaching in these schools, however, was very low. "The reigning spirit at Saint-Cyr", wrote one well informed historian, "was that of a badly run *collège* rather than a great military school."[23]

The evidence appears to corroborate this judgment. Not until 1852 was a cadet required to have earned his *bachelier ès sciences* before admission to the Ecole Spéciale Militaire at Saint-Cyr. He learned little afterward. First year courses, wrote Captain Pech de Cadel, reviewed what students already knew, and the second year science courses consisted of the arid memorization of names and technical terms which the cadets quickly forgot. Practical lessons relating to the service they would perform in the army were so few that an officer needed to work for years "if he wanted to acquire the knowledge he had missed."[24] Alumni later recalled their vapid course of study and uninformative exercises.

Many too noted the anti-intellectual attitude of the *officiers galettes*, the smart and greatly admired social leaders among the cadets. These students disdained any study except that which strictly pertained to the military craft; they took pride in the bad grades they received.[25] Dash, luck, and good social connections, they thought, would get them promoted, and so they sneered at the able students, one of whom, as he records in his memoirs, took refuge in the infirmary where, by feigning illness, he could find a quiet place to get some work done.[26] In 1860 Minister of War Marshal Randon appointed a commission to evaluate the school. Its report gave the institution and its product low marks. Cadets showed little interest in work or study, it said; there was nothing distinguished about the knowledge, manners, sentiments, or military *esprit* of the students. "The consequences of this state of affairs menace the army in the future."[27] Yet its recommendations for reform, like those of subsequent reports of the 1860's, were ignored.

Many officers had not received even this amount of instruction.   The Saint-Cyr Law of 1818 stipulated that one-third of the commissions granted each year should be given to noncommissioned officers. By 1870 nearly three-fifths of the commissioned officers had risen from the ranks of the enlisted men. Such military education as these men received was imparted in schools maintained by regiments.   These institutions, however, were essentially primary schools designed to provide recruits with basic literacy and noncommissioned officers with a bit of history, geography, and simple accounting. The schools varied in quality, but few seem to have provided any professional training for officers, and many failed to function effectively as elementary schools. Attempts in the 1860's to improve them came to little, and most of the officers who rose from the ranks remained woefully lacking in even the rudiments of knowledge.[28] One stark fact reveals the educational deficiencies of many of these men: the Prussians discovered a high rate of illiteracy among officers whom they took prisoner in 1870.[29]

Experience did little to change this situation.   Combat experience was largely gained in North Africa, the Crimea, and Italy. In the latter two cases, victory vindicated their training; the kind of war conducted in the former was irrelevant to the strategies and tactics being developed in Europe by the 1860's. At home the training of large bodies of troops and their officers was formal and sterile. From 1857 on officers occasionally attended summer maneuvers at the Camp of Châlons where, briefly, regiments had been gathered into brigades and divisions. These exercises, however, consisted of parade ground drills, simulated siege operations, and open field maneuvers with pre-arranged results. Discussion of strategic problems was limited. In the 1857 maneuvers, for example, the marshals and generals met in Imperial Headquarters where, in the presence of Napoleon III, they heard accounts of the battles of the First Empire from Thiers' work on the Consulate and Empire. "This was", an observer lamented many years later, "the only intellectual nourishment--and how thin it was--that Napoleon III offered his future lieutenants."[30]

None of these shortcomings mattered much to French officers, because the procedure by which they obtained promotion had little to do with professional competence. Laws governing a soldier's promotion to the commissioned ranks guaranteed his rank, pay and pension, carefully spelled out his rights, and circumscribed the means by which he might be separated from the service. These measures, according to William Serman, provided stability for officers, but stability had its price. "...It encouraged (officers) into looking for sedentary or sheltered assignments; it reduced their taste for taking risks; it prompted them to set their sights on nothing more than lifelong mediocrity."[31] Advancement in the French army, noted one close observer, was chiefly a matter of luck and age.[32] By the laws passed from 1832 to 1838 the army had to make two-thirds of its promotions to the rank of major on the basis of seniority, and even above that rank seniority reserved one-half of the promotions. Generally this system meant that for most officers who remained in the system promotion was slow. In 1867 the average age of a lieutenant was thirty-seven years; of a captain, fifty-five years. Not all officers, to be sure, had to endure such long waits. In the Second Empire France went to war twice, and these campaigns gave a man the opportunity to perform brilliantly on the battlefield. They also liquidated some of his rivals and opened positions in higher ranks. The Algerian campaigns offered similar opportunities.

Even without combat experience, some officers found ways to obtain promotions. Good looks, good health, and the correct attitude counted. Independent wealth and a good marriage improved an officer's chances of promotion because his pay was insufficient to cover the incidental expenses that increased as he rose in rank.[33] So too did social connections with the court of Napoleon III. There was no French equivalent to the Prussian military cabinet to keep records on each of the officers. The emperor had to rely on the advice of his friends when the promotion lists were prepared. In these circumstances officers spent their time better by reading the *Annuaire Militaire* ("Military List"); its lists of officers' seniority gave a man a more profitable means of calculating his chances for promotion than any experience in the field or reading of a volume on military theory.

In these circumstances it is no surprise that French officers held expertise and professional improvement in contempt. "Study was in disfavor, the coffee house in favor", recalled one veteran officer; "officers who stayed home to work were suspected of (trying to) live apart from their comrades."[34] One recalls Col. Ardent du Picq's celebrated failure to elicit any meaningful response to his questionnaire on combat experience; clearly officers deemed giving any thought to the subject worthless.[35] Even relatively uncomplicated intellectual tasks were ignored by officers. Map reading was one. Geography, topography, all that, scoffed a cavalry general in 1870, "is a pile of crap (*foutaises*).... Do you want to know what topography during a campaign is? All right! It's a peasant you place between two cavalrymen; you say to him, 'My boy, you are going to take us to such and such a place and we'll give you a little glass of ratafia and a pretty coin worth one hundred *sous*. If you take the wrong road, you're looking at two guys who will blast your head open with our pistols...'"[36]

The French general staff was equally deficient in leadership capabilities. The French *état-major* was not comparable to the Prussian general staff. It consisted mainly of clerks, dispatch riders, secretaries, and a few topographical officers. Its function was to provide the French army with map-makers and administrative assistants to commanders in the field. Although the staff was selected through competitive examination, the talent thus obtained was never adequately exploited. The education of French staff officers consisted of training for routine and semi-mechanical staff duties. They spent only a brief time in active service, the only time they ever made any contact with the realities of army life. When they returned to the staff, they remained there permanently, advancing through seniority. At no time did they play a part in preparing or directing military operations. They were unfit to co-ordinate military activities in wartime and were in no way ready to supply the army the articulation it so urgently required.[37]

Nor was this leadership forthcoming from the staff of the Ministry of War. Adequately staffed to provide for the needs of the army in peacetime, the Ministry's seven principal *directions* operated independently of one another and received no overall direction from above. The last two war ministers of the Second Empire, Marshal Adolphe Niel and General Edmond Leboeuf, took considerable interest in introducing reforms into the French army; neither, however, paid attention to the regular operations of the War Office or of its activities in wartime. Lacking co-ordinated direction from above, administrators adopted practices which seriously hampered the maneuvers of the army in 1870. In the crisis of 1870 each of the bureaus, assuming its needs had priority over all others, acted independently of the others and flooded army officials with orders these men frequently had neither the time nor the competence to obey. Some departments tended to collect their equipment in central warehouses, even though, as in the case of the *Intendance*, they were informed in 1868 that it would take several months to remove the equipment.[38] And without energetic direction from above administrators not surprisingly displayed a lack of initiative, responsibility, and imagination. In 1869 Napoleon III wanted to create peacetime units above the regimental level but dropped his project after War Office officials expressed their opposition. In 1870 during the mobilization of the army many of these officials failed to issue necessary orders until they had been authorized to do so from their superiors and thus deprived the army of services when they were most vitally needed.[39]

Perhaps the most astounding fact about French military administration in 1870 was that it repeated the same errors it had committed in 1854 and 1859. In both cases the army went into battle in a state of excessive disorder. When the French landed in the Near East in April 1854, supreme commander Marshal de Saint-Arnaud noted that the artillery was unprepared, the men were short of their *biscuit* supply, and other supplies were lacking because they were shipped on sailing vessels rather than steamships.   Five years later in the Italian campaign, similar complaints were expressed, yet little was done to eradicate these problems in the future. France had, after all, won both wars, and victory vindicated one of their favorite military maxims. *"L'on se débrouillera toujours"* (We'll always muddle through) was a popular line in the French army; out of it soldiers constructed their *Système D*, the indefinable way French soldiers made up for the shortages which they had learned to expect.

THE SHORTCOMINGS OF A MILITARY REFORM MOVEMENT, 1866-1870

The French army which took up arms in 1870 was not entirely the inefficient, unprofessionally led, ill-managed force that this portrait thus far seems to depict. It was also the product of attempts to reform its structure and practices, some of which had taken hold by the outbreak of war in July 1870. It was, therefore, better prepared to confront the Prussian challenge than it had previously been. The efforts undertaken are instructive. They show what strides had been taken to transform the army into a more mobile, articulated force, and they illustrate some of the reform impulses which came from within French military society before 1870. They also underscore the limitations placed upon these efforts, for many significant reforms came to naught.

The impetus for the reform movement was provided by the stunning reversal of the balance of power in central Europe caused by the battle of Königgrätz in 1866. France expected to be an arbiter in the 1866 war; instead it was a dazzled bystander unable to influence the re-organization of Germany undertaken by Prussia. Few observant officials could fail to note the reason why: it was Prussia's overwhelming military superiority, and this was a factor French military men now had to take into account. The question was, what needed to be done?

Napoleon III thought he knew. At conferences held with important civilian and military leaders in November and December 1866, he stated that an increase in the number of trained men was imperative and set an army of one million men as an objective. Most of these, he proposed, were to be constituted as a trained reserve. The military disagreed. What counts, suggested Minister of War Marshall Randon, is the men actually serving under the colors, and he recommended either increasing the existing draft or lengthening the term of service to nine years.   To Randon's objections, the civilians added political liabilities: any change in the size of the army had to be approved by the *Corps Législatif*, and such a policy at the moment would be unpopular.[40]

Unpopular it was, but the emperor intended to have his larger army. He could easily overcome the war minister's objections. In January 1867 Napoleon asked for Randon's resignation; in his place he appointed Marshal Adolphe Niel, a professional soldier whose grasp of French military problems suited him well for the task of reorganizing the army. Niel agreed that more soldiers were required. Neither he nor the emperor, however, was able to overcome civilian objections. They never got their one million man army, and what they did obtain may in some ways have been harmful to the army's interests.

Niel had *thought* he had a good scheme to obtain more manpower in France. He would revive the *Garde Nationale* (it had been abolished in 1851) and let it serve as a reserve force for men who had completed their service and also as a body to provide a minimal amount of training for men who otherwise avoided service entirely. In this way he could preserve the small annual draft yet give all able bodied men some training. France would have, he calculated, a mobilized army of over 800,000 men with 400,000 more in the *Garde*, a total well over the emperor's ideal figure.

Overcoming civilian proposals to these objections proved to be nearly impossible. The regime, said historian Jean Casevitz, who thoroughly studied the history of Niel's proposals, could not convince the country that reform was necessary. Important segments of support from the middle classes, especially from Catholics and from industrialists, were not forthcoming because these people had been alienated by other policies of the regime. Liberals, long suspicious of the authoritarian nature of a regime whose "liberalizing" trends were both too recent and too incomplete, found the debates in the *Revue des Deux Mondes* exciting and informative. Writers in the review found that some of the reforms were required but severely criticized Niel's recruitment proposals. Particularly notable was an article by General Nicolas Changarnier, a former supporter of Napoleon III. Changarnier argued, both convincingly and with some good reason, that numerical superiority did not necessarily convey advantages to the army which held it, that reserves could be a liability as well as an asset, and that the Prussian Army's quick victory in 1866 concealed serious faults in organization and weapons. The Niel laws, he hinted, risked creating a "flabby" military system, and the solution, he suggested, lay in better generalship, tighter organization, and wiser allocation of funds. If the army needs to increase its manpower, he argued, it can do so during an emergency when volunteers and draftees will readily and willingly learn their duties.[41]

The regime failed to make any adequate response to these criticisms. Thus the political elites of the nation rejected the Niel proposal. Meanwhile, the rest of the nation, most notably the peasantry, remained hostile. To them any measure increasing military liabilities was merely raising the blood tax, and that obligation had weighed most heavily upon them. The government, wrote Casevitz, did not inform the people of its needs or the reasons for them, and furthermore, it could not do so without discrediting itself in the eyes of its firmest supporters.[42]

Thus the *Corps Législatif* would have little of the Niel proposals, and the "Niel Law" it passed in January 1868 was a defeat for both Napoleon III and Niel. In effect the Soult Law of 1832 was nearly resurrected. The system of small annual contingents and *bons* and *mauvais numéros* remained untouched; the annual contingent was still to be divided into two *portions*, the first being required to serve a full five years with an additional four in the reserve, and the second undergoing five months training before release into the reserve. "Exoneration" as provided for by the 1855 law was abolished, but conscripts still retained the means of avoiding military service. The system of hiring substitutes was restored. The practice, writes Bernard Schnapper, flourished, and a new commerce in locating substitutes quickly developed.[43]

In the 1868 law all that remained of Napoleon's and Niel's schemes was the requirement that all men who escaped service enroll in a *Garde Nationale Mobile*.   This proved to be, however, a paper force of untrained and undisciplined citizens. The law limited Garde exercises to a minimum of two weeks a year--or rather fourteen separate days, for the army was not allowed to house a single member of the *Garde* in barracks overnight. As matters turned out, budgetary restrictions and the indifference of army officers conspired to prevent enforcement of even these provisions. Only the *Garde* units of the Paris region ever received as much as paper organization, and none of these underwent training. What few efforts Niel made to organize the *Garde* were discontinued after his death in 1869; his successor, General Leboeuf, despised the institution and did not protest when the *Corps Législatif* allocated funds which were insufficient for its training and administration.[44]

Because the conscription law was a political issue as well as a military one, the failure to increase the number of trained men can be partly attributed to majority opinion in the *Corps Législatif*. There were other changes the army could undertake without legislative ratification, and both Niel and Leboeuf did take an interest in improving the combat capacity of the regular army. Although some of their measures do not bear directly on the subject of mobilization, it is fair to mention them in passing, because they illustrate the scope and commitment of the army to internal reform. The most notable of these was the adoption of the *chassepot* rifle, which was superior to the Prussian needle gun in range and accuracy. The army also adopted use of a primitive machine gun, the *mitrailleuse*, which when effectively used in 1870 earned the respect of the Prussians.   Furthermore in 1870 the army undertook the manufacture of a seven-pounder breech-loading artillery piece which, when eventually but belatedly used, showed evidence of superiority to the Krupp guns in use in the Prussian army.

None of these changes was fully satisfactory. The *chassepot* was excellent, but there were only one million of them in 1870, enough for the summer of 1870 but insufficient for the total number of men *ultimately* armed in that war. The *mitrailleuse* was developed and tested in such secret that even responsible army officials remained ignorant of its existence. In the mobilization of 1870, wherever the one hundred ninety-two available *mitrailleuses* were sent, the men trained to use them were posted elsewhere. Finally the adoption of a new gun had only recently been undertaken, and none of the new pieces were used in the decisive stages of the war. Consequently the French depended on their four pounder and twelve pounder muzzle-loading bronze guns which were obsolete by comparison with the breech-loading steel guns in use in the Prussian army.[45] They had to depend too upon an inadequate and outdated doctrine regarding the use of these guns.[46]

Mobilization too was one of Niel's concerns. In a report drafted for Napoleon III in 1868, Niel recommended both the formation of permanent brigades, divisions and corps and the appointment of an army commission to study the military use of railroads. "Recalling the insufficient preparations revealed at the beginning of the Crimean, Italian, and Mexican expeditions", the report concluded, "the commission points out the need for drawing up a series of arrangements for the *rapid assembly* of an army in the theatre of war for the conduct of operations."[47]

The report was at least in part implemented, and one of the most important results obtained concerned the recall of reservists. Prior to 1868 the French recalled reservists by a system so cumbersome as practically to prevent the reincorporation of any reservist at all. By this system, the commander of each recruitment bureau, at the outbreak of war, was to submit the names of the reservists living in the region to sub-prefects, who were to fill out recall orders and forward these to the prefect's office whence they were sorted out by commune and mailed to the mayors who were responsible for their delivery to each individual soldier. Niel abolished this practice by removing the services of the civilian administrators and postal authorities. Henceforward the recruitment bureau kept recall orders readily filled out except for the date of dispatch which was then added upon the outbreak of war; the local *gendarmerie* then delivered the papers to the reservist.

This was, like so many of these measures, a partial reform. The change, one contemporary military expert observed, saved the army six to eight days. But Niel did not follow through: army officials made no arrangements to transport reservists from their domiciles to their depots nor did they abolish the practice of garrisoning regiments apart from the depots. The reincorporation of reservists, as we shall see, remained a time-consuming process.[48]

There was a similar attempt to improve the combat readiness of the artillery, and the results were similar. In the 1859 Italian campaign the artillery had arrived slowly because all of the guns had to be mounted on their carriages after war was declared. In spite of this, no change was made until 1867 when Niel ordered the preparation of all artillery, field and fortress, for quick mobilization. In 1868 he could report that ninety batteries had been mounted and distributed among the principal arsenals of France, that fifty-eight more could be ready on two week's notice, and that each artillery garrison possessed enough harnessing equipment to serve its needs during mobilization. Events proved him wrong on this last item, however, and the task of preparing fortress artillery, whose diverse guns, carriages, and shells did not necessarily fit one another, was not completed by 1870. The field artillery, furthermore, was mobilized more slowly than expected in 1870, and few army corps possessed their full complement of artillery when the first battles were fought.[49]

Partial as each of these changes were, they do represent a return on efforts made. There were three others which yielded no results. Each of these efforts touched upon a matter vitally important to the rapid deployment of a mobile, articulate field army; to each of these some thought was given; and in the end no significant changes were made. It is worthwhile to detail each, for together they illustrate both how comprehensive were the attempts to improve practices in the French army and how limited the results ultimately proved to be.

The first of these concerned the military transport services (*Train des Equipages Militaires*). As has been noted the army stored this equipment in a central warehouse in the Paris suburb of Vernon. Workers needed several weeks to remove all of it. Realizing the vital importance of the transport services to a field army, Napoleon III in 1867 requested Niel to prepare the wagons for immediate use during a campaign. Niel responded with proposals to distribute the transport equipment among eight bases and with the emperor's approval ordered the change to be made. Neither, however, followed the matter through, and in 1870 most of this equipment still lay in Vernon.[50]

Napoleon III was also disturbed, he later said, by the nagging problem of peacetime organization of the army. He had long hoped, he said, to create units above the regimental level but had always encountered opposition from officials in the Ministry of War. In 1867 he called on the services of the imperial *aide-de-camp* General Barthélemy Lebrun to prepare a study of the resources of the French army and to estimate the number of army corps France could put into the field. The study, completed in 1868, indicated that France could deploy eleven corps, a force of 435,657 men, and still leave 54,000 troops behind for service in Algeria. Eight of these corps he allotted to three field armies, leaving the remaining three behind for garrison duty within France.[51] On the basis of this report Niel's assistants patched regiments together into paper brigades, divisions, and army corps. Never once, however, did they try to translate these sketches into real permanent units complete with infantry, cavalry, artillery, engineer corps, *Intendance* officials, and transport services; nor did they think about the commands and staffs to lead these units. In 1870 as in 1859, in spite of Napoleon III's fretting and Lebrun's work, all these had to be assembled in confusion in the zone of concentration.

Of all measures considered by the army but put aside, perhaps none was more important than the establishment of a civil-military railroad commission. In 1869, upon the advice of the director of the *dépôt de guerre*, General Louis Jarras, Niel appointed a special central railroad commission composed of three generals, two engineers from the Ministry of Public Works, and the directors of the major railroad companies. He charged them to consider several significant matters: the size of troop transport trains, their speed, the amount of daily traffic a line could bear, the time required to load and unload supply trains, and the revision of the seemingly obsolete 1855 military railroad regulations. He also called for the establishment of subcommissions, one for each major railroad line and consisting of both staff and engineer corps officers and representatives of the railroad companies. Their charge in peacetime was to survey the equipment maintained by each line and keep the list up to date and in wartime to implement such troop transport regulations as were to be adopted by the central commission.[52]

Little came of all these efforts, however. The central commission drafted an interim report, but it labored in vain. Niel died shortly after the commission began its deliberations, and Leboeuf, his successor, showed no interest in its work. He adopted none of its proposals and after January 1870 ceased to call upon its services. Thus, at a time when the Prussians, as shall be noted, were improving their arrangements for military use of railroads, the French lost their opportunity to co-ordinate the direction of railroads during wartime.[53]

A note of 15 July 1870 in the *registres* of the Paris-Lyon-Méditerranée Railroad Company underscores the dimensions of the problem. Called upon to provide professional engineers and laborers to the Ministry of War, the *Directeur de l'Exploitation* pointed out that the PLM alone had served the army with its equipment and personnel in the 1859 war and that no measures had been taken by military authorities since to organize wartime military railroad services in the event of another war. Now the burden would be upon the Compagnie de l'Est although it could rely upon the assistance of the PLM.[54] His gesture was generous, but the reader is left to infer the obvious. A thoroughly inexperienced Compagnie de l'Est was going to have to organize military transports without any meaningful direction from the Ministry of War and probably not much advice from the PLM either.

* * * * *

In spite of the efforts of military reformers after 1866, the French army of 1870 remained essentially the armed force which had emerged in the two decades after 1815. It was still manned by long-service soldiers detached from the nation they served and commanded by an officer corps whose *élan* hardly compensated for its general ignorance of the changes in warfare and its inability to prepare for a campaign or assemble widely-scattered units into a cohesive fighting force. The administration, adequate to maintain the army during peacetime, prevented rapid mobilization and concentration during wartime. The reforms undertaken were far too partial and limited. The adoption of the *chassepot* yielded significant results, but the adoption of the *mitrailleuse* was far less impressive. The only significant change in recruitment policy was the *Garde Mobile*, and this proved to be an untrained paper force of no military value to France in 1870. The efforts the army made to effect a more rapid assembly of forces against the enemy were incomplete. A more efficient system of recalling reservists and the preparation of the artillery for a campaign were worthy efforts. But when administrators dropped their attempt to put their transport equipment in a state of readiness and ignored the work of the civil-military railroad commission, they condemned themselves to committing the same mistakes which had plagued them in 1854 and 1859.

Still there was a feeling of accomplishment among French leaders in 1870, and Leboeuf's claim of readiness "down to the last gaiter button" was not all empty rhetorical flourish. The four years that separated Königgrätz from the Ems Dispatch had not been entirely wasted; they were years of hard work. Given six weeks, the French army might well have been mobilized, a far better record than their dismal performance in Northern Italy in 1859. The problem was whether or not it was thereby prepared to respond to the specific challenges confronting it in 1870. One challenge was a reform of military institutions in Prussia which had begun six years before the French reforms and had resulted in Königgrätz. A second was the need to reach a clear definition of the objectives for which the French army was to be used in 1870. A third was the threats and opportunities offered by the ways the Prussians mobilized and concentrated their army for the War of 1870. France's fate lay in the way its army had met these challenges.

NOTES

1. This chapter was largely written before the publication of Richard Holmes, *The Road to Sedan: The French Army 1866-70* (London: Royal Historical Society, 1984). This excellent volume extensively analyzes the structure and doctrine of the French army on the eve of the Franco-Prussian War.

2. Michael Howard, *The Franco-Prussian War* (London: Rupert Hart-Davis, 1961), p. 23.

3. Ibid., p. 13. These arguments are also summarized in Richard Challener, *The French Theory of the Nation in Arms, 1866-1939* (New York: Columbia University Press, 1952), pp. 14-16

and Pierre de la Gorce, 7 vols., *Histoire du Second Empire* (Paris: Plon, 1899-1905), V, pp. 321-324.

4. Douglas Porch, *Army and Revolution: France 1815-1848* (London: Routledge and Kegan Paul, 1974), pp. 13-14 and 66-69.

5. The text of the bill is printed in *Archives parlementaires de 1787 à 1869: recueil complet des débats législatifs et politiques des chambres français imprimé par ordre du Sénat et de la Chambre des Députés*, Series II, 106 vols. (Paris: Librairie Administrative Paul Dupont, 1862-1902), XX, pp. 220-224. Texts of the debates on this subject follow in vols. XX and XXI. The debates and terms of the Saint-Cyr Law are summarized in Bernard Schnapper, *Le Remplacement militaire en France; quelques aspects politiques, économiques et sociaux du recrutement au XIXe siècle* (Paris: S.E.V.P.E.N., 1968), pp. 34-41.

6. For discussions of recruitment policies and practices see Challener, *The French Theory of the Nation in Arms*, p. 13; Joseph Monteilhet, *Les Institutions militaires de la France, 1814-1924* (Paris: Alcan, 1932), Chaps. I and II; Arpad Kovacs, "French Military Institutions before the Franco-Prussian War", *American Historical Review*, LI (January, 1946), pp. 222-223; Barthélemy Edmond Palat, *Histoire de la guerre de 1870-1871*, Part I: *La Guerre de 1870*, 6 vols. (Paris: Berger-Levrault, 1903-1908), I, pp. 153-167; and Jean Casevitz, *Une Loi manquée: la loi Niel, 1866-1868; l'armée française à la veille de la guerre de 1870* (Paris: Cardot, 1960), pp. 1-5.

7. Schnapper, *Le Remplacement militaire en France*, pp. 55-57.

8. Ibid., pp. 74-77.

9. Louis Jules Trochu, *L'Armée française en 1867* (Paris: Amyot, 1868), p. 59. See also Schnapper, *Le Remplacement militaire en France*, pp. 231-243.

10. "Registre," 1869, Compagnie de l'Est, AN, Paris, 13 AQ 129, p. 23.

11. Schnapper, *Le Remplacement militaire en France*, pp. 207-208 and 218-224.

12. Ibid., p. 220. See also La Gorce, *Histoire du Second Empire*, V, p. 320; Monteilhet, *Les Institutions militaires de la France*, pp. 20-27, 33.

13. Trochu, *L'Armée française en 1867*, pp. 12-13.

14. Monteilhet, *Les Institutions militaires de la France*, p. 60.

15. See in particular the discussion of the intent, terms, and effects of the Soult Law of 1832 in Porch, *Army and Revolution*, pp. 62-67.

16. The army as a whole was not involved in the coup of 1851 even though a few officers were. For a lively and controversial discussion of the politics of the army--or lack thereof--see Raoul Girardet, *La Société militaire dans la France contemporaine* (Paris: Plon, 1953), especially p. 144 for the 1851 period.

17. See especially Porch, *Army and Revolution*. pp. 79-127 passim. William Serman in *Les Officiers français dans la nation (1815-1914)*, (Paris: Aubier Montaigne, 1982) discusses the political attitudes of officers on pp. 65-84.

18. These figures are based on my collations of tables in Aristide Martinien, *La Guerre de 1870-71. La Mobilisation de l'armée: mouvements des dépôts (armée active) du 15 juillet au 1er mars, 1871* (Paris: L. Fournier, 1912). For a discussion of military budgets see Howard, *The Franco-Prussian War*, p. 14 and Palat, *Histoire*, Part I: *La Guerre de 1870*, I, p. 168.

19. The effect of the Crimean campaign is discussed by Le comte de La Chapelle, *Les Forces militaires de la France en 1870* (Paris: Amyot, 1872), p. 3 and Napoléon III, *Oeuvres posthumes et autographes inédits de Napoléon III en exil*, ed. by le comte de La Chapelle (Paris: Lachaud, 1873), p. 121. Monteilhet, *Les Institutions militaires de la France*, p. 38 shows how Prussian mobilization in 1859 affected the Italian campaign, and in Palat, *Histoire*, Part I: *La Guerre de 1870*, II, p. 130 the reader can find the number of reserves reportedly available to the French army in 1870.

20. Girardet, *La Société militaire dans la France contemporaine*, p. 89.

21. Recruitment of men and assignment of membership in a regiment on a national basis reflected more than just numerical needs of each regiment. They also corresponded to the way

Frenchmen read their own history and interpreted what they thought was the unique French *race*. A regiment was an *amalgame* of men from throughout France, and the *amalgame* was at the root of French military superiority in 1793 and 1794. Furthermore the French "type," so ran the theory, derived its peculiar qualities from the variety of peoples who made up the nation. The *amalgame* was, therefore, not just merely a convenient grouping of men; it was a way of expressing and exploiting the finest qualities of a diverse yet mystically united French race. See these ideas expressed and thus the regimental system defended in A. Laugel, "Les Institutions militaires de la France: Louvois, Carnot, Saint-Cyr," *Revue des Deux Mondes*, LXVIII, livre 1 (March 1, 1867), pp. 5-52. See also Joseph Revol, *Histoire de l'armée française*, (Paris: Larousse, 1929), p. 174.

22. There were two exceptions in 1870. The Imperial Guard, an elite force, was the size of an army corps. The 2nd Corps of the Army of the Rhine was made up of infantry and cavalry units assigned to summer maneuvers at the Camp of Châlons when war broke out. It had, however, no artillery, engineer, or transport units. Palat, *Histoire*, Part I: *La Guerre de 1870*, II, p. 62.

23. Ibid., II, p. 91.

24. Captain F. Pech de Cadel, *Histoire de l'école spéciale militaire de Saint-Cyr par un ancien Saint-Cyrien*, 2nd ed. (Paris: Delagrave, 1893), p. 140.

25. See especially A. Teller, *Esquisses de la vie militaire en France. Souvenirs de Saint-Cyr*, 2 vols. (Paris: Henri Charles Lavauzelle, 1886), I, pp. 39, 181 and Eugene Titeux, *Saint-Cyr et l'Ecole spéciale militaire en France* (Paris: Firmin-Didot, 1898), p. 407.

26. Teller, *Esquisses de la vie militaire en France*, I, pp. 109-111.

27. Titeux, *Saint-Cyr*, pp. 408-410 and General R. Desmazes, *Saint-Cyr, son histoire, ses gloires, ses leçons* (Paris: La Saint-Cyrienne, 1948), p. 115.

28. Holmes, *Road to Sedan*, pp. 180, 190-191.

29. See Girardet, *La Société militaire dans la France contemporaine*, pp. 57, 60-61; Howard, *The Franco-Prussian War*, p. 16; and Eugène Carrias, *La Pensée militaire française* (Paris: Presses Universitaires de France, 1960), pp. 232-235, 251. Crown Prince Frederick was far more kind; he noted an illiteracy problem only in the case of one Zouave officer: Friedrich III, German Emperor, *Diaries of the Emperor Frederick during the Campaign of 1866 and 1870-71*, (London: Chapman and Hall, 1902), p. 204.

30. Henri Bonnal, *La Manoeuvre de Saint-Privat, 18 juillet - 18 aout, 1870*, 2 vols. (Paris: Chapelot, 1904), I, p. 7. A brief account of summer maneuvers at the Camp of Châlons may be found in Holmes, *Road to Sedan*, pp. 195-196.

31. Serman, *Les Officiers français dans la nation*, pp. 12-13.

32. Trochu, *L'Armée française en 1867*, p. 125.

33. Serman, *Les Officiers français dans la nation*, pp. 165-171, 203-226 discusses both an officer's marriage prospects and his expenses. Personal wealth and a good marriage often went together. "The better his chances of promotion, the better his chances of getting married," writes Serman on p. 166. One's chances of promotion were best if he came from the families of the *grands notables* of France, and they were still reasonably good if he were born into a high-ranking military or a middle class family. See Ibid., pp. 17-18.

34. Quoted in Revol, *Histoire de l'armée française*, p. 172. See also Serman, *Les Officiers français dans la nation*, pp. 214-215.

35. Stefan F. Possony and Etienne Mantoux, "Du Picq and Foch: the French School," *Makers of Modern Strategy*, Edward M. Earle, ed. (Princeton: Princeton University Press, 1943), p. 209.

36. Quoted in Girardet, *La Société militaire dans la France contemporaine*, p. 110.

37. For a discussion of this see Dallas D. Irvine, "The French and Prussian Staff Systems before 1870," *Journal of the American Military History Foundation*, II, No. 4 (Winter, 1938), pp. 200-201. See also William Serman, *Les Origines des officiers français, 1848-1870* (Paris: Publications de la Sorbonne, 1979), pp. 19-20.

38. Napoleon III, *Oeuvres posthumes*, p. 190.

39. A table of organization in the French War Office is printed in France, Armée, Etat-major, Service historique, *La Défense nationale en province* in *La Guerre de 1870-71*, 35 vols. (Paris: Chapelot, 1901-1903). See also Napoleon III, *Oeuvres posthumes*, p. 190 and Le comte de La Chapelle, *Les Forces militaires de la France en 1870*, p. 59.

40. These points of view are summarized in Casevitz, *Une Loi manquée: la loi Niel*, pp. 15-29; Germain Bapst, ed., *Le Maréchal Canrobert: Souvenirs d'un siècle*, 6 vols. (Paris: Plon, 1898-1913), IV, pp. 57-66; and Emile Ollivier, *L'Empire libéral: études, récits, souvenirs*, 18 vols. (Paris: Garnier, 1895-1918), X, pp. 314-381.

41. Nicholas Changarnier, "Un mot sur le projet de réorganisation militaire," *Revue des Deux Mondes*, LXVIII, livre 4, (15 April, 1867), pp. 874-890. See also André Cochut, "Le problème de l'armée, réorganisation de la force militaire en France," Ibid., LXVII, livre 3, (1 February, 1867), pp. 645-677.

42. Casevitz, *Une Loi manquée: la loi Niel*, pp. 134-135.

43. Schnapper, *Le Remplacement militaire en France*, pp. 260-261.

44. Casevitz, *Une Loi manquée: la loi Niel*, pp. 43-68 for debates on the project and pp. 120-122 for its provisions; Challener, *The French Theory of the Nation in Arms*, p. 13; Revol, *Histoire de l'armée française*, p. 188; and Col. E. R. Rocolle, "Anatomie d'une mobilisation," *Revue Historique des Armées*, No. 2, 1979, p. 39; Montheilet, *Les Institutions militaires de la France*, p. 94.

45. For a discussion of weapons adoptions in the French army before 1870 see Bapst, *Le Maréchal Canrobert: Souvenirs d'un siècle*, IV, pp. 48-49, 73-74; Palat, *Histoire*, Part I: *La Guerre de 1870*, II, pp. 116-117; Victor Dérrécagaix, *La Guerre moderne*, 2 vols. (Paris: L. Baudoin, 1885), I, p. 400; and France, Assemblée Nationale, *Enquête parlementaire sur les actes du Gouvernement de la Défense Nationale: dépositions des témoins*, 5 vols. (Paris: Germer-Baillière, 1872-1875), I, p. 45.

46. Holmes, *Road to Sedan*, pp. 229-231.

47. Bapst, *Le Maréchal Canrobert, souvenirs d'un siècle*, IV, pp. 62-63.

48. Dérrécagaix, *La Guerre moderne*, I, p. 400.

49. Charles Antoine Thoumas, *Souvenirs de la guerre, 1870-1871* (Paris: Librairie Illustrée, n.d.), pp. 4-5; Napoleon III, *Oeuvres posthumes*, pp. 185-187.

50. Ibid., pp. 191-192, 208; Le comte de La Chapelle, *Les Forces militaires de la France en 1870*, pp. 71-73, 90.

51. The report is seriously flawed. Surely he overestimated the size of the army, and for some reason he overlooked the two infantry regiments, one cavalry regiment, and supporting artillery stationed in Rome. The report is reproduced in Napoleon III, *Oeuvres posthumes*, pp. 148-157. See also Ibid., p. 178; Le comte de La Chapelle, *Les Forces militaires de la France en 1870*, p. 59; and Palat, *Histoire*, Part I: *La Guerre de 1870*, II, p. 73.

52. AN, Paris, 48 AQ 3328, folder 4.

53. On railroads see François Jacqmin, *Les Chemins de fer français pendant la guerre de 1870-1871* (Paris: Hachette, 1872), pp. 32-48 and Louis Jarras, *Souvenirs du Général Jarras* (Paris: Plon, 1893), pp. 18-19.

54. "Registre: Procès-verbaux du Conseil d'administration," Compagnie du Chemin de fer de Paris à Lyon et à la Méditerranée, AN, Paris, 77 AQ 183, p. 183.

3

The Challenge

In spite of its shortcomings, the French army of 1870 appeared to some contemporary observers to be a splendid, well-armed, well-trained force, perhaps the finest France had ever assembled. Events proved the observers wrong, but their confidence was not entirely misplaced. Many of the officers were the equal of their Prussian counterparts. As has been noted, most of the troops were seasoned veterans carrying an excellent rifle. The problem was that the army was not prepared to respond to the specific challenges confronting it that July.

There were three. One was the Prussian army which had undergone significant changes during the past decade and had already passed two tests of its mettle. The French ignored these reforms at its peril. Another was derived from the serious errors which even this improved Prussian army committed in the 1870 campaign. They presented the French with splendid opportunities they needed to exploit. But to do so was a third challenge. The French required a clearly defined objective and a well-drafted plan of military action against Prussia. They had neither. In the end the French army's inability to respond to these challenges condemned it to frustrating, purposeless, and destructive maneuvers.

PRUSSIAN MILITARY REFORMS, 1860-1870

In 1859 observers thought that the Prussian army was dangerously weak. When it was mobilized during the Franco-Austrian War of that year, the number of trained regulars was very small; the *Landwehr* battalions, according to a British observer were unfit to take the field; and the supply services were in disarray. The Prussian ruler, Regent (later King) William I, himself a professional soldier, deemed this situation intolerable. He sought to create an efficient armed force, and he found two able assistants to second his efforts. Albrecht von Roon, whom he appointed Minister of War in 1859, provided him with the blueprints for reform and proved to be a competent administrator. Helmuth von Moltke, chief of the Prussian General Staff, transformed that institution into the corps of expert planners and military advisors who prepared and executed the Prussian victories in 1864, 1866, and 1870. By drawing lessons from their own mistakes and the activities of other belligerents at the time, they were able to turn the Prussian army into the strongest military force in Europe.[1]

The keystone of the reforms was embodied in a proposal of Roon to William as early as 1858. He recommended expanding the size of the regular army by the imposition of seven years of military service upon all men beginning at the age of twenty. Part of this service was to be filled by a term in the regular reserve. Since this reform involved increased army control over the militia or *Landwehr*, a political crisis ensued. To the liberals who dominated the Prussian Landtag the *Landwehr* was a citizens' army led by local notables and manned by all the able-bodied citizens of Prussia not enrolled in the army. The regular army by contrast was regarded as the symbol of royal authority and political reaction.

A deadlock occurred when neither the king, who insisted on having his reform without modification, nor the Landtag, which refused the funds necessary to implement it, compromised. It was broken by the appointment in December 1862 of Otto von Bismarck as William's principal minister. Bismarck's contempt for parliamentary institutions and his skill in maneuvering among political groupings resulted by 1867 in wearing down the opposition of the liberals. By then Bismarck had illegally collected the unappropriated funds and used them to effect reforms in the army. The army in turn fought the two successful campaigns which brought all of Germany north of the Main into a single state, the North German Confederation. To many German nationalists, the moment of national unity seemed close at hand. Since many of the liberals were firmly committed to the ideal of national unity, they were willing to compromise on constitutional issues. In 1867 they helped to pass the so-called "indemnity bill" which sanctioned Bismarck's actions. In the same year they also helped pass the law which was the basis of the Prussian system of recruitment.

The 9 November 1867 Law gave Prussia the most formidable army in Europe. It provided that male citizens with few exceptions were to be drafted into the army at the age of twenty. After three years of training, these men were to be released into the regular reserve for four years during which time they could be recalled to active duty in an emergency. Thereafter they were to pass into the *Landwehr* for five additional years, during the first year of which they were still liable for active duty. Since similar recruitment laws were enacted by the three remaining independent south German states, Germany possessed a powerful military force. The North German Confederation alone had 982,064 men available for service in 1870, and with the aid of the South German states it could confront France with 1,183,389 trained men--one of the largest armed hordes Europe had ever known.[2]

All this manpower was given organization and cohesiveness by being incorporated into the existing Prussian military system. In 1867 the North German Confederation was divided territorially into twelve districts called "corps". Each corps was of sufficient population to raise a field army corps of two infantry divisions, a Jäger battalion, a regiment of field artillery, and various supporting units. Each corps enjoyed considerable autonomy: it raised, trained, and maintained troops locally and was responsible for their mobilization. The peacetime corps was the basis of the wartime corps; its command responsibilities and staff organization already existed; its units were stationed permanently at the same base; its reservists generally resided in the vicinity. When war broke out, the ranks of the army could be filled within two weeks.[3]

The responsibility of articulating this huge force and giving it greater mobility in the field was assigned to the Prussian General Staff. In 1870 it was unique among European armies for the rigor of its training, the advanced level of its technical skill, and its high *esprit de corps*. For several decades staff candidates had undergone a program which rotated formal study of staff functions with service in the ranks, thus imparting a sense of the day-to-day "friction" of army life to these officers. In the 1860's the staff came to reflect the attitudes of its chief, Helmuth von Moltke, who transformed it into an independent institution responsible for the planning and general direction of military operations. Although he was no innovator--he did not found the staff, create its functions, or establish its training routine--he made two significant contributions to it. By selecting candidates only from the leading graduates of the *Kriegsakademie* and by promoting only a portion of these to the most advanced levels of the training program, he developed the staff into a corps noted for its high level of intelligence and its superior skill. By rendering expert advice to commanders in the field in 1864 and masterfully organizing the concentration against the Austrians in 1866, the general staff rarely had its command role questioned afterward. Through Moltke's influence, the Prussian General Staff later became the object of deserved, if often far too uncritical, admiration of military experts throughout Europe and the United States.[4]

This exalted status, Moltke knew, imposed grave responsibilities upon the staff. In peacetime these included the drafting of mobilization schedules and railroad timetables, and making decisions about where most advantageously to concentrate Prussia's armies in wartime.   The General Staff collected information about the military potential of its neighbors, carefully drafted detailed maps, and kept abreast of developments in international politics.

Little illustrates better the work Moltke put his staff to doing than their study of the military use of railroads. Under his direction they closely observed

French use of railroads in the 1859 war and their own in 1859, 1864, and 1866. They also noted the role of railroads in the American Civil War. It was this conflict in particular which illustrated how well-organized utilization of railroads permitted a state rapid concentration and regular maintenance of its armies over vast distances. The Prussian officer who observed the Civil War grasped this point, and the general staff paid close attention to his report. From these sources they derived valuable lessons which they applied to their own military transports in 1866 and again in 1870.[5]

The kind of detailed study and meticulous planning which Moltke trained his staff to do first bore fruit in the campaign of 1866 against Austria. A salient feature of the Battle of Königgrätz was the timely concentration of three Prussian field armies on the battlefield as the combat was in progress, and the result was an overwhelming Prussian victory and a quick and favorable conclusion to the war. It can be argued that this outcome was made possible by the mobilization proceedures and railroad timetables prepared in advance by the General staff. At the time such did not appear to be the case. Prussian mobilization had begun on 3 May, nearly six weeks before the declaration of war and nine before the battle. Thus it looked as if Prussia had been allowed a seemingly leisurely time to mobilize, transport, and concentrate their forces for what proved to be the decisive event.

Moltke clearly thought differently. He was keenly aware of the mobilization and its place in the war. The official Prussian General Staff history of the 1866 campaign, written under his direction, pointed out, perhaps for the first time, the place of mobilization in warfare. The message conveyed was drawn from the experiences of that war. Mobilization, the text asserted, is a disruptive process which interferes with both civil and military affairs and intrudes upon the lives of all citizens of the state. Because it is scheduled in advance authorities ought not to alter plans with partial or successive mobilizations, for these would require "special regulations, which must differ from those already laid down." Nor ought mobilization to be halted once it is undertaken. "Of old," says the text

> it was possible to prepare the Prussian Army for war without actually calling it into action. This can hardly ever now be the case. In 1866, certainly, everyone was convinced that if the Army in its entirety was once called out it could not be dismissed without a struggle. The mobilization of the Army was then in fact war, and for that very reason every possible delay was made in speaking the decisive word, for even in May the hope that hostilities might still with honour be avoided had not entirely been abandoned.[6]

The crisis which provoked the 1866 war grew out of disagreements between Prussia and Austria regarding the administration and disposition of two German states, Schleswig and Holstein, which the two had wrested from Denmark in

1864. While the details of that dispute lie beyond the scope of this study, some points of the chronology are relevant.   The arrangements made by the two powers for the temporary administration of the conquered territory began to fall apart in January 1866. Prussia in particular charged Austria with violating the terms of the agreements, and when in February 1866 the Austrians failed to respond satisfactorily to Prussian allegations, the Prussian cabinet for the first time discussed military measures they should take if the two broke relations. The Austrians, however, were the first to begin arming.   In early March they reinforced their garrisons in Galicia and Bohemia and continued to do so thereafter.   General mobilization orders were issued in Vienna on 21 April. Prussia, on the other hand, did not take a clear measure of mobilization until May, and their declaration of war upon Austria and its allies was not delivered until the middle of June.

For Moltke the delay between the onset of Austrian preparations and the beginning of Prussian mobilization was a cause of serious concern. Even though the Austrians had not planned their mobilization and required several weeks to prepare for a campaign, their reinforcements in Galicia and Bohemia were menacing. Not merely did they threaten both Silesia and Brandenburg, they also upset Moltke's mobilization projects. Since 1860 he had been planning measures to take in case of a war against Austria. The ones he drew up in the winter of 1865-1866 show that he had been calculating the times required of Austrian as well as Prussian mobilization.   He had also been considering the effect an alliance of Austria and the small German states could have exerted upon Prussian strategy. Having taken these factors into account he was quite precise about the timing of mobilization:

> If we are to succeed (in our projects), we must not mobilize
> before we declare war, but the first day of mobilization must
> be the day on which war is declared; moreover as soon as any
> one of our neighbors begins to arm we must at once mobilize
> and declare war in order to secure the initiative.[7]

He did not have his way. The Austrians were taking up arms, but Prussian King William I was unwilling to respond in kind. For two months Moltke fretted, and he took every opportunity he could to impress upon his superiors the need to match Austrian measures. Sent to Italy in early March 1866, he reported that Italy could not deploy troops against Austria until four weeks after Prussia decided to go to war. "This," he added, "is the weak point of the whole business..."[8] His point was that if Prussia wished to seize the advantages Italian participation would provide, the Prussian government ought to take military measures as soon as possible. What he merely implied in that note he made explicit in later weeks. On 28 March he recommended immediate mobilization of the entire army as soon as Prussia received news that the Austrians were buying up horses in large numbers and dispatching reservists to Italy. Convinced the Austrians were fully arming, he informed War Minister von Roon that the Austrians would hold a numerical advantage in mobilized troops over the Prussian army for two-and-a-half weeks if both began their general mobilization on the same day.   Only thereafter would Prussian numbers predominate. In a memorandum of 2 April, he analyzed the relative strengths of the Austrian and Bavarian armies. He believed the railroad network available to the Prussians permitted them to counter the threat posed by an alliance of these two, but he added a condition: "...we shall have the advantage of the initiative, provided we mobilize our army at once." He repeated this conclusion three days later in a memorandum to Roon.[9]

When Prussia began the mobilization of its army on 3 May 1866, the cabinet may well have been influenced by a note from Moltke to Roon the day before. "No longer possible to doubt that the mobilization of the Austrian army which has been gradually begun and carried on will shortly be complete," he wrote on that occasion.[10] Even then William I, still reluctant to take up arms against Austria, did not order full mobilization. On 3 May mobilization orders went out only to the cavalry and artillery of the III, IV, V, and VI Prussian Corps; two days later the rest of these units and all of the VIII Corps were issued mobilization orders. Thereafter mobilization took place in batches; it required orders on 8, 10, and 12 May 1866 before the entire army was mobilized. Thus Moltke did not get the general mobilization he so persistently urged. Instead he had to direct the complicated and difficult "partial or successive mobilization" he had hoped to avoid.[11]

By comparison with the mobilization of the Prussian army in 1870, the mobilization of 1866 appears to have been slow. It for some units like the 51st Line Infantry Regiment (IV Corps), the process of calling back and incorporating reserves and forming combat battalions and depot cadres took nine days, others usually required two weeks. This was true even though reservists generally resided in the same district as their regiment. Why this was so is not clear, but the official history does admit that the transportation of reservists was "more spasmodic than maturely planned." Likewise, as the same source notes, railroad companies required eight to ten days to convert from peacetime to wartime operations and thus were unready to transport reservists to their regiments upon a moment's notice.[12] Whenever reservists had to be called in from everywhere in the kingdom, as was the case of the Prussian Guard, the process consumed nearly three weeks.[13] But if the mobilization took time, it was far more efficient than the Austrian. There was nothing notably disorderly or confused about the recall of active reserves or of members of the Landwehr. Similarly the mobilization of supplies and support services took place without problems.[14]

The subsequent concentration of the army was determined by the political situation and by the location of Prussian railroads.   The Prussian military believed it could station small concentrations of troops to cover its Rhenish provinces; the small states in the west and south posed no significant military threat in that region.   The principal enemy was Austria, and Prussia had to eliminate its military strength in order to prevail in the conflict.   The position of Saxony complicated the strategic picture.   It lay between Bohemia and Prussia, and its government for a time remained neutral.   Thus, while the Austrians could threaten Prussian Silesia from Moravia, Saxony blocked the Prussian army's route into Bohemia and served as a dangerous salient from which an enemy could menace Berlin.   Furthermore important railroad lines ran through Dresden, the Saxon capital.   Prussia eventually found a pretext to declare war on Saxony, but until the Prussian Elbe Army entered its territory on 16 June, its roads and railroads were denied to the Prussians.

Moltke effectively employed existing Prussian lines safe in their own hands to counter these threats.   Whereas the Austrians possessed only one line to effect their concentration, the Prussians had five.   These lines permitted him to deploy three field armies, but the widespread location of the lines caused these armies to be dangerously dispersed when the troops disembarked.   The initial concentrations left these armies so far distant from one another that essentially they covered an arc roughly two hundred seventy miles long from the upper Elbe River in the west to Silesia in the east.

The transportation by rail of these three armies began on 16 May and was completed three weeks later on 5 June.   Although the concentration of the army was begun, like France's in 1870, while the entire mobilization was still taking place, there were significant differences.   The units first transported to the frontiers were the ones first mobilized.   More importantly railroad transportation caused no confusion.   Prior to the war the army had established commissions to co-ordinate and define the duties and responsibilities of both military and railroad officials.   An executive commission in Berlin managed the overall effort; it consisted of a general staff officer and an official of the Ministry of Trade. Each corps too had its own joint commission, each too consisting of both military and civilian officials.   These were responsible for arranging the concentration of their respective formations in accordance with directives from Berlin.

The transportation of a Corps from its base to its destination consumed from nine to twelve days.   In three weeks the five Prussian lines carried 197,000 men, 55,000 horses, and 5,300 wagons to the disembarkation points along the Austrian-Saxon frontiers.   Because other troops reached the zones of concentration on foot, the total number of troops available for the campaign numbered 280,000.   Subsequent movements were accomplished by marches.   At first these involved sidestepping designed to reduce the distance between the three armies facing Austria.   Not until 22 June did they begin the advance into

Bohemia, but this movement culminated with the decisive concentration of the First, Second and Elbe Armies on the battlefield at Königgrätz.[15]

In terms of logistics the concentration of the Prussian army in 1866 accomplished far less impressive results. Once soldiers detrained and moved beyond the railheads they were gradually cut loose from logistical support. Of the trains that deployed the three field armies opposite Austria and Saxony not one was a supply train. These were dispatched subsequently, but because there were few officials and no overall direction to organize the unloading and distribution of supplies, some 17,920 tons of goods lay in freight cars blocking the lines at the railheads. Nor were the military transport services prepared to forge a link between the rail depots and troops as they advanced in the field. Crowded off roads by combat troops, unsupervised by the military police, their columns bloated with unauthorized vehicles, the military trains lost contact with their troops on 29 June. They did not catch up with them until after the Battle of Königgrätz. For the Prussians the logistical predicament was serious, but the victory on 3 July rescued the army from suffering the consequences. The war ended soon afterward.[16]

Königgrätz was a stunning military reversal. Before the engagement experts thought the two forces were no better than evenly matched, but the result was an overwhelming Prussian victory. A key factor leading to that result was the organization of the Prussian mobilization. It permitted the Prussians to overcome the advance in preparations they had yielded to the Austrians. But the mobilization was far less dazzling than the skillful use of five railroad lines for the deployment of three field armies. Furthermore because these two processes had taken nearly six weeks, this fact, more than the careful, painstaking work which managed the mobilization and concentration of 1866, impressed outside observers. The misconception had its uses: after the 1866 war the Prussian General Staff learned how to accelerate mobilization, but French and Austrian observers did not think the Prussians could do so. What impressed them was not how quickly Prussians had raised and deployed their forces, but how slowly, and they anticipated similar results in the next campaign. To be sure dispatches from French military attaché Baron Eugène Stoffel warned that the Prussians were learning from their experiences of 1866 and were likely to improve upon that record.[17] His view did not prevail, however, and French and Austrian experts preferred to measure Prussian mobilization capabilities by what they had accomplished in 1866.

Moltke did not, and in planning for war against France he sought to improve upon the 1866 experience. He assigned the task of preparing timetables to the Railroad Section of the General Staff. The information it had long been assembling and the experiences of the most recent campaign were sources from which planners could draw up schedules. The problems were larger than before, for now the entire German railroad network was at their disposal. In all there were fifty-one different railroad companies whose activities needed to be co-ordinated in wartime. Overall direction was now turned over to a six man Central Commission composed of three high-ranking officers, including one from the General Staff, and three civilian representatives from the Ministries of Commerce and the Interior. The Commission was responsible for supervising and controlling troop transports during mobilization and concentration and of directing military transports for the duration of the war. It delegated most of the mobilization tasks to the commanders of each of the army corps, limiting itself only to the relatively minor matter of arranging transport for reservists who had long distances to cover to rejoin their units.

For the more difficult task of preparing the troop and supply trains the commission called upon the Lines of Communication Department of the General Staff. From this office came the special timetables and all the decisions regarding the size of trains, the number of each to be sent along each major line each day, the dispatch of supply trains, and the points of disembarkation.[18] Such planning did not eliminate all errors, but it prepared the army to handle foreseeable problems and gave it the time and experienced personnel to cope with emergencies.

THE MOBILIZATION AND CONCENTRATION OF THE PRUSSIAN ARMY IN 1870

All these measures were put to the test by the Prussians when they mobilized, transported, and concentrated their forces against the French in July 1870. For many years afterward the Prussian mobilization and concentration measures were held up as models of superbly efficient execution of well-drafted, carefully detailed plans, and there is much to recommend this point of view. The army was far more efficient than it had been in 1866 and far better mobilized than the French. There were, however, several imperfections, particularly in the concentration of the Prussian armies on the French frontier. Moltke and his staff quickly learned that they had not in fact perfected the organization and operation of supply columns. They also discovered that commanders were in the position to make ill-considered decisions that not only upset Moltke's plans but disrupted the army's approach march and exposed it to defeat.

With respect to war plans Moltke had sought carefully to match military objectives with a sound estimate of Prussian potential. Starting at first with a purely defensive scheme, he was able by 1869 to evolve a plan allowing Prussia to seize the initiative from the beginning. It was based on a remarkably accurate assessment of French strength and Prussian advantages. The essential point of Moltke's plan was the rapid concentration of ten army corps of 330,000 men in the Rhenish-Palatinate. He proposed to distribute these forces so they could both counter any French thrust into German territory and assume the offensive. The main force, called the "Second Army," was to contain 131,000 troops and assemble around Neunkirchen. Moltke assigned command of this force to Prince Frederick-Charles, a nephew of the king and a competent and well-known soldier. To the right of Frederick-Charles was a smaller "First Army" of 60,000. It was to be concentrated near Wittlich under the command of Friedrich von Steinmetz, a hero of the 1866 campaign. The "Third Army" on the left of the Second was to be formed near Landau and Rastatt in the Bavarian Palatinate. Because this army--it was nearly equal in size to the Second--was to consist of units from both the North German Confederation and the South German states, its command was diplomatically assigned to the Crown Prince of Prussia, who like his cousin was reputed to be an able soldier.

Moltke distributed this strength as unequally as he did because of his assessment of French railroad capacities and French manpower capabilities. The way French railroads ran dictated a dual French concentration around Metz and Strasbourg, and this implied that the French possessed the capacity to invade both north into the Palatinate and east into the South German States. The six major rail lines serving the North German Confederation, however, afforded Moltke the opportunity to check this threat with a heavy concentration of forces just beyond the Alsace-Lorraine frontier. Moltke also correctly assumed that Prussia held an advantage in numbers; France could, he thought, and he was nearly correct, assemble only about 250,000 men in this region in three weeks time.

By these calculations, Moltke was confident that Prussia and its allies could upset whatever plans the French might have. If the French crossed the Rhine into South Germany, the Third Army was strong enough to fall upon their flank. If they invaded the Palatinate, they would collide with the Second Army, which in turn was protected by the First Army on its flank (and by the Third as well if the French threw all their strength into the Palatinate). On the other hand if the Prussians were to be the first to attack, Moltke expected the First and Second Armies to engage the French frontally while the Third Army turned the French right flank and severed them from their base in Paris.

Once Moltke had established this plan, the Prussian Army worked out the arrangements for executing it. Above all this meant the careful preparation of the mobilization, transport, and concentration of the army. Moltke left the responsibility of implementing the details of mobilization to the commanders of each army corps. Under their direction officials prepared the orders for recalling reservists and putting transport and supply units into operation. All that was needed to carry out these directives was authorization from the King and a date of expedition. Meanwhile the General Staff prepared the military railroad schedules and designated the routes of each unit of the army was to follow during the concentration. When, on 15 July, 1870 at the end of a diplomatic crisis with France, William I authorized the mobilization, the Prussian army was adequately prepared to put these processes into effect.[19]

"... Because of the harmonious and intelligent cooperation of all those called upon to play a role, mobilization took place successfully." So states the official historian of the Prussian mobilization.[20] His judgement appears sound. A Prussian mobilization plan contained a chart detailing the composition of the active army on a war footing. It showed the number of men who were expected to be present at the outbreak of war and listed the measures required to bring units up to full strength. The plan also determined in advance which troops would be assigned to the field armies, which to depots, and which to garrison duty. It determined where all troops were to be initially posted and supplied detailed instructions regarding matériel, horses, transport equipment, uniforms, arms and munitions, and tools. It also provided for the replacement of peacetime territorial commanders who would now be assigned to duty in the field army, thus assuring that the normal peacetime activities of the army would continue to be performed during the war. Finally it assured the means by which civil authorities would co-operate with the military to carry out the mobilization plan.[21]

Careful planning produced impressive results. So too did the fact that, unlike 1866, the mobilization was general from the first day. Military and civil authorities delivered recall orders to reservists and members of the *Landwehr*. Within three days of receipt of their orders reservists reported promptly to the recruitment centers and were rapidly reincorporated into the ranks. This process caused little strain even upon the still-operating peacetime schedules of the railroads. The flaws in the mobilization were noteworthy because they were so rare. There were a few cases of disobedience in Polish and Danish speaking regions and in areas like Hannover which had come under Prussian rule in 1866. In some regions there were too few reservists, and the wartime ranks had to be filled out by borrowing men from nearby corps. There were the expected laggards among the reservists; several trains ran behind schedule. The remount services could not obtain transport because none had been scheduled for them, and railroads fell short of rolling stock. Even so the process was completed in about two weeks. It proved to be so uneventful that Minister of War von Roon was later heard to remark that he had never spent a fortnight so free of care with so little work to do in his entire public career.[22]

The transport of the troops to the zones of concentration likewise caused Roon little worry. In addition to the six major lines available to the North German Confederation there were three more available to its South German allies. Railway equipment was in ample supply, and the schedules avoided the mingling of army corps along the same line at the same time. By calculating the most efficient use possible for both single-track and double-track lines, the army was able to transport each army corps (31,000 men) from its bases to its point of disembarkation within between three and a half to five and a half days. Except for temporary problems involved in crossing the Elbe and the Rhine at points where there were no bridges--one solved by the use of steamers, the other by a bridge of barges--the Prussian army encountered no serious difficulties transporting its men to the zone of concentration in 1870.[23]

By contrast the process of concentrating the Prussian army was accomplished with great difficulty. Once separated from its railheads, the army proved to be as cumbersome as armies before the industrial era had always been and were to remain even into World War I. The principal fault in this respect lay in the organization of the supply services; they proved to be as unready to fulfill the demands made upon them as they had been four years earlier.

The Prussian system of supply in the field was elaborate and awkward. It was called the *Etappen* (or staging) system. The idea behind it was that the army, instead of dragging bulky and lengthy convoys along with it, replenished its needs from continuously advancing supply bases close to the rear which in turn were linked to a road and railroad network securely in Prussian hands. As the army advanced, so too, presumably, did the supply base through the formation of a new "stage" once the army had outdistanced the old base. Between each army corps and its mobile base there were to be fourteen columns, five carrying food and forage and nine bringing up ammunition to the troops.[24]

This system proved to be an inadequate response to the army's needs. Moltke had based the *Etappen* system upon experiences derived from the 1864 and 1866 campaigns, but these the Prussians had not adequately assessed. In both wars they had encountered nagging difficulties in bringing up supplies, but the campaigns had reached successful conclusions before the faults of the system had really taken their toll.[25] The Prussians had won in spite of and not because of their supply organization.

The result was there were numerous problems they had not solved by 1870. For example, once the army was concentrated the Prussians deployed most of their combat troops prior to forwarding their supply services, but then they advanced their troops, thus lengthening the distance between the supply bases and the men. To be sure each combat battalion brought extra ammunition along with it, and each soldier carried three days provisions in his pack, but neither of these made up for the shortcomings in organization. There were no headquarters to coordinate the gathering of supplies and their transport to the zones of concentration; nor were their sufficient laborers and wagons at the unloading sites. Consequently there were snags throughout the system, and the goods reached the men slowly and inadequately, if at all.

Even the task of procuring supplies from civilian contractors proved to be cumbersome. These contractors had received requisitions and were expected to deliver goods to wherever the army directed them. When war broke out, however, the railroad companies regarded these goods as peacetime supplies and refused to ship them without prior authorization of the Line Commission of the General Staff. Once this difficulty was overcome, the contractors forwarded the most expensive items first rather than necessarily the most needed ones. The army had never given them priority lists.

The distribution of supplies was equally disorderly. These were frequently dispatched to depots with inadequate facilities to process them. There, quartermaster corpsmen wasted days sorting them out. Furthermore, because these same workers had too little space to store supplies, they regarded freight cars as movable magazines and failed to unload them at all. Thus the cars remained in railroad yards where they congested lines and caused shortages of available rolling stock. Worst of all, perhaps, was the burden placed upon the Inspector General of Communications whose job it was to supervise the shipment of men and matériel and establish new supply depots. He was also responsible for procuring horses, supervising prisoners of war, maintaining roads and telegraphs, keeping daily journals, and preparing reports.[26]

By effecting an alteration of his deployment plans, Moltke himself exacerbated these organizational faults. Although he had originally intended to disembark the three armies close to the French frontier, Moltke on 23 July told them to detrain on the right bank of the Rhine and march to the points of concentration. This change derived from Moltke's understandable, if misplaced, fears of a rapid French mobilization, thrust into the Palatinate, and consequent disruption of the Prussian concentration. He also believed he could run more troop and supply trains per day if the army were to deploy further to the rear than originally intended.[27] His decision was ill-considered. The First and Second Armies disembarked at Mainz, Bingen, and Coblenz then had to pick their way fifty to eighty miles along hilly, second rate roads to reach their zones of concentration. The supply convoys had to move along these same roads, and because of distance and intervening bodies of troops, they were often unable to reach their destination.

As it was, the dispatch of supply columns began later than originally scheduled, and this too resulted from another modification of plans by Moltke. He had intended to station three army corps in the east to counter a possible threat from Austria, who, he thought, might seek to gain revenge for the 1866 defeat by allying with France. Then, on 26 July, Moltke, seeking the greatest troop strength in the west (and relieved by Russia's threat to mobilize should Austria do the same), ordered these three corps transported to the Rhineland. This decision further delayed the distribution of supplies because of the Prussian practice not to dispatch supply trains until troop transport was completed. Not until 1 August were any provision trains run, and by then, the army, marching away from its railroads and consuming much of the food it carried, had separated itself from its supply columns.

How seriously any of these problems exposed the Prussians to defeat is difficult to say, given the results of the war, but nobody can maintain, as the official German General Staff history of the war implies, that the mobilization and concentration went smoothly without any serious problems.[28] A far sounder assessment is that of a later writer who, though asserting that the Prussian *Etappen* system was efficient, hedged by adding, "it must be remembered that the enemy's inefficiency in supply made an excellent foil for (the Prussian system)."[29]

Only by comparison with the French did the Prussian concentration appear to be well executed. At the time it caused Moltke enormous vexations. German armies on the march in 1870 averaged only ten miles a day, and even at this rate they outran their supply columns. At the very beginning of the campaign this situation disrupted Moltke's plans. He had expected the Third Army to make the first thrust at the French. Only by attacking through Alsace before the First and Second Armies invaded Lorraine could he hope for a rapid strategic encirclement of France's main force. Once the Third Army had been strengthened by the armies of the three South German states, Moltke had reason to believe his strategy would work, and on 30 July he ordered the Third Army to begin operations. Impossible, answered the Third Army's chief of staff von Blumenthal; the Prussian units, he reported, were still short of batteries and supply convoys, and the Bavarians had none at all. The Third Army would not be ready, reported one of Moltke's assistants, until at least 3 August.[30]

This left the initiative to the First and Second Armies. Here too, however, the concentration of the armies did not take place as smoothly as had been anticipated. Part of this situation was due to the distances the Second Army had to cover in order to reach the Saar valley. Even by 6 August when its advanced guard engaged the French south of Saarbrücken, the Army remained stretched thirty miles in column to the rear. Its supply columns extended even further. Worse yet, the Second Army was unable fully to concentrate its forces because General Steinmetz, commander of the First Army, had impetuously pushed his own troops directly across the path of the Second Army, effectively barring its route into France.

The selection of General Friedrich von Steinmetz to command the First German Army was no doubt due to his reputation for stubbornness. In 1866 he proved he could maneuver effectively against a force of superior numbers. His conduct at Nachod on 27 June 1866 helped greatly to prepare the subsequent victory at Königgrätz. Here clearly was the soldier who could exercise the potentially most perilous command in 1870. The First Army was the smallest and weakest of the three. Containing only two army corps, it needed a resolute leader who was capable of responding to an attack by superior forces.

As matters turned out the selection of Steinmetz was unfortunate. At the age of seventy-four Steinmetz was the product of an earlier age. Tenacity and initiative were meaningful to him; Moltke's strategy and the duty to follow the instructions of the General Staff were not. The function of the First Army was to cover the Second Army's right as it concentrated around Saabrücken; the First was to gather further downstream at Saarlouis and then operate against the French left. Steinmetz failed to understand this point. While the Second Army was painstakingly making its way through the Palatinate, small units from the French 2nd and 3rd corps attacked the garrison forces covering Saarbrücken on 2 August. When they failed to press their attack across the Saar, Steinmetz concluded that they were weak and sent a portion of his own men in the direction of Saint-Avold to counter the French attack. In so doing, he seized the initiative, but he also threw his men across the path of the Second Army, disrupted their concentration, and wrecked Moltke's strategic plans.

By maneuvering the way he did on 2 August, Steinmetz could no longer be expected to fall onto the French left flank. He could merely participate in a frontal attack with the probable result of aborting the intended encirclement of the French Army. What is certain is that Steinmetz' impetuousness caused units of his army to become entangled with the advanced guard of the Second Army on 3 August. Orders issuing from royal headquarters betray Moltke's concern for this problem. Not until 9 August, he said, would the army begin operations. He ordered the Second Army in the interim to complete its concentration and units of the Third Army to draw closer together.[31] One suspects that Moltke needed this time to extricate the First and Second Armies from the predicament Steinmetz' refusal to follow orders had caused.

Meanwhile, the concentration of the Third Army was less vexing, but as late as 5 August it was still unprepared for combat. Neither the commander of this force nor its chief of staff evinced much confidence in the force they led. Crown Prince Frederick thought the South German units were hostile to the Prussians, and he had little respect for their training. Chief of Staff von Blumenthal believed that supply deficiencies could not be corrected quickly, thus precluding operations before 7 August. Yet Moltke's strategy implied that the Third Army had to begin operations before the First and Second did, so on 1 August they crossed the Rhine and concentrated around Maxau and Landau, five miles north of the Alsatian frontier. Forming into three columns roughly in a pentagonal shape, they approached the frontier. On 4 August the advanced guard of the left column crossed the border and fell upon the Abel Douay Division of the 1st French corps at Wissembourg, a frontier village thirty-six miles north of Strasbourg and eleven west of the Rhine. In a brief skirmish the Germans routed the French.

The victory was unimportant. All that had been defeated was a French outpost, and in the aftermath the Third Army failed to determine the location of the main body of French troops. German positions occupied by the night of 5 August betrayed this ignorance; they faced in three directions. The II

Bavarian corps faced southwestward along the road from Wissembourg to Bitche, a fortress city fifteen miles beyond. The XI Prussian corps was bivouacked along the Haguenau-Strasbourg road; thus it looked directly south. The V Prussian corps camped around the village of Preuschdorf and looked westward across a small valley toward heights dominated by a village named Froeschwiller. There they perceived some French camps. Not until the next day did they learn that they were observing the entire French force in lower Alsace. To the rear of these three positions lay the I Bavarian corps and the Baden and Württemberg contingents. The Crown Prince and Blumenthal had admirably sited their army, for in case of attack each corps lay within supporting distance of the other. But there can be no doubt that these positions were taken by the Third Army because its commanders remained in the dark about the whereabouts of the French.

These dispositions of the entire German forces on the night of 5 August 1870 provided excellent opportunities for the French to exploit. Steinmetz' march on Saarbrücken was a tactical error which would, in Moltke's words, "have exposed the First Army to defeat."[32] For 5 and 6 August, at least, Moltke's observation was correct: on that day the French enjoyed numerical superiority over the Prussians near Saarbrücken. A resolute attack by a well-organized French army against scattered German forces still collecting their trains and batteries offered the reward not merely of a defeat of the First Army but also a thorough disruption of the concentration of the Second Army.

Likewise the Third Army, although better concentrated on 5 August than the other two, was still short of supplies, and its intelligence had served it poorly. It was unaware that it was close by the main French force in Alsace. The French had the opportunity to lure the Third Army onto an assault on the Froeschwiller Heights and inflict serious damage upon it. Prussian dispositions in both Lorraine and Alsace offered the French army splendid occasions to halt the German advance. To do so, however, required initiative and excellent organization. It also required in the first instance a clearly defined strategic objective without which no mobilization or concentration of an army can be meaningfully effected.

FRENCH WAR PROJECTS, 1866-1870, AND THE ARMY OF THE RHINE

One of the most serious indictments of French policy in 1870 is that the government of Napoleon III declared war on Prussia without seriously considering what its military objectives were. Although it is not within the scope of this monograph to assess the responsibilities for the outbreak of the war, it is necessary to point out that it was France who issued the declaration of war and that it did so at the conclusion of a crisis involving the succession to the Spanish throne in which the French had won a diplomatic victory over the Prussians. Yet there were no concrete plans for a war against Prussia. There were projects and vague ideas, as shall be examined, but there was nothing comparable to the work so carefully completed by Moltke: no clearly stated strategic objective based on a careful assessment of their own and their enemy's capabilities.[33]

Still Napoleon III and his advisors knew that war with Prussia was possible. Between 1866 and 1870 three significant projects for war against Prussia were considered by responsible French officers. Two were never seriously discussed by the Emperor and his military aides; none was adopted; but worst of all elements of each influenced the way France deployed its forces at the commencement of war in 1870. Having defined no objective, the French were condemned to implementing three, each of which contradicted the other.[34]

The first of these projects was drawn up in a memorandum drafted by General Charles Frossard in 1867. A distinguished military engineer, Frossard possessed a practiced eye for fortresses and strong positions (belles positions). Calculating that the Prussians would have 470,000 men at their disposal at the outbreak of war, he recommended that the French assume the defensive against this superior force. Specifically he called for four armies. One, a 60,000 man "Army of Alsace" was to occupy a nine to ten kilometer long ridge in northern Alsace upon which the village of Froeschwiller was an important point of resistance. A second "Army of the Moselle," consisting of 140,000 soldiers, was to be drawn up along a plateau in Lorraine stretching from Forbach to Sarreguemines, a position called the Cadenbronn Line. These two armies, although numerically inferior to the Prussians, would be strong enough, he believed, to bar the routes to Strasbourg and Metz. Meanwhile two reserve armies, together totaling 120,000 men, were to be established at Châlons-sur-Marne and Rheims, though for what purpose is uncertain. Frossard's sketch clearly is defensive in nature and states no objective for the French other than shutting France's door in Prussia's face.[35]

Frossard's plan never received official sanction, yet it exerted some influence on operations in 1870. When Marshal MacMahon concentrated the 1st French corps in Alsace on 5 August, he occupied the Froeschwiller ridge. One of the officers under his command, General Auguste-Alexandre Ducrot, had been in communication with Frossard.[36] On the same day another army corps took up position in the Spicheren Heights, a forward post of the Cadenbronn Line, and the commander of that corps was General Frossard.

The second project, one which revealed some of Napoleon III's strategic thinking, was sketched by the emperor and his aide-de-camp, General Barthélemy Lebrun. In 1868 they assembled a project entitled Composition des armées en 1868 in which they estimated that the army had 490,000 men ready for service as of 1 July 1868.[37] This number, they thought, allowed for the assembly of three field armies and three reserve corps. The first of these, the "Army of Lorraine," was to be concentrated in three corps totalling 130,000 men around Metz and to be under the command of Marshal Achille Bazaine, who had directed the recent expedition in Mexico. The second, called the "Army of Alsace," was to gather 121,000 men in three corps near Strasbourg under the command of Marshal Patrice de MacMahon. The third army, to be led by Marshal Certain Canrobert, was to assemble two corps, a total of 87,000 soldiers, at the military base near Châlons-sur-Marne. Until 1870, the war ministry assumed that this project reflected Napoleon III's intentions and, based upon it, drew up paper brigades, divisions, and army corps. In July, 1870 when the Spanish succession crisis broke out, the war ministry began preliminary mobilization with this project in mind. What Napoleon intended to do with this force, however, is unclear. What is significant is that he never arrived at any clear definition of a strategic objective for these three armies.[38]

By July 1870, however, another idea had evolved in the emperor's mind. Although the 1868 project did not state a military objective, its overestimate of the number of trained men available to the French prompted Napoleon III to envisage an offensive into South Germany. The idea was attractive. It accorded well with the French tradition of the offensive, and it afforded the French the advantage of the initiative. It also threatened the alliance between the North German Confederation and the South German states. The latter, where some influential persons were deploring the looming influence of the Prussians, might conceivably be intimidated into neutrality by the French. Furthermore an offensive strategy also raised a third possibility, that of a military alliance with Austria and possibly also Italy. Discreet discussions of such a disposition were raised in 1869 by Austrian foreign minister von Beust through the intermediary of the Austrian ambassador to Paris, Prince von Metternich. So discreet were these conversations that the Duc de Gramont, French ambassador to Vienna at the time, later claimed he did not know about them until after he left that post to become French foreign minister in May 1870.[39] Part of the initiative involved a visit by the Austrian Archduke Albert, commander of the Austrian Army, to France in March and April of 1870.[40]

During this visit Archduke Albert discussed both the possible alliance and his ideas about a plan of joint Franco-Austrian military operations against Prussia. No copy of these plans has been found in French army archives, but General Barthélemy Lebrun, one of Napoleon III's closest associates, recorded both what he knew about these conversations and an account of subsequent negotiations with the archduke. A somewhat jumbled manuscript version of his notebooks has been deposited in the archives of the French army's *Service historique* in Vincennes;[41] his report of 29 June 1870 to Napoleon III was printed in his memoires in 1895.[42] According to Lebrun, Napoleon III revealed Archduke Albert's proposals to a small circle of military advisors on 19 April

1870; besides Lebrun the group included General Leboeuf, General Frossard, and General Louis Jarras.[43] Subsequently Lebrun was assigned to continue the conversations with Archduke Albert, which he did in Vienna on five separate occasions between 7 and 14 June 1870.

The archduke's "plan," Napoleon III told his advisors, involved the formation of three armies of 100,000 men each, a French one called the "Army of Alsace," an Austrian one, and an Italian one, which, he asserted, King Victor Emmanuel was willing to promise if the aim of the three powers was "to act in common to resist the ambitious projects of Prussia."[44] The campaign was to start with a French incursion into South Germany, and the objective was to detach the South German states from their alliance with Prussia and to secure a base of operations in Franconia on the line Würtzburg-Nuremberg-Amberg. From here the three allies, having by now joined forces, would be able to follow a route similar to the one adopted by Napoleon I in the Jena campaign of 1806.[45] In the meantime another French army, this one called the "Army of Lorraine," was to draw the Prussians away from the decisive theatre of operations by invading the Palatinate with twelve divisions on the fifteenth day of mobilization.[46]

Along with the slavish and naïve reference to the strategy of the first Napoleon, the archduke's plan abounded with other weaknesses. One of these the archduke himself noted at his first conversation with Lebrun in Vienna. He told his guest that these discussions were to be considered "solely from a military point of view," or as he also more emphatically put it, *"from an academic point of view."* (Italics Lebrun's)[47] How hypothetical in fact these discussions in fact were is evidenced by other details Lebrun noted. The campaign was to begin in the spring, mobilization being ordered in mid-March and operations starting a month later. Although the Italians might mobilize 100,000 men, thought Archduke Albert, only half of them would be available for service in Germany. Furthermore there would be a role for Denmark to play in this alliance as well, and yet nobody had invited Danish diplomats or generals to participate in the discussions.[48]

Equally weak were the speculations about mobilization capabilities. Influenced by what he knew about the Prussian experience of 1866, Archduke Albert said it would take two weeks to mobilize an army corps in Prussia and another three to five weeks to concentrate it, depending on the number of other corps using the same railroad line. In the meantime, the French, according to the archduke, could be ready in two weeks time. He was probably more correct in his estimate of Austrian and Italian mobilization; the former required six weeks and the latter could not be calculated. But when in light of these estimations Lebrun demanded that all three powers begin their mobilization at the same time, Archduke Albert doubted this could be done.[49]

The archduke was telling Lebrun that if France went to war with Prussia it would have to campaign alone for at least several weeks without assurances of allied military support.   This point was underscored by Emperor Francis-Joseph in an interview he granted to Lebrun on 14 June 1870. Austria would be pleased to join France in a campaign against Prussia, he assured the general, but Austria could not declare war at the same time France did. A convincing pretext was necessary, and this situation would obtain when France had occupied the South German states posing as their "protector" against Prussia. Austria then would be able to do the same.[50]

Lebrun thus came home with little more than speculation: a theoretical military project, uncertain assurances of an alliance and those only if the French produced victories, and unrealistic mobilization schedules that made these victories unlikely. In his own notebook Lebrun remarked that Archduke Albert was underestimating the time required for French mobilization and concentration.[51]   In fact even by the time he had arrived in Vienna he must certainly have had doubts about the Archduke's projects. He had been present at the 19 April meeting when Napoleon III first revealed them. Before the meeting broke up, according to General Jarras in his memoirs, the four military personnel present examined the project. They concluded that given both the likely disposition of French forces at the beginning of operations and their estimates of the time Prussia required to mobilize and concentrate its forces, the French would be unable to secure significant victories during those weeks when Austria would presumably still be mobilizing its army. This put an end to the discussions of the project, said Jarras. Certainly afterward nobody adopted measures intended to put the archduke's ideas into effect.   Furthermore, according to Jarras, nobody ever hinted to him that the proposal had officially been adopted, and after war was declared nothing was done to suggest to him that the principal mission of the French army was to cross the Rhine.[52]

Jarras was probably mistaken. Other evidence suggests that the archduke's proposal was indeed the project that most influenced Napoleon III's strategic thinking in July 1870. General Leboeuf later testified that the emperor expected to cross the Rhine and asked him to select the best crossing point. In a book attributed to Napoleon III and published in 1871, there is the claim that the "Army of Alsace" was expected to secure the neutrality of the South German states and subsequently join forces with the Austrians and Italians.[53]

If this were so, it illustrates one of the fatal weaknesses of French policy in July 1870. France was mobilizing its army to pursue an ill-defined military objective based on a nonexistent alliance system. Simply put, when war broke out, France had concluded no formal arrangements with either Austria or Italy, nor, in spite of what French leaders may have hoped, were there any firm assurances that France could count on the assistance of either power. The evidence pointed in the other direction. As the diplomatic crisis of July 1870 unfolded, the French believed they could get the diplomatic support of Austria,[54]   but when they made threatening gestures, the Austrians understandably held back. On 8 July 1870 Gramont made intemperate remarks to the Corps Législatif regarding Prussia and the Hohenzollern candidacy to the Spanish throne. Austrian foreign minister von Beust was appalled. He warned the French that they were presuming too much. "I have dispatches here from Metternich," he told the French *chargé d'affaires*, "which talk about armament and troop movements, which say we and our effective alliance can be counted on." There is no such alliance, he pointed out. What was needed, he added--and here he was echoing what Emperor Francis-Joseph had told Lebrun--was for Prussia to appear as the aggressor bullying the South German states. This would serve as a pretext for Austrian intervention, as the plans of the campaign have been arranged "or rather are in the process of being set up *(ou plûtot en projet)."*[55]

These were not the words of an ally with whom a power has concluded a plan of military operations. They were saying that Austria is not yet an ally and that military strategy is still in the planning stage. Furthermore they imply that since Prussia was not in fact being aggressive against the South German states, the pretext for Austrian support did not exist either. Nor were assurances of help forthcoming after the declaration of war. On 20 July 1870 French *chargé d'affaires* de Cazaux wired Gramont from Vienna that he had just learned that Austrian council had resolved to "put the army on a war footing" but would not do so before six weeks to two months.[56] Whatever French officials may later have claimed--namely that there was, in fact, a reasonable hope of an Austrian alliance--the signals they were receiving from Vienna in July 1870 were hardly the sort to justify a policy of invading South Germany and of a hastily organized mobilization of their available forces for the purpose of undertaking so risky a venture.

Even more uncertain was the idea of an Italian alliance. With the Austrians there had at least been informal conversations. With Italy there was not even this.   Instead matters pointed to Italian nonintervention.   One issue alone strained Franco-Italian relations: the continued French military presence in Rome. As long as the French were there, there was no satisfactory solution to the "Roman Question." Napoleon III favored an arrangement whereby the Pope could be guaranteed his sovereignty inside the Vatican while the rest of Rome was absorbed into the Kingdom of Italy, but circumstances in France prevented him from realizing this policy.[57] Yet until the problem could be solved to the satisfaction of the Italian state, a Franco-Italian alliance was out of the question. In the crisis of July 1870 French inquiries regarding Italian support thus received noncommittal responses. Italy would not be an adversary, their foreign minister told French ambassador Malaret on 8 July 1870, but beyond that he was not willing to express his opinion. Malaret's advice to his foreign office was direct:

if France wants the aid of Italy, "it must dress the wound it has inflicted upon Italian *amour propre*," and that, he stated, was to settle the Roman question.[58]

In any event Italy was not prepared for war, and it is unlikely France could have counted on significant Italian military assistance even if the Roman issue had been settled. Dispatches from Malaret were warning the French government that this was the case. Earlier in the year Malaret had reported on the financial stringencies being imposed on the Italian army. He cited the Italian Minister of War who had told parliament that because Italian finances were in disarray, the government had to reduce its allocations to the army, so much so, in fact, that Italy had become incapable of raising a force equal to the one they mobilized during the 1866 war.[59] Italy, wrote Malaret on 16 July, had "an army barely sufficient to assure the security of the interior of the country, and was also lacking a navy, money and credit."[60] Under these circumstances the 100,000 men projected in Archduke Albert's project were an impossibility; it is unlikely that the 50,000 he more sensibly projected later on could have materialized either.

Such was the level of military planning the French had accomplished when on 4 July 1870 the diplomatic crisis which resulted in the Franco-Prussian War began. Almost at once Minister of War Leboeuf began last minute preparations. There was plenty to do. Dispatches from Colonel Stoffel in Berlin warned of increased military activity there. These were hints the Prussians were taking preliminary steps prior to mobilization; they suggested how intense and serious the crisis was.[61] Generals were ordered to return to their posts: "There may be urgent orders to execute," stated the telegrams. The Minister ordered officials to check mobilization slips, collect and load munitions onto wagons, prepare the transport of troops from Algeria, and purchase draught horses. All this was busy work which long since should have been done. More to the point, Leboeuf occupied himself with these details, working on the assumption that the 1868 Napoleon III-Lebrun sketch reflected the emperor's intentions: there were to be three field armies over which Napoleon III was to exercise nominal command. Leboeuf was sure he could put 250,000 men in the field in two weeks, and on 6 July he affirmed this to the council of ministers.[62]

Leboeuf had mistaken the emperor's intentions. On July 11, Napoleon III told Leboeuf that he intended to form a single "Army of the Rhine" under his personal command as he had done in Italy in 1859. This announcement disrupted Leboeuf's last minute activities; it also revealed that the emperor, in fact, had no clear plans at all. "The Army of the Rhine" was at best cosmetic. Lebrun told Leboeuf: "The emperor intends to exercise command only for a short time after which we shall form the three armies the way he indicated in the work he did in 1868."[63] The objective of this "short time" Army of the Rhine was irrelevant; Leboeuf had nevertheless to create an entirely new chain of command. With so casual a decision Napoleon III thus threw out even the paper organization of the army drawn up two years earlier and violated the spirit of the military project he and General Lebrun had discussed with Archduke Albert. In the process he had made the French mobilization and concentration even more chaotic.

What emerged was a cumbersome, incoherent organization, which, even on paper, was difficult to comprehend. The "Army of the Rhine" was to consist of eight corps. The three marshals who had by this stroke been reduced to mere corps commanders were to be compensated by being given corps consisting of four divisions apiece whereas the remaining five corps consisted of three divisions each. There was no sense to this scheme at all except to mollify three supposedly outraged soldiers. The major effect of Napoleon's decision was to create confusion in the war office where the order of battle had to created from scratch. For three days and nights the French General Staff worked feverishly, dumbfounded by the emperor's decision, to remake the army according to whim.[64] As far as possible the seven corps were created by simple shifting of units at points where they were supposed to be concentrated. The major problems were to reassign personnel to new duties, create new commands and staffs, and reallocate the artillery and the supply services. By 14 July the work appeared to be completed.

As commander of the Army of the Rhine, Napoleon III selected his own staff. The job of *Major-Général*, a post analogous to Moltke's, went to Leboeuf, but since Leboeuf was simultaneously to serve as Minister of War, he was somehow expected to carry out the duties of a Roon as well. For assistance the emperor called upon Lebrun and Jarras, each of whom assumed the rank of *Aide Major-Général*. Lebrun worked closely with Napoleon and Leboeuf in the formulation of operational plans, while Jarras served as chief secretary who transmitted orders to the army. None of these positions was an enviable one. The emperor, who had left much to be desired as a commander in 1859, was now suffering badly from a gallstone which left him physically unfit for command. Leboeuf, who had never commanded infantry nor done any staff duties, was chief of staff to a commander who was constantly changing his mind. Although Lebrun and Jarras, like Leboeuf, worked hard to organize and execute operations, they too lacked the staff experience needed to articulate the masses of men and supplies collecting in Alsace and Lorraine.

Napoleon's selection of corps commanders was as easily made as his decision to assume personal command. Reliable accounts assert that he selected his men from among court favorites, usually *aides-de-camp*, and the criteria for court favoritism were dash, gallantry, and the ability to please.[65] Four proved to be able commanders: General Frossard (2nd Corps), Marshal Canrobert (6th Corps), General Felix Douay (7th Corps), and General Bourbaki (Imperial Guard). General Ladmirault (4th Corps) was reasonably competent; serious doubts remain about the rest. Marshal MaMahon (1st Corps) was a capable and courageous corps commander at Froeschwiller (6 August, 1870), a defeat for which he was not responsible. But later as commander of the "Army of Châlons," he displayed his incompetence as commander of the army which surrendered at Sedan. General de Failly (5th Corps) proved to be weak, indecisive, and disobedient. Marshal Bazaine (3rd Corps) was later unjustly held responsible for the entire defeat. To do him justice, however, is not to cover up his own incompetence. He simply was no army commander.[66]

Nor were staff arrangements which had been hastily reshuffled, satisfactory. The Imperial general staff, for example, was too large for its functions, but corps and divisional staffs were short of officers. In some cases, staff officers were assigned to commanders who had little confidence in them. Canrobert frequently complained about the men designated to serve him; he developed a strong dislike for his chief of staff who, he claimed, was an intimate of a personal enemy. Likewise General Ladmirault, who did not obtain the services of the officer he requested, refused to place confidence in the man assigned to him.[67]

Such then was the state of planning and organization of the Army of the Rhine when France's formal declaration of war was delivered in Berlin on 19 July. By declaring war on Prussia, the French had made themselves the aggressor in a conflict for which they had no plans. Even at this most fundamental level the French had failed to meet the challenge. In the dark about objectives, General Leboeuf was clear about one thing: he knew that the rapid mobilization and concentration of France's armed forces was necessary. He thought too that time favored the French and told the cabinet that the French army could undertake operations within two weeks of mobilization.[68] Since the French mobilization had begun on 14 July, Leboeuf expected the army to take the offensive on 28 July. Due to the Niel reforms and his own work over the past year, he thought the army was prepared to go to war on so short a notice.

Leboeuf was correct in one respect: speed was necessary. If the French had any chance of defeating the Prussians at all, they had to recall their reserves, gather their supplies, and transport all these to the zone of concentration for operations within the two allocated weeks. What Napoleon III and Leboeuf were to learn was that two weeks was insufficient time. Why this was so is the subject of the following chapters.

NOTES

1. Michael Howard, *The Franco-Prussian War* (London: Rupert Hart-Davis, 1961), p. 12; Walter Goerlitz, *History of the German General Staff, 1657-1945*, Translated by Brian Battershaw (New York: Praeger, 1953), pp. 57, 66; Martin Van Creveld, *Supplying War: Logistics from Wallenstein to Patton*, (New York: Cambridge University Press, 1977), p. 78.

2. The text of the law may be found in Eugen von Frauenholz, *Entwicklungsgeschichte des deutschen Heerwesens*, 5 vols. (Munich: Beck, 1941), V, pp. 575-580; Germany, Army, Generalstab, Kriegsgeschichtliche Abteilung, *The Franco-German War*, Translated by F. C. H. Clarke, 5 vols. (London: Her Majesty's Stationery Office, 1874-1884), I, i, p. 46, (cited hereafter as G. G. S.); Gustav Lehman in *Die Mobilmachung von 1870-71* (Berlin: E. S. Mittler, 1905), p. 154 cites a lower figure: 1,025,151.

3. G. G. S., I, i, p. 36; Barthélemy Edmond Palat, *Histoire de la Guerre 1870-71*, Part I: *La Guerre de 1870*, 6 vols. (Paris: Berger-Levrault, 1903-1908), II, p. 221.

4. See Goerlitz, *History of the German General Staff*, pp. 53, 58-59, 82-86; see also Dallas D. Irvine, "The French and Prussian Staff Systems before 1870," *Journal of the American Military History Foundation*, II, No. 4 (Winter, 1938), pp. 192-196.

5. Jay Luvaas, *The Military Legacy of the Civil War: The European Inheritance* (Chicago: University of Chicago Press, 1959), pp. 122-123.

6. Prussia, Army, Generalstab, Kriegsgeschichtliche Abteilung, *The Campaign of 1866 in Germany* (London: Her Majesty's Stationery Office, 1872), p. 11, (cited hereafter as *The Campaign of 1866 in Germany*).

7. Helmuth von Moltke, *Moltke's Projects for the Campaign of 1866 against Austria* (London: His Majesty's Stationery Office, 1907), p. 30. Moltke's various war plans are found on pp. 3-32.

8. Ibid., p. 33.

9. Ibid., pp. 35-39, 42-43.

10. Ibid., p. 41.

11. *The Campaign of 1866 in Germany*, p. 12. Perhaps Moltke himself contributed to this situation. In a note of 30 March he minimized the threat posed by the Austrians at that time. To counter it he recommended a partial mobilization of two corps for as long as Prussian policy still forbade general mobilization. This was to endorse the very measure he found so abhorent. Se Moltke, *Moltke's Projects*, p. 42.

12. *The Campaign of 1866 in Germany*, p. 505.

13. The mobilization of sample units is compared in Eugène Stoffel, *Rapports militaries écrits de Berlin, 1866-1870* (Paris: Garnier, 1871), pp. 457-463.

14. *The Campaign of 1866 in Germany*, pp. 12-14; Henri Bonnal, *Sadowa, étude de stratégie et de tactique générale* (Paris: Chapelot, 1901), pp. 11-20.

15. There is a discussion of the organization and role of railroads in the mobilization and concentration of the Prussian army in 1866 in *The Campaign of 1866 in Germany*, pp. 18-30 and especially 505-507; see also Bonnal, *Sadowa*, pp. 13-31. Prussian and Austrian mobilization and concentration are compared in Craig, *The Battle of Königgrätz*, pp. 27-42.

16. For a discussion of the logistical plight of the Prussian army in the 1866 campaign see Martin Van Creveld, *Supplying War: Logistics from Wallenstein to Patton* (New York: Cambridge University Press, 1977), pp. 79-85. The campaign of 1866 in Bohemia has been extensively analyzed in *The Campaign of 1866 in Germany* and more succinctly in Craig, *The Battle of Königgrätz*. Moltke's strategic concepts and their application in 1866 have been examined by Hajo Holborn in "Moltke and Schlieffen: The Prussian-German School," in Edward Meade Earle, ed. *Makers of Modern Strategy: Military Thought from Machiavelli to Hitler* (Princeton, N.J.: Princeton University Press, 1943), pp. 172-186. The section on Moltke has been reprinted as "The Prusso-German School: Moltke and the Rise of the General Staff," in Peter Paret, ed. *Makers of Modern Strategy from Machiavelli to the Nuclear Age* (Princeton N.J.: Princeton University Press, 1986), pp. 281-295.

17. Stoffel, *Rapports militaires écrits de Berlin*, pp. 178-184.

18. A description of the Lines of Communication Department may be found in Germany, Army, Generalstab, Kriegsgeschichtliche Abteilung, "The Railroad Concentration for the War of

1870-71," reprinted in *The Military Historian and Economist*, III, No. 2 (Jan. 1918), pp. 2-10, (cited hereafter as G. G. S., "Railroad Concentration").

19.   On the evolution of Prussian plans and the details of Moltke's plans see G. G. S., I, i, pp. 49-56. See also Helmuth von Moltke, *Moltke's Military Correspondence 1870-71*, Part I: *The War to The Battle of Sedan* (Oxford: Clarendon Press, 1923), pp. 28-33.

20.   Lehmann, *Die Mobilmachung von 1870-71*, pp. 40-41.

21.   See Jules-Victor Lemoyne, *Notices militaires. La Mobilisation. Etude sur les institutions militaires de la Prusse.* (Paris: Berger-Levrault, 1872), pp. 10-13.

22.   See Lehmann, *Die Mobilmachung von 1870-71*, pp. 40, 47-50 and G.G.S., "Railroad Concentration," pp. 13, 20-27. The Prussian mobilization has also been carefully detailed in Lemoyne, *Notices militaires. La Mobilisation*, pp. 80-128.

23.   G. G. S., I, i, pp. 58-59.

24.   G. C. Shaw, *Supply in Modern War* (London: Faber and Faber, 1938), pp. 78-80; Van Creveld, *Supplying War*, p. 97.

25.   Ibid., p. 84.

26.   Numerous sources treat this problem. See especially Ibid., pp. 77-105; G. G. S., "Railroad Concentration," pp. 49-55; Wilhelm von der Goltz, *The Nation in Arms: A Treatise on Modern Military Systems and the Conduct of War*, Translated by Philip A. Ashworth, 2d ed. revised, (London: Hodder and Stoughton, 1915), pp. 257-258; Edwin A. Pratt, *The Rise of Rail Power in War and Conquest, 1833-1914* (Philadelphia: Lippincott, 1916), pp. 107-111.

27.   Van Creveld, *Supplying War*, pp. 89-90; G. G. S., "Railroad Concentration," pp. 51-52.

28.   None of the difficulties described in this section are cited in the official staff history. The authors either ignore them or leave the reader with the impression that somehow the problems that arose were solved. See G. G. S., I, i, pp. 34-76, notably pp. 36-37, 56-59, 75-76.

29.   Shaw, *Supply in Modern War*, p. 85; for an account of the German mobilization see G. G. S., I, i, pp. 34-82.

30.   Howard, *The Franco-Prussian War*, p. 85.

31.   G. G. S., I, i, pp. 105-106, 147. The correspondence between Moltke and Steinmetz is translated and reprinted in Moltke, *Moltke's Military Correspondence*, Part I: *The War to The Battle of Sedan*, pp. 69-73.

32.   Quoted in Howard, *The Franco-Prussian War*, p. 89; see also *Extracts from Moltke's Correspondence*, p. 190.

33.   Throughout the 1860's French officers drafted several memoranda detailing dispositions to take in the event of war against Prussia. Most of these projects were filed away and ignored. They have been discovered and examined in Richard Holmes, *The Road to Sedan: The French Army (1866-70)* (London: Royal Historical Society, 1984), pp. 165-179 and are convincing evidence of the amount of often intelligent thought the French military put into war preparations prior to the Franco-Prussian War. But none of this work was translated into policy or concrete war plans. Hence there were no attempts to prepare the mobilization of the French army with the objective of implementing any one or the other of these projects.

34.   Palat, *Histoire*, Part I: *La Guerre de 1870*, II, pp. 199-208; Howard, *The Franco-Prussian War*, pp. 47-48; Louis Le Gillou, *La Campagne d'été de 1870* (Paris: Charles-Lavauzelle, 1938), p. 99.

35.   This plan may be found in France, Armée, Etat-Major, Service Historique, *Préparation à la guerre* in *La Guerre de 1870-71*, 35 vols. (Paris: Chapelot, 1901-1903), pp. 79-115, (cited hereafter as Guerre followed by the title of the particular volume to which reference is made).

36.   Palat, *Histoire*, Part I: *La Guerre de 1870*, II, p. 201; Auguste-Alexandre Ducrot, *La Vie militaire du Général Ducrot d'après sa correspondence*, 2 vols. (Paris: Plon Nourrit et cie., 1895), II, p. 174.

37.   Barthélemy Louis Joseph Lebrun, *Souvenirs militaires, 1866-1870. Préliminaires de la guerre. Missions en Belgigue et à Vienne* (Paris: E. Dentu, 1895), p. 42; Napoleon III, *Oeuvres*

posthumes et autographes inédits de Napoleon III en exil, ed. by Le comte de la Chapelle (Paris: Lachaud, 1873), pp. 149-157; Palat, *Histoire*, Part I: *La Guerre de 1870*, II, p. 147.

38. Ibid., IV, p. 148; "Projet de composition de l'armée," 8 July 1870, SHAT, Vincennes, Lo 2 and 3.

39. MAE, Paris, Papiers Gramont, I, fol. 63-65.

40. *Les Origines diplomatiques de la guerre de 1870-71. Recueil de documents publié par le Ministère des Affaires Etrangères.* 29 vols. (Paris: Charles-Lavauzelle, 1910-1932), XXIV, pp. 359-361 and XXVII, pp. 445-446.

41. "Cahier du Général Lebrun," SHAT, Vincennes, 1 K 25.

42. Lebrun, *Souvenirs militaires*, pp. 151-173.

43. Ibid., p. 71.

44. Ibid.

45. Ibid.

46. Palat, *Histoire*, Part I: *La Guerre de 1870*, II, pp. 203-204; this matter is also discussed in Louis Jarras, *Souvenirs du Général Jarras* Paris: Plon, 1892), pp. 106, 151, 153, 170.

47. "Cahier du général Lebrun," SHAT, Vincennes, 1 K 25, "Chapter II." General Lebrun's notes are not paginated, but sections are divided according to "chapters."

48. Ibid., "Chapter III."

49. Ibid.; Lebrun, *Souvenirs militaires*, pp. 77, 93-96.

50. Lebrun, *Souvenirs militaires*, pp. 82, 146-149.

51. "Cahier du général Lebrun," SHAT, Vincennes, 1 K 25, "Chapter III."

52. Jarras, *Souvenirs de Général Jarras* pp. 43-51. I found no evidence in the French army archives at Vincennes to refute his claim.

53. France, Assemblée Nationale, *Enquête parlementaire sur les actes du Gouvernement de la Défense Nationale: déposition des témoins*, 5 vols. (Paris: Germer-Baillière, 1872-1875), I, p. 151, (cited hereafter as D. T.); Napoleon III (?), *Campagne de 1870. Des Causes qui ont amené la capitulation de Sedan* (Brussels: J. Roses, n.d.), p. 4.

54. Dispatch, Chargé d'affaires de Cazaux to Gramont, 9 July 1870, MAE, Paris, CP Autriche 502, p. 262.

55. Ibid., p. 265.

56. Ibid., p. 352.

57. Georges Dethan, "Napoleon III et l'opinion française devant la question romaine (1860-1870)" *Revue d'histoire diplomatique*, LXXII, (April-June 1958), pp. 118-134 examines this issue.

58. Dispatch, Ambassador Malaret to Gramont, MAE, Paris, CP Italie 28, p. 410, 417-425.

59. Dispatch, Ambassador Malaret to Gramont, 27 May 1870, MAE, Paris, CP Italie 28, pp. 282-290. See an earlier discussion of this same problem on pp. 447-452.

60. Ibid.

61. Dispatches, 7 to 13 July 1870, MAE, Paris, CP Prusse 379, pp. 45, 128, 191, 211, 247.

62. D. T., I, p. 41. Carton Lo 2 and 3 in the French army archives contains many copies of orders putting these activities into effect. Copies of telegrams in the records of the Imperial household, then in residence at the Palais de Saint-Cloud, contain similar evidence: AN, Paris, AB XIX 1710 and 1711.

63. Lebrun, *Souvenirs Militaires*, p. 80.

64. Germain Bapst (ed.), *Le Maréchal Canrobert: Souvenirs d'un siècle*, 6 vols. (Paris: Plon, 1898-1913), IV, p. 140.

65. Howard, *The Franco-Prussian War*, p. 65; Palat, *Histoire*, Part I: *La Guerre de 1870*, II, p. 74.

66. Recent authors have revised Bazaine's reputation. Edmond Ruby and Jean Regnault in *Bazaine, coupable ou victime? A la lumière de documents nouveaux* (Paris: Peyronnet, 1960) dispel any doubt about Bazaine's honesty and relieve him of the responsibility for the defeat. In Maurice

Beaumont, *Bazaine, les secrets d'un maréchal (1811-1888)* (Paris: Imprimerie nationale, 1978), Bazaine emerges as a conscientious corps commander upon whom supreme command was thrust in August 1870. Beaumont attributes the defeats in the Metz sector on 16 and 18 August 1870 to the shortcomings of his subordinates, notably Frossard and Ladmirault. See especially pp. 107, 110-121. Even so there is little in this volume to suggest that Bazaine had the talent to command an army.

67. Palat, *Histoire*, Part I: *La Guerre de 1870*, II, p. 154; Le Gillou, *La Campagne d'été de 1870*, p. 89; Bapst, *Le Maréchal Canrobert: Souvenirs d'un siècle*, IV, p. 150; Beaumont, *Bazaine, les secrets d'un maréchal*, p. 113.

68. Emile Ollivier, *L'Empire libéral, études, récits, souvenirs*, 18 vols. (Paris: Garnier, 1895-1918), XIV, p. 100. Texts of the orders setting the mobilization process in motion in the French army in 1870 are stored in SHAT, Vincennes, Lo 4 and 5.

4

Mobilizing Manpower

Of all the mistakes committed by the French army in 1870 few were more visible than the utter confusion in which French manpower resources were mobilized for war, and few results were more catastrophic than the paltry results obtained. All commentators then and since have noted the stark contrast between the Prussian mobilization, which appeared to be efficient, and the French one, which seemed to symbolize the sorry state into which France's military system had fallen. Many of these same commentators have attributed France's defeat to the insufficient numbers of men France mobilized. For Marshal Leboeuf the dismal reports from the daily muster rolls of the Army of the Rhine were sufficient proof that the army was not as well prepared as he had thought.

Turning his duties as Minister of War over to an assistant, Leboeuf on 26 July assumed the title of *Major-Général* of the Army of the Rhine and set out for Metz to inspect the force in process of formation. Early news reports were encouraging. *Le Constitutionnel* in particular depicted an army being rapidly assembled. "The work of setting up the two divisions designed to act first is finished," it informed its readers on 20 July. In ensuing days the paper printed equally optimistic news: "Never has France put so fine an army in line so rapidly," it said on 22 July. "The French army is in the best of conditions to wage war; it is well-armed, well-equipped," it added three days later.[1] And some official messages seemed to confirm these reports. A note Leboeuf received on 23 July informed him that by 30 July the concentration of the army would nearly be completed and that several reserve detachments would be on their way to the Army of the Rhine.[2]

Leboeuf might well have taken note of words such as "nearly" or "several" in that message. They were telling him that not all the detachments were on their way and that the optimistic reports were misleading. Not long after he arrived in Metz he learned the truth. He quickly sensed that the army would not be ready as soon as he anticipated. One of the first problems to come to his attention was how slowly reservists were returning to the ranks.[3] What was wrong, he did not know, but within a few days, the messages he received from commanders throughout France gave him his answer. Troops criss-crossed France, lost their way, and failed to find transportation. Because the officers in charge of them had received no orders to dispatch them to the Army of the Rhine, many were remaining in their regimental depots. Branches of the army which depended on horses were unable to perform effectively because there were not enough available. Finally, the *Garde Nationale Mobile*, parts of which were mobilized, proved to be of no help to the army. The *Garde* had few officers, little training, no weapons, no uniforms, and no available funds. In sum, Leboeuf learned that the army would contain far fewer than the 300,000 to 330,000 men he had hoped for.

LEBOEUF'S EXPECTATIONS

Leboeuf hoped to call on about 1,142,000 men for service in 1870. Of these, 500,000 were enrolled in the *Garde Mobile* and 75,000 more were of the 1869 contingent which had not yet entered the army. This left the regular army, he thought, with 567,000 men. From this latter number Leboeuf hoped to create the Army of the Rhine. After subtracting troops for service in Algeria and Rome as well as depot troops and noncombatant categories, he counted on 231,000 available for service in the Army of the Rhine.[4] By adding reserves from the 173,000 he expected to join the colors within a few days of the order of mobilization, he believed he could concentrate between 300,000 and 330,000 men on the frontier for the beginning of operations. To this number, he anticipated adding the auxiliary services of at least a part of the national guard.

Leboeuf believed, furthermore, that this force would be ready by 1 August. A memorandum distributed by the War Ministry and entitled *"Delai strictement nécessaire pour la mise en route des militaires de la réserve et des jeunes soldats de la 2e portions des contingents"* outlined the War Minister's intentions. He allotted five days for dating and distributing the individual order slips which had been so carefully prepared since 1868. He assigned three more days to allow reservists to reach the capital of the department. From there they were to be sent within two days to the depot of the unit to which they were attached. Here they were to be "armed, clothed, and equipped" and sent on to the *portions actives* of the regiment, a process which required five more days.[5]

The recall of the 173,000 reservists for whom this schedule had been prepared became a source of great annoyance to them, their commanders, and the nation. Obliged to find their way from their homes to the regimental depot and on to the regiment often without an officer in charge, the reservists scandalized the country with their drunkenness and lack of discipline. Many of them believed their early release had in fact liberated them from all further obligations and expressed their resentment by feigning sickness, destroying their ammunition, or refusing to obey orders. A witness riding on a train with reservists on their way to Châlons took special note of the sullen behavior of the men. One soldier, with only a few weeks left before his final discharge and with plans of marriage, broke out in tears saying, "Now they are going to put me up front for the slaughter". The circumstances may have been exceptional in this man's case, but his attitude summarized the feelings of many reservists in 1870.[6]

Unhappy as they were to serve, their officers were even more displeased to have them. Most of these men had been released before the adoption of the *chassepot* and had to be trained to use it. Very often this training took place within the theater of operations. So unsatisfactory was the performance of these men that many officers openly stated their preference to fight without them.[7]

The manpower Leboeuf was counting on, however, was not limited to the regular army and its reserves. In the two weeks following the call of the reserves, the war office took the time to prepare the mobilization of other men. The classes of 1869 and 1870 were called into service. The Ministry of War sent out directives governing the incorporation of volunteers, putting the Marine Light Infantry on a war footing, and bringing customs officials and state foresters under its orders. The *gendarmerie nationale* was mobilized; its purpose was to accompany the Army of the Rhine and serve as a police force for the protection of civilian populations.[8] Imperial decrees allowed the formation of foreign battalions and of corps of *franc-tireurs*.[9] Even the Paris fire brigade was called into service.[10] Few of these formations saw much active service. Nobody was prepared to receive, train, and equip them; and any attempt to do so was to waste time and energy needed elsewhere. All that these measures betrayed was a growing uncertainty over numbers. France's numerical inferiority was beginning to take its toll of nerves in the war office.[11]

Of more importance to the army than the above steps was the decree of 16 July which mobilized the *Garde Nationale Mobile* in Paris and the northern and eastern departments. A subsequent decree, issued 10 August following the defeats of Froeschwiller and Spicheren, extended the mobilization of the *Garde* to the rest of the country.[12] These measures suggested too that the French high command was already disturbed by the shortage of trained soldiers. By law, the *Garde* could not be ordered into battle, but there was nothing to prevent army officials from assigning guardsmen to duties that would liberate trained regulars for service on the front.[13]

The French high command quickly found uses for mobilized guardsmen. In messages to Ladmirault and Canrobert on 18 July, *Aide Major-Général* Lebrun recommended that the staffs of the 4th and 6th Army Corps obtain secretaries from the *Garde Mobile*.[14] *Aide Major-Général* Jarras sent a similar note to Bazaine two days later. In it he informed the marshal that by the emperor's orders nobody was to be taken from the ranks of the Army of the Rhine and that all accessory personnel must be taken from volunteers of the *Garde*.[15] Several messages of 25 July recommended the use of guardsmen in military convoys.[16] By 1 August, the need for additional personnel had become so urgent that the War Ministry asked the prefects of all departments to seek from guardsmen a long list of professions which included bakers, butchers, barrel-makers, masons, carpenters, joiners, locksmiths, and blacksmiths. This was to make official military policy what Leboeuf had already recommended to Napoleon III.[17] Thus began the mobilization of a previously unorganized branch of the French armed forces.

THE MEN JOIN THEIR UNITS

The French command had good reason to want auxiliary troops for the regular army. Aware of an acute shortage of manpower, the commanders of the eight corps of the Army of the Rhine had, by 27 July, forwarded messages to Imperial Headquarters in Metz urging the staff to bring up reserves as quickly as possible. Their ranks, they warned, had not been filled up, and no operations could be undertaken without more men.

The general causes of these shortages have been known since 1870. Few books which treat the opening weeks of the War of 1870 fail to mention the chaos and confusion that followed Leboeuf's call for the reserves on 14 July. In two weeks French recruiting officers dispersed some one hundred sixty-three thousand reservists to the regimental depots scattered throughout France. These men congested railroad stations while they awaited the transportation nobody had ever scheduled for them. Their presence aggravated the confusion already caused by the simultaneous transporting of men, guns, horses, wagons, munitions, and supplies, which were converging helter-skelter from bases, depots, and arsenals upon the zones of concentration. Oftentimes these reserves crossed paths with regiments they were eventually to join. Their departure from the depots was frequently delayed because they lacked necessary equipment and because officers in charge had received no orders to send them forward. In the case of the Meurthe military subdivision the territorial command refused to release reservists to regiments based there or passing by their depots in the region on their way to the zone of concentration.[18] Their transportation by detachments to the frontier caused further strain on the railroads which, again, were not prepared to take on this added burden.   Under these circumstances, some detachments of reserves never reached their destination at all; those that did arrived much later than anticipated.[19]

There are still other reasons to explain the gaps in the ranks of the Army of the Rhine. The cavalry, the artillery, and the auxiliary services encountered special difficulties that prevented them from appearing at full manpower strength in the zones of concentration. The mobilization of the *Garde Nationale Mobile* was the source of even further delays. Taken together these problems help to illustrate how faulty the French mobilization of 1870 was. They suggest, furthermore, what can happen without adequate preparation, for each of these problems required several months of planning of a kind that was noticeably lacking in the French army of 1870.

The failure of the reservists to reach their units in the time or number expected was a fault, in the first place, of the Ministry of War. One of the most serious mistakes made by Napoleon III in 1870 was to appoint General Leboeuf as his Chief of Staff (*Major-Général*), simply because now the administrative apparatus of the French army had to be turned over to a new man. On 26 July, the job went into the hands of Leboeuf's able assistant, General Dejean, but Dejean merely assumed the position of Interim War Minister, a status that created some question in his mind as to the full extent of his authority. "We have decided," he informed Leboeuf on 27 July, "that all correspondence from army corps commanders who address correspondence to the central war administration will go to you first."[20] Moreover, he needed time to accustom himself to operating the cumbersome machinery of the war office, and the tasks he was asked to perform simultaneously would have broken a weaker man. He did his job well, but political problems arising from the defeats of 6 August, contributed to his replacement on 13 August by the Count of Palikao, who, at least, enjoyed full authority as War Minister. But for the second time in a month, the war office suffered from change of direction at the top.[21]

To coordinate the activities of the French Ministry of War in July and August 1870 was, in any case, an impossible task. Officers who paid a visit to the *rue Saint-Dominique* recall the bustle and confusion evident in each room; above all they noted the lack of central direction to guide all the activity.[22] Since the mobilization of the army had gone virtually unplanned, each *bureau* of the war office had ample opportunity to issue orders and make requests with little regard to overall operations. Confusing in their variety, contradictory in their intent, and often vague in meaning, these orders were dispersed throughout France: they set trains in motion, halted or diverted them; they distributed supplies or held them back; and they moved men in bewildering directions. The military archives are full of telegrams requesting explanation of orders or greater precision on unclear points. Units of reservists were often sent to the wrong places, thus adding the extra burden of answering demands from irate officials who did not know how to handle unwanted and unexpected hands. Quite often officials held reservists in their depots until express order to send them to the

Army of the Rhine came through from the Ministry of War; yet such orders were sent only after urgent request from Imperial Headquarters.[23]

Compared with the chaos in the Ministry of War, the eighty-four recruitment centers of France dispatched their duties with relative efficiency. Nevertheless, there were snags which delayed the movement of the reserves. The peculiarities of the regimental system assured recruitment officers several sleepless nights. They had to find trains to take men to their depots, but they frequently discovered that railroad transport was not readily available. Moreover, even before they sent reservists on, they had to sort these men out by regimental detachment. Since, furthermore, these centers were understaffed, the process of sorting and sending consumed time, and the longer the work took the greater the problems, for in the meantime the reservists had to be fed and sheltered. Little had been prepared for the care of reservists in the departmental capitals.[24] Under these circumstances, it is a wonder that the men were processed at all, but by 24 July, the latest date Leboeuf had allowed for transportation of reserves to the depots, recruitment centers had in fact dispatched 141,500 men.[25]

There was a third factor that delayed the arrival of reservists in the active ranks of the Army of the Rhine: far too many were retained at the depots. The depots had two responsibilities: putting the combat battalions of the unit on a war footing and maintaining a trained manpower reserve as a source both of replacements within the unit and of experienced cadres for completely new units.[26] As reserves reached the depots, officers saw to the clothing, arming, and equipping of these men, and they formed them into detachments ready to be sent to the frontier. But this was all they had orders to do. They had received clear instructions not to forward the detachments to the zone of concentration until expressly ordered. "This," explained Dejean to MacMahon, whose complaints about the shortages of manpower echoed several that arrived in Paris during the opening weeks of the war, "is to prevent congestion and errors of destination."[27]

Between 15 and 19 July, each infantry regiment of the French army also received orders to create a reserve battalion. At first these "fourth battalions" were to be made up of reserves and the cadres of two companies from each of the three combat battalions.[28]   Later orders, however, prescribed the incorporation of any soldier, active, "first portion" or "second portion," into these units. The results of these orders were doubly disastrous. The depots used trained men as the nucleus of these reserve units and sent men of the "second portion" forward. In the meantime, while the depots retained large numbers of men, the army, partly because of numerical inferiority, suffered its first defeats.[29]

As the depots filled with men, both depot officials and commanders in the field requested permission from the war office to transport troops to the Army of the Rhine. For officers in charge of the depots, the matter was urgent.

Supplies were running low, and the depots could not accommodate all the men present.[30]   For the field commanders, the matter was equally pressing. The offensive, they understood, was to begin soon, but wartime battalions were not yet at full strength. In response to these requests the War Ministry, beginning on 26 July, dispatched several telegrams instructing depot officials to forward detachments of men. On 27 July alone the Ministry of War dispatched messages to fifteen regiments of infantry ordering the movement of detachments totaling 5,692 troops.[31] As the days went by the tone of these messages became more desperate. More and more they stressed the need for immediate compliance. The depots responded with as many men as they could put onto trains.[32]

After the mobilized men left the depots for the front, still a fourth problem created delays. A few detachments lost their way, largely due to the lack of transport. If there was no train to take them to their destination, the men hitched a ride to a point as close as possible to their unit. In other cases, they were sent to the wrong place. The detachments of the 27th, 48th, 68th, and 86th infantry regiments were all sent by mistake to Metz. Failing to reach their units, they were incorporated into *ad hoc* units raised to defend the town. Still other detachments were sent off to units stationed in Rome and Algeria. Irate at having the garrisons at Brest and Lorient emptied, the commander of the Sixteenth Territorial Division (Rennes), independently secured detachments from the units previously stationed there. His orders were quickly countermanded.[33]

These, then, were the chief obstacles which hindered the movement of the reserves in the summer of 1870. The Ministry of War tried to keep as close to Leboeuf's schedule as it could. But between administrative chaos and the operation of the regimental system, Leboeuf was forced to accept results he had not anticipated. In the five days he expected reserve detachments to be dispatched to the Army of the Rhine depots yielded far fewer soldiers than he needed, perhaps as few as 63,642 if figures supplied a few years later by the historian and military analyst Victor Dérrécagaix are to be accepted.[34] For the 6th Corps detachments began to arrive in significant numbers only on 1 August. During the first three days of August its first division alone reported the arrival of 2,138 reservists, but by then the 6th Corps, theoretically in reserve behind the Army of the Rhine, was immobilized for lack of troops and was located too far to the rear to be of use in the coming days.[35] The Army of the Rhine counted at most 280,000 combatant troops as of 1 August, a number far lower than the figure the *Major-Général* promised Napoleon III two weeks previously.[36]

In mobilizing the required numbers of men for war in 1870, all units of the French Army suffered from the delays which prevented reservists from reaching the Army of the Rhine within the two to two and a half weeks Leboeuf had counted on. Some branches of the army, furthermore, had to solve problems special to their arms, and these problems, too, contributed to the shortage of manpower in the Army of the Rhine.

There were, for example, enough trained troops to fill the ranks of every cavalry unit sent to the frontier in 1870, but there were too few horses. In July 1870, according to the custom adhered to each summer, the number of men serving each cavalry unit was close to wartime strength.[37] The same was not true, however, for the number of horses. No cavalry unit kept enough of them during peacetime to provide mounts for all cavalrymen in wartime. When war broke out, the officers in charge were obliged to obtain horses by whatever method they could devise. The cavalry obtained 11,000 horses from the *gendarmerie*, thereby retarding the mobilization of this organization which now too fell short of horses.[38] The number the cavalry got, however, was insufficient, and officers had to resort to purchase. Such an expedient proved to be unsatisfactory. Not until after the beginning of the mobilization was there a decision to establish a purchase commission to help the cavalry obtain horses.[39] The steeds available turned out to be too small and too poorly bred to be of significant value to the cavalry, and there was not enough of these inferior animals to allow squadrons to attain full strength. As a result, in spite of the availability of trained men, the cavalry squadrons in the Army of the Rhine averaged 126 mounted men, a figure much lower than the 171 set by regulations.[40]

Like the cavalry, the artillery was short of horses. It possessed enough guns, carriages, and supply wagons to mobilize 396 batteries in the summer of 1870, but this force also required 51,500 horses. The French artillery had on hand only 17,000, a number insufficient to mobilize the 154 batteries it was expected to send to the Army of the Rhine.[41] As in the cavalry, artillery officers had to resort to purchase, and the quantity as well as the quality of available draught-horses left much to be desired. To make matters worse, it was discovered that the supply depots were also short of harnesses. As a result, barely enough matériel could be gathered to equip the divisionary batteries of the Army of the Rhine. The reserve artillery parks never reached their full complement of men and equipment, and all other batteries similarly were unable to take full advantage of the firepower they were supposed to have.[42] Thus, the disadvantage in range and accuracy under which the French artillery already labored was aggravated by its inability to realize whatever potential it did possess.[43]

Of the other branches of the army, the engineer corps and the *Intendance* encountered no serious difficulties in mobilizing the manpower they had trained. They simply had not trained enough men in the first place. The *Train des Equipages Militaires*, on the other hand, had sufficient manpower, but when Leboeuf arrived in Metz he learned that very few of these men were serving the Army of the Rhine. The reason is not difficult to ascertain: in the military archives there are several telegrams dated from 28 July to 6 August to the *Train* depots ordering that the mobilized companies of this organization be dispatched to seven corps of the Army of the Rhine. Obviously, the Ministry of War had overlooked these vital units when sending the rest of the army to the frontiers. As late as 2 August Imperial Headquarters was sheepishly assuring the commanders of the seven corps of the Army of the Rhine that it was taking measures to speed up the dispatch of *Train* workers to the frontiers.[44]

The effect of this oversight upon the mobility of the army was not missed by Marshal Canrobert. His report of 27 July was pointed and caustic. Most of his combat troops had arrived, he noted, but, he added, "There are in our military organization very useful accessories about which the 6th Corps currently knows nothing and without which putting this corps in motion is simply not possible: I am speaking of administrative troops."[45] In the meantime, other commanders of the Army of the Rhine, equally short of workers to drive wagons, purchase and deliver supplies, and perform miscellaneous labor duties, began to rely on civilian help. Dependence on non-military aid, however, has one great disadvantage: civilians are not subject to military discipline. They may come and go as they please.

MOBILIZATION OF THE *GARDE NATIONALE MOBILE*

Of all the measures taken to increase the manpower available to the French army in 1870, none was more futile than the mobilization of the *Garde Nationale Mobile*. Since it was virtually unorganized, its mobilization required enormous amounts of time and effort to make up for the years of work in fact necessary to raise and train it for the duties expected of it in 1870. It must be admitted that the French command could not foresee quick defeat and that they, therefore, thought the army would have sufficient time to train the *Garde*. Similarly, it must be remembered that the army was critically short of service troops. The attempt to use the *Garde Nationale Mobile*, however, brought out all the faults of French military planning and organization in 1870.

There were several difficulties in raising the *Garde* in the summer of 1870. In the first place, the war office had to call upon the cooperation of prefects, military intendants, and territorial commanders to organize the *Garde* into units and to find officers to lead it. The directives the ministerial bureau in charge of the *Garde* distributed to responsible officials suggest how great the task was. All individual mobilization order blanks had to be filled out and then sorted before delivery. Officials, furthermore, were asked to submit the names of men they thought fit for commission as officers and were told to watch the *Journal Officiel* for lists of those nominated. Leboeuf told the commander of the third territorial corps that the emperor allowed a few officers of the regular army to assist in the organization of the *Garde Nationale Mobile*. These officers, he added, would organize the cadre of officers, select noncommissioned officers, and oversee the training and equipping of the troops.[46] Qualified officers, however, were difficult to obtain, and on 30 July Leboeuf had to inform Dejean that the arming of the *Garde* in the Metz region was hindered by the lack of available officers, particularly from the artillery and the engineer corps.[47] In the meantime, the war office had to obtain funds to finance the operations of the *Garde*; it also had to determine the amount of pay guardsmen were to receive.[48]

For officials responsible for the mobilization of the army, the added burden of overseeing details of raising and equipping the *Garde* proved to be unusually irritating. A mere glance at the notations by the commander of the Third Territorial Infantry Brigade in Arras in his daily *registre* reveals how vexing these problems were. Besides coping with the detachments of reserves in the regular army and attending to the seemingly endless supply demands of its depots, this harassed individual found his own physical and mental resources strained by the simultaneous needs of the hitherto unorganized battalions of the *Garde*. Where was he to billet *gardes*? Did he have the authority to issue them arms? To what work duty should they be assigned? Did this include work in hospitals? And what should he do about those *gardes* discharged as unfit but not yet sent home? Their continued presence, he noted, was irregular and harmful to the interests of the state, a roundabout way of saying that their contagious rebelliousness was causing a severe discipline problem. Nor was his concern for the morale and the morals of the *gardes* limited to this matter. In the midst of a clearly busy work load he also found the time to have a *maison de tolérance* shut down and to order authorities to put surveillance upon a lady of doubtful reputation.[49]

Other records reveal how widespread and all encompassing these organizational problems were, for clearly nothing had been done to prepare for the mobilization of the *Garde*. These were matters that concerned not just the Ministry of War but the Ministries of the Interior and of Public Works as well. "Must I call out everybody in the *Garde Nationale* as the figures sent to me indicate or just well-selected artillery companies as the dispatch states?" so inquired the Prefect of the Ardennes to the Minister of the Interior on 26 July.[50] At the same time the railroad companies had their own problems to sort out with the *Garde*. Not until somebody raised the issue after the start of the mobilization were *gardes* assured that they could travel by rail to their bases at the same reduced rate as regular soldiers. Furthermore lines affected by the mobilization obtained exemptions for their workers inscribed on the rolls of the *Garde*, but the general call-out of the *Garde* on 10 August threw this privilege into doubt. It took special assurances from the Minister of Public Works that all railroad workers remained exempt from duty in the *Garde* to allay these fears.[51] Meanwhile authorities noted inconsistencies in instructions in the nomination of officers in the *Garde*; others, most notably Marshal Canrobert, complained about the large numbers of units of the *Garde* arriving on the scene unannounced and expecting food and billeting.[52]

Well might officials like Canrobert have lamented the unexpected arrival of *gardes*, for supplying them was beyond the means of the army in the summer of 1870. There were serious shortages of food, uniforms, and tents and camping equipment. Little transportation was prepared to deliver them to army camps; nobody had regularized the means to pay them. Medical authorities lacked the time to examine them and release those unfit to serve.[53] Nor could they be adequately armed. The supply of *chassepots* was sufficient for the regular army. Members of the *Garde* were issued rifles from a supply of 800,000 older model weapons adapted to 1870 standards, but these proved to be heavier and less accurate and could only be fired at a slower rate of fire. Many guardsmen openly grumbled about the inferior weapons they received.[54]

For the *Garde* units of the Paris region, which had been organized into battalions prior to the outbreak of war, the problem of mobilization lay elsewhere. The Paris *Garde* had received little or no training, and when it descended upon the training camp at Châlons on 29 July, it brought with it a lot of indiscipline and disorder that alternately shocked and delighted both inhabitants of the region and the press. Upon their arrival most Paris guardsmen marched in order into the Camp of Châlons where they set themselves up as best they could in spite of the shortages of nearly everything. The effect was more like a jamboree than a military encampment. Men milled about, performed chores more according to their jobs at home than to any military necessity, organized entertainments, gave Parisian street names to the alley ways in the camp, and posted their names on their tents, the better to facilitate the arrival of the large number of civilians who, according to reports, daily visited the base.[55]

Work assignments were quite another matter. Guardsmen refused to perform KP duty, garbage detail or sweeping-up work. And for a very noticable minority any sign of order was an anathema. Some of these men disembarked from their train, took an omnibus by assault, and rode it into the camp; others broke rank and overran the cafés and drinking spots of the town of Mourmelon which lay just outside the gates of the camp.[56] Others joined regulars of the 6th Corps in acts of vandalism which appeared to have political connotations. One of their targets was the statue of the Prince Imperial which they overturned and smashed while, as the reports put it, they uttered "cries of sedition."[57]

Marshal Canrobert, whose 6th Corps was assembling in the Camp of Châlons and who was responsible for order in the camp, found the situation alarming. A tactful man, he sought to exercise the charm for which he was known to coax guardsmen into accepting discipline. He inquired into their well-being, and his messages to Paris reveal a genuine concern about the deplorable shortage of supplies for these men. On 1 August he tried to display his concern by passing the *Garde* in review, but he got a rebellious demonstration as a reward. Thirty troops of the Belleville battalion were arrested for hurling insults at him; other troops were heard to shout anti-government slogans. To cheers of "Long Live the Emperor." guardsmen responded with "*Un*! *deux*! *trois*! *merde*!" With no way to control these men Canrobert had to post pickets along with the *gendarmerie* to patrol the peripheries of the camp. Later on, when he began to move his own troops forward to make contact with the Army of the Rhine, he had to leave a battalion of veteran regulars behind to guard the supplies he was unable to take along with him. Canrobert's solution to the discipline problem was to disperse the Paris *Garde* among frontier posts, and this he recommended to Dejean. Empress Eugénie agreed--just so long as not one unit was returned to Paris. Nobody took up Canrobert's recommendation, and the Paris *Garde* remained in Châlons until late in August.[58]

In the northern and eastern departments, the mobilization of the *Garde* was almost as disorderly. Officials echoed Canrobert's requests with telegrams demanding the removal of the Guardsmen. Here the cause of discontent was shortage of supplies. Overwhelmed with the work of supplying the regular army, the *Intendance* claimed it was not responsible for the *Garde Mobile*. As a result, little was available for the Guardsmen. Alsatian Guardsmen found, upon arrival at Belfort, that they could not even expect to find billets for the night.[59]

Similar difficulties attended upon civil and military authorities when the mobilization of the *Garde National Mobile* was extended to all remaining departments after 10 August. Messages instructed prefects to gather *gardes* in the seat of each arrondissement by 18 August and have the men ready for departure to the departmental capital the following day. These authorities were also told to expect temporary shortages of uniforms but to count on a plentiful supply of rifles. They were to keep the men in good order and lodge them adequately until such time as army officials took charge of the *Garde*, presumably on 24 August. But no message instructed prefects on measures to take should the army be unprepared to receive units of the *Garde*.[60]

As soon as the units began to assemble, officials were overwhelmed by the same shortcomings and problems that had plagued their counterparts in the northern departments the previous month. Nobody knew which tasks were to be performed by civil or which by military personnel. In the *Garde* there were too few commissioned and noncommissioned officers and too many guardsmen. Discipline suffered accordingly. Several *gardes* claimed exemption from service; nobody had the time to verify these claims. As predicted, guardsmen could not be issued uniforms at once.   Men who obtained them received ill-fitting, ill-matched remnants, and frequently they still ran short of accessory equipment, most notably shoes.   The promised rifles, meanwhile, did not regularly materialize. When they arrived they were the out-of-date makeovers referred to above. Housing fell short of needs. Disorder was endemic. In Blois notably, angry guardsmen vented their feelings upon a passing clergyman whom they insulted mercilessly. When a policeman tried to intervene, he was roughed up and chased away. Later on the same day, many guardsmen got drunk and milled about the streets irritating the prefect by shouting republican slogans. Elsewhere there were similar outbreaks of this kind of sullen behavior.[61]

Such problems make it understandable why the mobilization of the *Garde Mobile* appeared so disappointing to those who expected it to perform significant auxiliary services to the Army of the Rhine. In fact the *Garde* was in no way ready to assist regulars in the upcoming campaign. In the meantime, the army had wasted valuable time and effort seeking to call upon the services of the *Garde*.

It is impossible to measure exactly the effect mobilizing the *Garde* exercised upon the mobilization of the Army of the Rhine. Two results, however, clearly emerge. In the first place, the army was not able to call upon the *Garde Mobile* for garrison duty or for auxiliary services. "The *Garde Mobile* is of no use to us as team drivers for the *Train des Equipages Militaires*." So wrote Canrobert to the Ministry of War on 3 August. While the marshal's disappointment no doubt derives from the noisy *garde* demonstration of two days earlier, the essence of his message reflects conditions elsewhere in the French army.[62] The Army had to draw upon its own manpower for these duties; else they would never have been performed. Secondly, the operations of the 7th Corps of the Army of the Rhine were adversely affected by the call-up of the *Garde*. Units of the 7th Corps were garrisoned in Lyons, and until replacements arrived, these units could not join the rest of 7th Corps in Belfort. Army officials hoped to use a few battalions of the *Garde* to relieve the regulars in Lyons, but no *Garde* units were ever forthcoming. The army had to gather a small number of regulars from elsewhere for garrison duties, but not until 5 August did these men arrive in Lyons. By then it was too late for most of the 7th Corps to join Marshal MacMahon on the Froeschwiller heights where the Germans attacked him on 6 August.[63]

THE SIZE OF THE ARMY OF THE RHINE, 1 AUGUST 1870

It remains to be seen how many men actually were in service in the Army of the Rhine by 1 August. Information of this nature was a matter of concern to the staff of the army. The high command required officers to report daily the number of men in their charge. These reports, tabulated by corps, enabled Napoleon III, his *Major-Général*, and his staff at Imperial headquarters at Metz to keep watch of the growing strength of the army. The results they obtained were disappointing. On 28 July, the tallies enumerated only 200,795 men in the Army of the Rhine. By 1 August this number had risen to 251,127, a figure far short of the one Leboeuf had predicted.[64]

The statistics Napoleon III received were not reliable. They were often based on reports submitted two or three days earlier, and sometimes they included men who had not yet arrived from their depots or who were still held on their bases. Since 1870 no one list of totals on the Army of the Rhine has coincided with another. Leboeuf later claimed that on 1 August 1870 there were 243,171 men in the Army of the Rhine; General Lebrun wrote that there were 235,800 men on the same date; and the French army officially set the total at 251,130. One authority has even contradicted himself in the same work: on one page he cites 251,127, and on another he enumerates 264,499 men.   Two situation reports, both dated 1 August, cite two different figures.   One claims there were 244,828 present; the other, 263,962.[65]

The most authoritative source on the question of numbers is Aristide Martinien's study, *La Guerre de 1870-71: la mobilisation de l'armée.* This work is not a monograph. There is barely a word of text to it; all the information is in tabular form. Thus while it is not quite the full history of the mobilization of the French army in 1870 as the title might imply, every bit of the statistical data is indispensable. By consulting army correspondence, attendance reports, regimental records, and depot journals, Martinien painstakingly produced the most reliable information available on the number of men in every regiment in the French army in 1870. From his findings he was able to state as closely as possible the total number of men under arms on 15 July 1870 and again on 1 August 1870. He has shown that of the 173,000 reservists expected in 1870 only 144,618 had reached the depots by 1 August.[66]   Furthermore, by using the statistics he provided for each regiment, it is possible for us to reach the conclusion that the number of men in the infantry, cavalry, and artillery units of the Army of the Rhine on 1 August was 279,909, a figure which, although higher than figures reported at the time, was still 20,000 short of the minimum Leboeuf had predicted. In the following five days 24,299 more men of the same branches left their depots in detachments. This number is the highest the depots would yield during those days in spite of increasingly desperate requests from the war office.   Even if these late detachments had reached their destination by 6 August, and many did not, the Army would have numbered at best only 304,208. Of these, the total number of infantry and cavalry, officers and enlisted men together, could have been no more than 253,224.[67]

These, then, were the numerical results of France's faulty mobilization in 1870. They were instrumental in forcing postponement of the offensive that Napoleon III hoped to undertake by 1 August. There were, however, problems of a different nature that also compelled the French high command to delay operations, and these obstacles were as patent as the shortage of manpower. Shortly after Leboeuf arrived in Metz, he inspected units drawn up near the city. What he found caused him great concern: the Army of the Rhine was desperately short of matériel and provisions of all kinds. In this respect, too, he was to learn, *passage sur le pied de guerre* was not operating as smoothly as he had expected.

NOTES

1. *Le Constitutionnel*, 20 July 1870, p. 2; 22 July 1870, p. 1; 25 July 1870, pp. 1-2.

2. Note to the Minister of War, 23 July 1870, SHAT, Vincennes, Lo 4 and 5.

3. France, Armée, Etat-major, Service Historique, *Préparation à la guerre* in *La Guerre de 1870-71*, 35 vols. (Paris: Chapelot, 1901-1903, p. 54, (cited hereafter as Guerre followed by the title of the particular volume to which reference is made).

4. These numbers are taken from Victor Dérrécagaix, *Guerre de 1870* (Paris: Le Spectateur Militaire, 1871), pp. 50-51. Many other sources on the regular army report roughly the same figures; see Charles Fay, *Journal d'un officier de l'Armée du Rhin* (Brussels: Muquardt, 1871), pp. 15-16 and Louis Le Gillou, *La Campagne d'été de 1870* (Paris: Charles-Lavauzelle, 1938), pp. 85-86. The most authoritative source, however, is Aristide Martinien, *La Guerre de 1870-71. La Mobilisation de l'armée: mouvements des dépôts (armée active) du 15 juillet au 1 mars, 1871* (Paris: L. Fournier, 1912), and his figures show that LeBoeuf overestimated the size of the army. On p. 309 he shows that the army had 367,670 men on active duty on 15 July, 1870. To this figure we may add 173,000 reservists, which brings the total to only about 520,670 in the regular army.

5. France, Assemblée Nationale, *Enquête parlementaire sur les actes du Gouvernement de la Défense Nationale: déposition des témoins*, 5 vols. (Paris: Germer-Baillière, 1872-1875), I, p. 69 (cited hereafter as D.T.). Also see Victor Dérrécagaix, *La Guerre moderne*, 2 vols. (Paris: L. Baudoin, 1885), I, p. 404.

6. Useful descriptions of these situations may be found in German Bapst (ed)., *Le Maréchal Canrobert: Souvenirs d'un siècle*, 6 vols. (Paris: Plon, 1898-1913), IV, pp. 158-159 where, interestingly, we find Marshal Canrobert crediting a Col. Ardent du Picq with commendable handling of these morale problems in the 10th line regiment. See also Barthélemy Edmond Palat, *Histoire de la guerre de 1870-71*, Part I: *La guerre de 1870*, 6 vols. Paris: Berger-Levrault, 1903-1908), II, pp. 134-135; Le Gillou, *La Campagne d'été de 1870*, pp. 28, 83-84; Henry Brackenbury, *Les Maréchaux de France* (Paris: Lachaud, 1872), p. 23.

7. Le Gillou, *La Campagne d'été de 1870*, pp. 84-85; Palat, *Histoire*, Part I: *la Guerre de 1870*, II, 115, 135-136; Capitaine Dagneau, *Historique du 13e régiment d'infanterie* (Paris: Charles-Lavauzelle, 1891), p. 78; General Devauraix, *Souvenirs et observations sur la campagne de 1870* (Paris: Charles-Lavauzelle, 1900), pp. 40-41.

8. Orders and Circulars, SHAT, Vincennes, Lq 2.

9. Notes, letters, and circulars, SHAT, Vincennes, La 6, folders 18 and 21 July; La 7, folder 7 August; Lo 2 and 3, folder 13 July; and Xp 67, folder "Corps francs." See also Dérrécagaix, *Guerre moderne*; I, p. 409; Palat, *Histoire*, Part I: *La Guerre de 1870*, II, pp. 145-146.

10. Martinien, *La Guerre de 1870-71. La mobilisation de l'armée*, pp. 232-233.

11. Palat, *Histoire*, Part I: *La Guerre de 1870*, II, p. 138 has suggested this idea, and his point seems reasonable.

12. Decrees, 16 July and 12 August 1870, SHAT, Vincennes, Xm 52. See also J.O., 17 July 1870, p. 1267 and 11 August 1870, p. 1396.

13. Le Gillou, *La Campagne d'été de 1870*, p. 82.

14. Telegrams, Lebrun to 4th Army Corps Command and 6th Army Command, 18 July 1870, SHAT, Vincennes, La 6.

15. Telegram, 20 July 1870, AN, Paris, AB XIX 1711.

16. Telegram, Jarras to Bazaine, 20 July 1870, SHAT, Vincennes, La 6; Telegrams, 25 July 1870, SHAT, Vincennes, Lb 1; Note, 2 August 1870 SHAT, Vincennes, Lr. 8.

17. Circular, Minister of War to Prefects, 1 August 1870, SHAT, Vincennes, La 7. J.O., 22 July 1870, p. 1303.

18. Telegram to Ministry of War, 26 July 1870, AN, Paris, AB XIX, 1713.

19. There are several descriptions of the chaos which resulted from the simultaneous movement of active units and their reserves. The best are in Palat, *Histoire*, Part I: *La Guerre de 1870*, II, pp. 127, 130-133; Dérrécagaix, *Guerre moderne*, I, pp. 403-05; Michael Howard, *The Franco-Prussian War* (London: Rupert Hart-Davis, 1961), pp. 66-67.

20. Telegram, Dejean to Leboeuf, 27 July 1870, SHAT, Vincennes, Lb 1, folder 27 July.

21. Guerre, *Mesures d'organisation depuis le début de la guerre jusqu'au 4 septembre*, p. 4.

22. Barthélemy Louis Joseph Lebrun, *Souvenirs militaires 1866-1870. Préliminaires de la guerre. Missions en Belgique et à Vienne* (Paris: E. Dentu, 1895), p. 193.

23. Telegrams, Notes, SHAT, Vincennes, La 6, Lo 4 and 5.

24. Two good descriptions of conditions in recruitment centers may be found in Jean-Baptiste-Alexandre Montaudon, *Souvenirs militaires*, 2 vols. (Paris: Delagrave, 1898-1900), II, p. 59 and C. E. Bertrand, *Souvenirs de 1870: Notes d'un aide-major auxiliaire* (Paris: Baillière, 1900), p. 21.

25. See Appendix I. See also Palat, *Histoire*, Part I: *La Guerre de 1870*, II, p. 130. The number was 31,000 short of the 173,000 desired. Palat adds that 21,500 were sent in the next three days. The remaining 10,000 dallied along or never joined the colors at all.

26. Dérrécagaix, *Guerre moderne*, I, p. 410; Colonel E. R. Rocolle, "Anatomie d'une mobilisation," *Revue Historique des Armées*, No. 2, 1979, p. 39.

27. Letter, Dejean to MacMahon, 1 August 1870, SHAT, Vincennes La 7.

28. French infantry regiments in 1870 consisted of three battalions of eight companies each. The remaining companies served as reserve battalions and depot troops to which two more companies, "created out of nothing," were to be attached according to Colonel E. R. Rocolle, "Anatomie d'une mobilisation," *Revue Historique des Armées*, p. 39. Other branches of the army similarly left troops behind in the depots. Many of these formed the basis of the *régiments de marche* which made up the Army of Châlons and which surrendered at Sedan.

29. See the statistics for each regiment of the line infantry in Martinien, *La Guerre de 1870-71. La Mobilisation de l'armée*, pp. 26-191. See also Palat, *Histoire*, Part I: *La Guerre de 1870*, II, p. 138 and Le Gillou, *La Campagne d'été de 1870*, p. 87.

30. Telegrams, Commanders of the Fifth and Nineteenth Territorial Divisions to Minister of War, 27 July and 3 August, 1870, SHAT, Vincennes, La 6 and La 7.

31. Telegrams, Ministry of War to Commanders of Territorial Divisions, 27 July 1870, SHAT, Vincennes, La 6.

32. Scores of these messages may be found in SHAT, Vincennes, La 6 and La 7. The dates run from 27 July to 5 August.

33. Telegrams, 22 July 1870, SHAT, Vincennes Lo 4 and 5; Fabre de Navacelle, *Précis de la guerre franco-allemande* (Paris: Plon, 1890), p. 10; Le Gillou, *La Campagne d'été de 1870*, pp. 83-84.

34. See Appendix II below. The figure 63,642 is derived from the increase in reserves over the previous day for the period from 28 July to 1 August. Dérrécagaix's totals appear to be low, but even so the slow rate of increase in the number of men in the Army of the Rhine is cogently tabulated in these columns.

35. "Journal de marche...de la 1re Division du 6e corps," SHAT, Vincennes, Lb 64.

36. Figure based on Martinien, *La Guerre de 1870-71. La Mobilisation de l'armée*. It represents the number of infantry, cavalry, and artillery troops on the Army of the Rhine on 1 August 1870.

37. See statistics for war squadrons and depot troops on 1 August 1870 in Martinien, *La Guerre de 1870-71. La Mobilisation de l'armée*, pp. 234-284. See also D. T., I, p. 44 and Le comte de La Chapelle, *Les Forces militaires de la France en 1870*, (Paris: Amyot, 1872), pp. 92-93. Cavalry officers preferred to train men during the summer and release them from duty during the winter months.

38. "Gendarmerie nationale, ordre du jour no. 16," 26 July 1870, SHAT, Vincennes, Lq 2.

39. SHAT, Vincennes, Lr 8, folder 1.

40. Palat, *Histoire*, Part I: *La Guerre de 1870*, II, p. 140; Lieutenant-Colonel Bonie, *Campagne de 1870: la cavalerie française*, (Paris: Amyot, 1871), p. 4.

41. France, Assemblée Nationale, Année 1873, *Rapport fait en nom de la commission des marchés relatif à l'enquête sur la guerre* (Versailles: Cerf et fils, 1873), pp. 25-26. For the number of guns available see Ibid., pp. 24-25 and D. T., I, p. 44. See also Palat, *Histoire*, Part I: *La Guerre de 1870*, II, p. 141; Martinien, *La Guerre de 1870-71. La Mobilisation de l'armée*, p. 309.

42. Fabre de Navacelle, *Précis de la guerre franco-allemande*, p. 11.

43. Very soon after combat began many officers reached this conclusion. See, for example, Charles-Nicolas Lacretelle, *Souvenirs* (Paris: Emile-Paul, 1907), p. 256. Messages detailing the tardy and incomplete mobilization of the artillery abound in the archives of the French army in Vincennes, notably cartons Lo 4 and 5 and Lo 5 and 6. Like the infantry and cavalry, artillery units fell short of reservists. Others were misdirected to the wrong places in the zone of concentration. These problems, however, were less pressing, and the most serious problem confronting the artillery was the shortage of horses.

44. Telegrams, 28 July to 6 August 1870, SHAT, Vincennes, Lo 4 and 5, and Letters, General Jarras to Commander of Army of the Rhine, SHAT, Vincennes, Lb 4. To be sure, even if the companies of the *Train* had been ordered to Alsace and Lorraine, they would have been unable to get there fully equipped due to faults in the mobilization of supplies.

45. Report, Canrobert to Dejean, 27 July 1870, SHAT, Vincennes, Lr 8 and Lb 55.

46. Instructions, Leboeuf to Commander of the Third (Territorial) Corps, 16 July 1870, SHAT, Vincennes La 6. The *Garde* of the Third Territorial Corps (eastern France) was one of the first to be called.

47. Letter, Leboeuf to Dejean, 30 July 1870 SHAT, Vincennes, Lb 3.

48. The relevant letters and instructions may be found in SHAT, Vincennes, La 6, La 7, Lo 2 and 3.

49. "Registre, Third (Territorial) Infantry Brigade," SHAT, Vincennes, Lq 6, entries for August 1870.

50. Telegram, 26 July 1870, AN, Paris, AB XIX 1713.

51. "Registres" of the Compagnie de l'Est, AN, Paris, 13 AQ 54, entry for 21 July 1870 and 13 AQ 667, pp. 1242, 1306, 1373-1374, 1381; "Registres" of the Compagnie du Nord, AN, Paris, 48 AQ 17, pp. 94-95 and 48 AQ 102, entry for 19 July 1870.

52. "Cahier du correspondance du 6e Corps," 31 July 1870, SHAT, Vincennes, Lb 55; Telegram, 26 July 1870, AN, Paris, AB XIX 1712.

53. "Cahier du correspondance du 6e Corps," 25 July and 3 August 1870, SHAT, Vincennes, Lb 55; Letter to the Prefect of Calais, SHAT, Vincennes, Lq 6, folder 5; telegram, 25 July 1870, AN, Paris, AB XIX 1713.

54. Victor Moritz, *Froeschwiller, 6 août 1870* (Strasbourg: Dernières Nouvelles de Strasbourg, 1970), p. 175.

55. Much of this description is based in "Les mobiles au Camp de Châlons," *Le National*, 3 August 1870, pp. 2-3.

56. Ibid.

57. "Registre, 1re Division, 6e Corps," 31 July 1870, SHAT, Vincennes, Lb 65.

58. Howard, *The Franco-Prussian War*, p. 184; Bapst, *Le Maréchal Canrobert*, IV, pp. 150-153, 162. "Registre Canrobert," 6 August 1870, SHAT, Vincennes, Lb 55; "Correspondance:

Ministre et Major-Général," 6 August 1870, SHAT, Vincennes, Lb 55; "Journal de marche... de la 1re Division du 6e Corps," 3 August 1870, SHAT, Vincennes, Lb 64; "Registre, 1re Division du 6e Corps," 31 July 1870, SHAT, Vincennes, Lb 55.

59. Guerre, *Mesures d'organisation depuis le début de la guerre jusqu'au 4 septembre*, pp. 27-29; Emile Gluck, *Guerre de 1870-1871: 4e bataillon de la Mobile du Haut-Rhin, Journal d'un sous-officier* (Mulhouse: Meininger, 1908), pp. 7-8.

60. Telegram to prefects, 16 August 1870, AN, Paris, F⁹ 1257.

61. Material regarding the mobilization of the *Garde Nationale Mobile* may be found in AN, Paris F⁹ 1256 through 1259. These cartons contain reports and messages from prefects in several but not all the departments of France. The report on the behavior of the guardsmen in Blois is in carton F⁹ 1258, folder "Loir-et-Cher."

62. Telegram, Canrobert to Minister of War, 3 August 1870, SHAT, Vincennes, Lb 55. There is a similar type of message from the Intendant of the *Garde Nationale Mobile* to the Minister of War, 27 July 1870, AN, Paris, AB XIX 1713.

63. Nine battalions of infantry, nine squadrons of cavalry, and two batteries of artillery occupied Lyons on 1 August, Dérrécagaix, *Guerre moderne*, I, p. 428.

64. Dérrécagaix, *Guerre moderne*, I, p. 412. For a more complete summary of numbers of troops as they were reported to Imperial Headquarters, see Appendix II.

65. SHAT, Vincennes, La 7, folder 2 August; Ibid., Lb 4, folder 1 August. Leboeuf's figures are in D.T., I, p., 72. For the others see Lebrun, *Souvenirs militaires 1866-1870*, p. 197; Palat, *Histoire*, Part I: *La Guerre de 1870*, II, p. 403, and Dérrécagaix, *Guerre moderne*, I, pp. 412, 428.

66. Martinien, *La Guerre de 1870-71. La Mobilisation de l'armée*, pp. 309, 400, 409-410.

67. For a further breakdown based on Martinien's findings, see Appendix III. The figures for this table include only infantry and cavalry, the two branches most seriously affected by the failure to incorporate reservists in due time.

5

Mobilizing Supplies and Services

Of all the circumstances determining the fate of the French army in 1870 none was more ironic than the matter of logistics. While an undermanned and ill-supplied army went down to defeat, ample material lay just beyond its reach. France had, as it turned out, enough gaiter buttons--and rifles, ammunition, and other equipment as well. The French army, however, had not mastered a technique for distributing its equipment efficiently to men in the field. As a result corps and divisions wallowed helplessly, and the supplies which would have afforded them the mobility they so desperately required remained in warehouses and freight cars or got lost in transit.

Both Niel and Leboeuf had compiled a store of supplies which should have permitted the Army of the Rhine to campaign effectively in the summer of 1870. The army counted 1,037,555 *chassepots* and adequate supplies of ammunition--enough to maintain the army of 330,000 with which Leboeuf expected to undertake a campaign in late July.[1] Furthermore, during the Niel and Leboeuf ministries, French arsenals and warehouses had collected an impressive list of equipment that included uniforms, shoes, tents, blankets, and cooking utensils. After the war Leboeuf even declared with a precision so lacking in 1870 that the Army had stored 3,640,000 rations of *biscuit* (hardtack) for distribution.[2] When Leboeuf first arrived at Imperial headquarters, he thought his expectations were being met. "The 2nd Corps," he telegraphed to the Emperor on 25 July, "is complete, in good condition, well-supplied and ready to undertake a campaign."[3] Yet by the end of July 1870 corps commanders and intendants joined in showering headquarters with messages requesting delivery of all kinds of food and equipment.

After his arrival at Imperial Headquarters, Leboeuf spent days seeking remedies for the exasperatingly slow movement of supplies and auxiliary services to the army. Without these supplies and services, General Ladmirault (4th Corps) informed him, the army could not function.[4] Leboeuf responded by dispatching one of his aides, General Lebrun, to Paris to instruct officials on the organization of supply routes and special services.[5] Leboeuf's belated efforts were insufficient. In spite of the rich quantities of goods that piled up in the railroad yards in Metz, Forbach, and Strasbourg, the army possessed inadequate means of distributing these to the troops. Soldiers got along as best they could from day to day while they awaited the regular distribution of supplies. When the army transport workers arrived on the scene, they found few vehicles available, and the ones they obtained were in poor condition. As a consequence, the French army was even less mobile than the cumbersome German forces converging on it from the Rhine.

There were three general causes for this predicament. First, the *Intendance* was given duties it was ill-prepared to fulfill. Second, the auxiliary services, especially the transport services and the medical corps, faced insurmountable obstacles and performed unsatisfactorily. Third, there was no military unit at the railheads organized to unload trains and deliver supplies to the field army. As a result, the army had to resort to expedients and improvisations, so characteristic of the motto *"débrouillez-vous."* "Muddling through" worked in isolated instances, but it never compensated for the lack of meticulous planning, rational structuring, and careful distribution of supplies required of a massed force about to attack an equally formidable enemy.

THE *INTENDANCE*

For a service which has been described as the "grand master of morale for armies in the field," the French *Intendance* was remarkably unsuited to the duties it was asked to carry out in 1870. Its responsibilities covered several fields of administration, notably pay, food, uniforms, transport, military hospitals, and the medical corps.[6] Since the *Intendance* was short of personnel in 1870, these tasks were too numerous for it to oversee. Its organization, furthermore, prevented it from operating efficiently. In particular corps headquarters were top-heavy with *Intendance* workers while at the division level one *sous-intendant* and two adjutants were all that were available to administer the supply of six to nine thousand men.[7] During the mobilization of the French army in 1870, intendants became so confused and subsequently ineffectual that they must bear some of the blame for the French defeat.

Probably the worst shortcoming of the French *Intendance* in 1870 lay in its relationship within the chain of command. The activities of the *Intendance* were directed by *Intendant-Général* Wolff at his headquarters in Metz. Under Wolff one intendant and staff were assigned to each corps, and they in turn oversaw the work of the sub-intendants attached to each division. The *rapport* between these officials and the commanders whose corps they were to serve was limited and often strained. Leboeuf had warned intendants they faced exemplary punishment if they stood on formal regulations and refused supplies requisitioned by commanders.[8] Despite this they often tended to act independently of the command and looked upon themselves as delegates of the Ministry of War which had given them authority over the shipment of supplies. For example, *Intendance* workers in Strasbourg told General Ducrot, commander of the first division of the 1st corps, that he could not obtain camping equipment for two batteries of horse artillery without the signature of his intendant, who for the moment was unavailable. Generals, in turn, ignored these intendants to the point of failing to inform them where they expected to have supplies gathered; at times they left the responsibility of organizing convoys and itineraries to the intendants and then blamed them if supplies did not arrive on time.[9]

An equally serious deficiency of the *Intendance* was overcentralization of authority in the war ministry. Most supplies in the French army had been stored in six central warehouses from which goods were shipped upon order by the War Ministry. When commanders discovered their troops were short of matériel, they complained to their intendants, who retorted with the argument that until express permission had come from their superiors, they had no right to release anything. This kind of response betrays an attempt by intendants to evade responsibility, and it is evident even in the highest ranks. "I only transmit orders to ship or stop shipment of supplies. I do not take the initiative," wrote *Intendant-Général* Wolff to Dejean.[10] Even his orders were delayed, for intendants were unwilling to distribute what they had available without permission from Paris. Appeal to authority was an easy recourse for officials of the *Intendance*, indicating their unwillingness to take initiative in getting supplies to the army. The results were often preposterous: "May I have flannel belts delivered to those men who have none?" queried Bazaine, a Marshal of France, in a telegram sent to the war office.[11]

The operations of the *Intendance* in 1870 were also governed to too great an extent by mere habit. The French army was supplied in the same way it had been in the Crimean and Italian wars. In both these encounters, the record of the *Intendance* had been far from admirable. Yet no one attempted seriously to change its pattern of operations. The *Intendance* furthermore, was accustomed to supplying the demands of an army in Algeria. Here, unable to live off the country, the army depended on its convoys. Since the force in Algeria was rarely larger than 50,000 men, and since goods arrived regularly from France, they were able to keep the army well provisioned. In the Army of the Rhine, however, intendants had to deal with a force larger than they had ever cared for before. When supplies reached the field army more slowly than anybody expected, intendants were often at a loss to find a remedy. They certainly could have alleviated the crisis of food shortages by recourse to local requisition, but, writes one reliable historian, many intendants had forgotten how to requisition supplies. Clearly, then, little in the recent experience of the *Intendance* prepared its employees for the problems they had to solve in 1870.[12]

These shortcomings in the structure and performance of the *Intendance* were exacerbated by problems for which it was not responsible. The fact that generals sometimes failed to inform intendants of their marching route has already been cited. Infantrymen, too, caused intendants endless trouble. By regulation each soldier was supposed to carry his weapons, ammunition, four days' rations, cooking utensils, a change of uniform, an extra pair of boots, and his camping equipment in a pack on his back. These supplies the soldier was to obtain in the depots, but since depots were often short of these items, soldiers went to the front without many of the things they needed. Even soldiers who set out for war with a full load on their backs often marched into battle short of their personal supplies. A full load weighed seventy-five pounds, and because the months of July and August 1870 saw blazing heat alternate with heavy rain, exhausted soldiers often threw off a burden which had become intolerable to them.[13] Enterprising soldiers of the 2nd Corps found a profitable way to dispose of their unwanted equipment; they sold pieces of it to eager souvenir hunters of the town of Saint-Avold.[14]

There were still other problems for which the harassed officials of the *Intendance* were not responsible. The twin defeats at Froeschwiller and Spicheren on 6 August caused the 1st and 2nd Corps to abandon stores which, in spite of the confusion during mobilization, had actually been collected near these two corps. Further, several auxiliary services placed under the direction of the *Intendance* were unorganized at the outbreak of the war. Without them it was impossible to complete the task of mobilizing the Army of the Rhine.

THE AUXILIARY SERVICES

No document better illustrates how deficient the army was in organization of auxiliary services than a memorandum Napoleon III wrote to Leboeuf on 23 July 1870. It contained a list of instructions on the establishment of "branches of the services" to which attention had to be paid if the organization of the army was to be complete. There were eighteen items on the list, and these included such necessary services as a railway construction and repair corps, military telegraphists, an army staging system, military requisition officials, medical services, and army postal services. The emperor requested Leboeuf to "organize the means of transport for civil engineers, the telegraph service, chaplains, printers, employees of the Ministry of War who accompany the army, interpreters, orderlies, foreign officers, and authorized writers." These men, furthermore, were to receive arms, food supplies, tents, and uniforms. In the longest item on the list, Napoleon called for the establishment of an army staging system through which campaign kitchens, storehouses, ambulances, hospitals, military convalescent homes, veterinary hospitals, camp grounds, and prison camps would be carefully established. All of Napoleon's requests, some of which were very detailed, indicate the extent to which he understood military problems, for the provision of the services might have allowed for the more orderly advance of troops and trains and for well-established stopping places. 23 July 1870, however, was too late a date for the emperor to call anybody's attention to the fact that these services did not yet exist. In the opinion of Michael Howard, the French needed months if not years of preparation to avoid shortcomings like these.[15]

Of all the auxiliary services directed by the *Intendance* in 1870, none was more crucial to the mobility of the French army than the *Train des Equipages Militaires* (Military Transport Services). It was the responsibility of the *Train* to provide the horses and wagons that served to connect the army in the field to the railheads. The carrying of food, ammunition and other supplies required about 10,000 men and accompanying wagons to serve the Army of the Rhine in 1870. Marshal Niel stated in 1868 that the Army had a sufficient number of wagons to keep the army moving. The three regiments of the *Train* had trained enough men to run the transport services so that the army undertook no basic change in the organization of the *Train* after the War of 1870.[16]

In spite of these facts, the mobilization of the *Train* was very slow. Leboeuf had expected it, like all other services, to be ready by 28 July, but, by 1 August, only 3,930 troops of the *Train* had been sent forward from their depots.[17] On 23 July General Frossard, whose 2nd Corps had already been concentrated in Lorraine to serve as the "eye of the army", complained that, except for three wagons, his corps possessed no transport. "My corps," he wrote on the same day, "is no longer able to remain deprived of the mobility which circumstances may demand." Only a week later did conditions begin to improve. What held true for Frossard obtained in all the other corps of the Army of the Rhine.[18]

The causes for the lack of transport are not difficult to explain. Some of the shortages in manpower were due to the disorder of calling back the reserves; in other instances, companies of the *Train* did not move to the zone of concentration because they had received no orders from the War Ministry. Equally serious was the shortage of horses. Like the artillery and the cavalry, the *Train* did not keep a full complement of horses available during peacetime, a practice tailored to budgetary needs. Instead they like the artillery rented horses out to farmers. When war broke out, they, again like the artillery, encountered nearly impossible obstacles getting them back. The command of the peacetime territorial divisions was responsible for collecting the animals, but only on 17 July did they receive instructions on the procedures to follow.[19]   Then they found that farmers invoked clauses in the rental agreements or claimed they needed the horses for the upcoming harvest and refused to return them.   Others agreed to release theirs but only in the *arondissements* they lived in, thus requiring time of the military who had to go get them.[20]

Even if the horses had been available, the officials of the *Train* would not have been able to use them immediately.   Most of the wagons in the French army, as we have seen, were stored in a single warehouse whence they could be removed only with great difficulty.   Thus some units received theirs only after the campaign began.   Even then, several regiments discovered that their transport was unusable because of inadequate harnessing material and otherwise broken-down equipment.[21]   Consequently, even though the *Train* seemed to have sufficient numbers of men and wagons, its units were confined to their depots and rendered unavailable to the Army of the Rhine.

Similarly the corps of engineers (*Génie*) found itself nowhere near prepared to supply the Army of the Rhine with the technical expertise and skilled services required to make it mobile.   Reports of 27 and 28 July informed the high command that companies were short of officers, enlisted men, and horses.   Of those men present, so complained a message from the 6th Corps, many did not understand the nature of their duties.[22]   The telegraphic service was supposed to be supplied by the *Génie*, but its organization was undertaken only after the start of the mobilization.   Officials of the Compagnie de L'Est made forty cars available for this purpose on 20 July but had to ask the *Génie* as of that date how they wanted the space to be arranged.   There is no record of the answer, and one is entitled to assume that the company never received one.   Six days later the War Ministry informed LeBoeuf that the telegraphic service was being set up, but, it added, its "park is not yet constituted; it can do nothing useful for the army until its organization is completed."[23]

Almost completely unorganized at the beginning of the war was the medical corps.   Railroad companies, particularly the Compagnie de l'Est, put their facilities and medical personnel at the disposal of the army in order to help care for the wounded.[24]   The army could also count on the services of 1,147 doctors and 159 pharmacists to look after the sick and wounded, but this number was insufficient.   Furthermore, nurses were generally unavailable, and there were no stretcher bearers whatsoever to carry the wounded off the field.   Shipping ambulances to the army was a slow and difficult operation because the overworked and understaffed crew at the *Hôtel des Invalides* sought horses and harnesses in vain.   Faced with competition from the artillery and the *Train des Equipages*, the medical corps finished a poor third.   Many units of the army were without ambulances as late as the Battle of Sedan (1 September 1870).[25]   The French branch of the International Red Cross brought some aid to alleviate this situation, and the Compagnie de l'Est accorded its members access to transportation at the same rate as applied to the military.[26] Even so this organization found difficulty in gaining access to the zone of concentration. Temporary War Minister Dejean did not believe he had the right to grant commissions to Red Cross workers. These could be obtained, said Dejean, obviously unsure the extent of his authority, from "General Leboeuf, who is *Major-Général* of the Army of the Rhine and who, at the same time, is fulfilling the functions of Minister of War." But few doctors and fewer ambulance drivers ever reached the Army of the Rhine, and, as a result, wounded men went unattended until cared for by the Prussian medical corps.[27]

The medical corps possessed at least a rudimentary organization at the outbreak of war; railroad maintenance workers, by way of contrast, had none at all. For this the army had to turn to the railroad companies for advice and assistance, but it did not do so until after the beginning of the mobilization process. On 16 July the Ministry of War addressed a request through the Ministry of Public Works to the major railroad companies for assistance in organizing a special *corps franc* to maintain rail lines in the war zone and to exploit railways and coal mines in conquered territory. The Compagnie de l'Est readily accepted the charge to do so and by 6 August reported that it had recruited a company of 38 officers, 103 noncommissioned officers, and 940 enlisted men. Opportunity to serve in this special railroad corps was particularly welcome to railroad employees, because those who were enrolled in the *Garde Nationale Mobile* received permission to substitute their service in the *corps franc* for their obligations to the *Garde*. By the time this corps was organized, however, its reason for being had ceased. There were no conquered lines to exploit, and far from "following the army" as it was originally expected to do, it fell back along with the debris of the Army of the Rhine. The brief and uneventful history of the *corps franc* in 1870 is particularly eloquent testimony to the army's failure to plan for a rapid mobilization of all its components, and the contrast this makes with the Prussian effort in the same respect is all more striking.[28]

Besides these tribulations a host of minor problems also hampered the movement of the French army in 1870. For example, a remount service had to be created in order to purchase horses for officers without them.[29] The army needed interpreters, not only to interrogate German prisoners but also to provide communication with the Alsatian peasantry. There were attempts to create a spy service, which, had it been constituted, might have compensated for the reluctance of the French cavalry to undertake any reconnaissance missions. Nothing came of these attempts, and the French remained generally ignorant of the whereabouts of their enemy, who, incidentally, was equally uninformed about French positions. Finally, even such questions as when and how to pay the army had still to be settled. While financial officials accordingly evaded the responsibility of releasing funds, officers went without items like the revolvers, maps, and horses that they needed and were expected to purchase out of the personal "war indemnity" allotted to each officer.[30] Just as often the enlisted men required money; because of a shortage of food, soldiers sought to buy what they could in village stores or in restaurants. Without money, they were forced to resort to looting and pillaging, which occasionally they did, as a matter of fact. Others expressed their anger over inadequate food distribution in letters, some of which found their way into the newspaper *Le Peuple*. Authorities seized the issues printing these letters.[31]

In sum, the mobilization of both the *Intendance* and the auxiliary services was thoroughly unsatisfactory in 1870. To commanders in the field the deficiencies in the supply of all kinds of goods--from food to horses and wagons--were so serious that offensive operations were delayed far beyond the expected time. These commanders sent daily messages to Leboeuf, Wolff, and Dejean with requests to furnish them with provisions. "No sugar, coffee, rice, *eau-de-vie*, salt and very little lard and *biscuit* in Metz. Send at least a million rations to Thionville at once," wrote Wolff on 20 July, just as the units of four army corps were beginning to assemble around these cities. "No resources, no money...," gasped de Failly (5th Corps) the next day. "We need everything, in every respect." He probably added, as he did almost every day, that his men lacked cartridge belts. On 29 July Leboeuf, had to plea for *biscuit*, "...in order to move forward. Send everything you have in the interior *places* to Strasbourg without delay."[32] As late as 8 August, the *Intendant-Général* was demanding the shipment of more goods.

Such appeals make it clear why the army was unable to begin operations around 1 August. The mobilization of supplies and services was so slow that it prevented the army from taking the offensive; it also restricted the movement of most units, allowing only for slow and limited changes of position. The faults of the *Intendance* and the lack of *Train* personnel go far to explain this situation. No explanation, however, is complete without a description of conditions in the major railroad yards.

CONFUSION AT THE RAILHEADS

There are few descriptions of the mobilization of the French army in 1870 that fail to dwell upon the chaos in the Metz railroad center. Metz contained the principal railroad yards of northeastern France. With its eight depots and four miles of sidings, it had enough space to permit the simultaneous unloading of three hundred ten freight cars, and railroad officials believed the army could receive nine hundred thirty in one day. Between 16 July and 15 August 1870, the station received an average of seven hundred seventy-five cars per day, and these were enough to supply the four army corps which were assembling within twenty-five miles of Metz. Yet only a small quantity of the items shipped by railroad was distributed to the army during the mobilization. Most freight cars, in fact, were not unloaded at all. Units stationed in and around Metz obtained daily supplies of food and forage at the railroad yards, and some supplies were shipped ahead to Thionville and Saint-Avold in closer proximity of two of the four corps in Lorraine.[33]

In the meantime, military and railway officials were confronted with a crisis. As the days went by, more and more supply trains reached Metz, and fewer and fewer departed. Because the main lines were frequently blocked by troop transports or by supply trains, railroad dispatchers shunted incoming supply trains onto sidings, and there these trains remained. Since these sidings had no facilities for unloading, the army was unable to obtain the foodstuffs and munitions it so urgently needed. When Metz finally fell in October, the Germans captured 16,000 freight cars full of the items the French army had required for operations.[34]

There are three specific reasons which explain how and why confusion at the railheads developed and why intendants had to consume so much time to restore order. In the first place, the intendants on duty in Metz when the first supply trains arrived were not directed by the high command of the Army of the Rhine. Under the orders of the peacetime territorial command, they were responsible only for the everyday supply needs of the peacetime garrisons. They were instructed not to interfere with orders concerning transportation of matériel on the railroads.[35] Because they received no orders of any kind on what to do with incoming supplies, they were unable to perform services which could have helped to eliminate confusion.

In the second place, the intendants who were attached to the Army of the Rhine were reluctant to have freight cars unloaded. This situation arose from two factors. Unlike the Prussian army, the French army had no field transfer stations to store matériel for use by an army in the field. Further, since the army had no clear plan of operations, intendants were rarely sure where any given corps or any given division was going to be stationed on any one day. Under these circumstances, French intendants yielded to the same impulse that tempted their Prussian counterparts. They tended to look upon a freight car as a mobile storehouse. It was easier, they argued, to leave supplies in freight cars and unload them at depots nearer the troops. In any case, they added, they had received no orders to unload trains and thus had no right to do so. But since few freight trains were ever transferred from major railheads like Metz to intermediate stations closer to army units, the intendants' arguments proved to be unsubstantiated.

Finally, even when intendants were instructed to unload cars, they were often unable to do so effectively. Frequently, there was no labor hired to do the job, and until the army obtained civilian help and assigned soldiers to special work duty, nobody touched the freight cars.   Even after workers became available, intendants were unable to organize the task rationally.   One authority has pointed out that sometimes no military official was present to direct civilian laborers, and the implication is that these workers did not know which cars they had to unload or what they were supposed to do with items they did take from the cars.

It would have been impossible to deliver what commanders wanted anyway. Nobody knew what the freight trains contained.   They arrived without bills of lading; freight cars were unmarked.[36] Furthermore, because of a paucity of workers in the *Train des Equipages Militaires* it was frequently impossible to have supplies transported from railroad stations.   Lastly, intendants themselves tended to work at cross purposes.   For example, Palat in his authoritative work on the War of 1870 cites a case where one intendant ordered fodder unloaded for storage in Metz while another sent fodder from Metz to be loaded onto freight cars.[37]   The result was all sorts of disorder.   These "are creating obstacles for me," grumbled Intendant General Wolff, "or (they) are leaving me uncertain about what resources are available to me."[38]

With conditions so chaotic at the railheads, it is a wonder the Army of the Rhine obtained any food and matériel at all.   The extent to which the army corps were able to exist from day to day resulted not from careful planning and organization; it was the outcome of expedients.   The French, true to the slogan which had seemingly served them so well in the past, were once again trying to "muddle through."

DEBROUILLEZ-VOUS

When the first units of the Army of the Rhine began to move toward the zone of concentration on 19 July 1870, the generals assigned to their command probably knew that these corps would be required to overcome temporary shortages.   This situation was to be expected.   Since these units were entrained at the same time as supplies were being readied for shipment, field commanders could not expect these items for at least a week.   Furthermore, they had received warnings from intendants and from the Ministry of War not to expect to find everything ready for the army in the zones of concentration.   Goods will be short when the ranks fill up, the chief intendant in Metz told Marshal Bazaine (3rd Corps) on 18 July.   He assured him that this problem would soon be solved.[39] Similar messages reassured the other commanders: within a few days, a vague period of time never specified, there would be no shortages.

In the meantime, of course, the army had to live.   Getting along from day to day seemed to offer no special problems to officials of the war office; they told commanders and their intendants to resort to temporary expedients until regular services had been organized and supplies had arrived. Such messages were not new to the French army in 1870: they were merely suggesting that the Army of the Rhine *se débrouille* for a time as had its predecessors. What was decisive in 1870 was that "making-do" or "muddling through" became the principal way of organizing supplies and services during the mobilization.

Since the Army of the Rhine expected to have difficulties finding supplies for a few days, expedients could provide partial or short term solutions, and intendants, commanders, and staff officers found no end to ingenious ways to overcome shortages. The easiest and least inventive method officials used was to recommend to others that they obtain what they needed from some other source: "Your regimental transport is expected in Metz today," said a staff officer to a general. "If it doesn't get here before you leave, address yourself to Intendant Friand to get what you need,"[40] but the telegram did not indicate steps to take should Friand have none. It was always possible to secure administrative personnel from other posts, even if their procurement meant, as it did for the 5th Corps in Bitche, that no one would remain to look after the needs of units being concentrated near the Prussian frontier. Some intendants furthermore were simply unwilling to acknowledge difficulties; they merely averred that certain items should have been picked up by units on their way to the frontier: "All units under the orders of General de Failly were told to get their cantines before they left Lyons. Didn't they do this? . . .Wagons are on their way from Toul. . .. All generals and troops from Lyons where they had been stationed when war broke out should have gotten theirs before their departure."[41] General Colsen, Intendant of the 1st Corps, told Abel Douay, commander of its second division, that all his men should be provided with two pairs of boots and that there should be one pair in reserve, as if merely saying so made the boots materialize.[42]

Certain generals called on neighboring corps commanders for help. General de Failly sent messages to Marshal MacMahon (1st Corps) asking for money to buy supplies for his troops as well as for wagons, ambulances and cantines. Confronted with similar difficulties, MacMahon had none to spare. In fact, after the defeat of the 1st Corps at Froeschwiller on 6 August, he, in turn, had to call upon Marshal Canrobert (6th Corps in Châlons) for food and munitions, some of which Canrobert was similarly unable to supply.[43]

Not all measures, however, were thus aimed at evading responsibility and passing it on to others. Administrative personnel attached to the peacetime territorial command in Strasbourg received orders to supply the 1st Corps with meat and rations "until the company assigned with this duty is prepared to do so."[44] Troops stationed near Metz were sent out on special work detail to help unload supplies accumulating in the Metz railroad yards.[45] Companies of the *Train des Equipages Militaires* were divided among neighboring army units to permit each unit the use of a few service personnel until all companies of the

Train were mobilized. The Intendant of the 3rd Corps, having organized auxiliary administrative assistance for his own corps and confident that he would obtain sufficient transport, reported that he would assist the 4th Corps to do the same.[46] Officers purchased maps at their own expense. Civilians assisted in transporting supplies, unloading them, or even procuring them.

These expedients were helpful to the French army in 1870, but, given the dire need for long-term planning, they were not sufficient to assure the organization of services and the shipment and distribution of supplies. Even the best mobilized units of the French army still suffered from shortages and were thus held immobile.

One of these was the 2nd Corps, which had been partly organized as a corps before the war broke out. It consisted of infantry and cavalry units on summer maneuvers at the military camp of Châlons. On 15 July it was sent under the command of General Frossard to Saint-Avold, northeast of Metz, where it awaited its reserves, artillery, service corps, and supplies. All of these were slow in arriving. Even though the 2nd Corps took all available supplies from Châlons, it possessed far from enough.[47] No one gave orders to ship supplies directly after the departure of the corps or to prepare a forward depot for them. An adjutant was simply sent to Metz where he failed to find any supplies. When the intendants of the 2nd Corps arrived in Saint-Avold, they discovered that they had no services to unload supply trains and that the corps was critically short of food. An appeal to Intendant General Wolff produced no worthwhile results. Unable to provide either supplies or services, he told the Intendant of the 2nd Corps to look after its needs himself, and this meant that responsibility was delegated in turn to divisionary intendants. These officials, however, never succeeded in obtaining all that the corps required.[48]

Under the conditions of the mobilization of the French army in 1870, the intendant who carefully attended to all the needs of the units under his supervision encountered a series of frustrating experiences. Just acquiring adequate transport took many days of effort and often proved to be impossible. For example, when companies of the *Train des Equipages Militaires* arrived in Saint-Avold on 20 July, they were able to hitch only half of their equipment, and by 6 August, they were still sixty-six short of the two hundred thirty wagons they were supposed to have. Not even all of the available vehicles were used to supply the corps. The staff of the 2nd Corps, which had no transport of its own, resorted to the expedient of requisitioning regular corps transport. There were not enough horses for the remaining wagons, and the intendant, who tried to purchase horses locally, found few available: the remount service had already scoured the area around Saint-Avold. Between 27 and 31 July the 2nd Corps was ordered forward to Forbach, ten miles to the east. Without the aid of local farmers and lost reservists temporarily pressed into service, who together provided most of the transport, this troop movement would have been almost impossible.[49] Civilian labor also unloaded railroad cars belonging to the 2nd Corps. These workers were hired presumably to allow the intendants the extra time to plan the distribution of goods arriving at both Saint-Avold and Forbach. Since the cars were unmarked and their contents unknown until opened, however, intendants never got the extra time they needed. It was also impossible for intendants to give special consideration to top priority items, for, given the shortages of almost everything, no list of priorities could be drawn up.

Not long after the 2nd Corps assembled at Saint-Avold, the harassed *Intendance* officials encountered still another difficulty: they were unable to feed the troops. This was a matter they believed had been covered, for while still in Châlons, before the outbreak of war, they had concluded agreements with supply houses for the maintenance of the men. The intendants now found, however, that it was exceedingly difficult to transfer delivery to Saint-Avold. The government, they learned, had given priority on the railroads to troop movements. The enlisted men in the meantime consumed their reserve supplies of bread. Even the bakeries in Metz and Forbach were hard pressed to keep abreast of daily consumption, a problem which became worse once the reserves began to join the ranks. It thus became impossible to accumulate adequate supplies of bread, and there was no solution to the problem. The *Intendance* did make efforts to secure supplies of meat by local purchase, but the results were not impressive. There is no evidence that the men of the 2nd Corps went hungry, but all the sources make it clear that there were no reserves of food. This outcome is no surprise. There was, in the first place, no established system governing the purchase of food. Local merchants found it almost impossible to drive cattle to units which had ordered it. Soldiers clogged the roads and, because changes of position, however slight, were not reported to the merchants, they were often unable to locate their customers.[50]

There appeared to be little hope the 2nd Corps could solve its supply problems in short time. Georges Jeannerod, a war correspondent for *Le Temps*, reported on 30 July that while morale was high, the arrival of reservists was welcome since the overall troop numbers were weak. A serious problem, he remarked, was the supply system, which had "yet to be worked out, and I think it will still take more time."[51] On 3 August he wrote that "the administrative services still leave much to be desired." In particular he noted the poor system of distribution of whatever food supplies the *Intendance* managed to obtain. These were merely dumped on regiments in bulk, and distribution was left to the men. *Intendance* personnel left two or three boxes of *biscuit* behind, according to Jeannerod, and after that it was "*débrouillez-vous*." Meat delivery was even more casual. "They drop off one animal on the hoof, and the regiment does all the butchering," he reported.[52] He might well have added "whenever they could butcher," because changes in bivouac disrupted the process of butchering animals and preparing meat for cooking.

* * * * *

These nuisances were not unique to the 2nd Corps. The telegrams that abound in the military archives provide ample evidence of similar difficulties.[53] Together they point to a disastrous consequence: the inability of the French to bring their forces to bear against the weak points in the deployment of the Prussian army. Leboeuf stated the matter succinctly in a message to Dejean on 1 August: "When I took leave of you I thought that by the time I wrote this letter we would have undertaken operations. Unfortunately our administrative organization holds us back on the frontier, and I am beginning to fear that we shall not have the advantages and honors of taking the offensive."[54] Simply put, the Army of the Rhine was not being concentrated, it was assembling at seven different locations in Alsace and Lorraine along a front about two hundred miles long. Obviously a closer concentration of these forces was necessary in order to meet the growing Prussian threat looming to the north. But French commanders, unable to bring along the supplies they had succeeded in obtaining and fearful of occupying places where they could not get items still missing, hesitated to move their forces into closer contact with one another. For some the army appeared to be wallowing helplessly, and the cause was clear to them. The 6th Corps could not advance to Nancy on 5 August as ordered, lamented its intendant to Dejean. "Your Excellency knows that the 6th Corps is paralyzed by the failure of administrative personnel and matériel to get here in sufficient time."[55] As a result of this situation, the concentration of the French army on 6 August, far from having been completed, had just commenced.

NOTES

1. Germany, Army, Generalstab, Kriegsgeschichtliche Abteilung, *The Franco-German War, 1871-1872* Translated by F. C. H. Clarke. 5 vols. (London: Her Majesty's Stationery Office, 1874-1884), I, i, pp. 13-14, (cited hereafter as G.G.S.). Regulations required three *chassepots* per soldier. France, Assemblée Nationale, *Enquête parlementaire sur les actes du gouvernement de la Défense Nationale: dépositions des témoins.* 5 vols. (Paris: Germer-Baillière, 1872-1875), I, pp. 44-45, 50, (cited hereafter as D.T.).A report on matériel in the French army archives asserts there were only 1,019,265 *chassepots*: SHAT, Vincennes, La 44, Report on matériel, pp. 28-38.

2. D.T., I, p. 42.

3. Telegram, Leboeuf to Napoleon III, 25 July 1870, AN, Paris, AB XIX 1713.

4. France, Armée, Etat-major, Service Historique, *Préparation à la guerre* in *La Guerre de 1870-71*, 35 vols. (Paris: Chapelot, 1901-1903), pp. 55-56, (cited hereafter as Guerre followed by the title of the particular volume to which reference is made).

5. Louis Jarras, *Souvenirs du Général Jarras* (Paris: Plon, 1892), pp. 55-56.

6. A survey of the responsibilities and the shortcomings of the Intendance may be found in Barthélemy Edmond Palat, *Histoire de la guerre de 1870-71*, Part I: *La Guerre de 1870*, 6 vols.

(Paris: Berger-Levrault, 1903-1908), II, pp.86-69.   See also Charles Antoine Thoumas, *Les Transformations de l'armée française*, 2 vols. (Paris: Berger-Levrault, 1887), II, pp. 24, 26.

7. See, for example, the organization of the *Intendance* of the Garde Impériale, SHAT, Vincennes, Lhs 23, folder août 1870. The organization of the *Intendance* in the other seven corps was similar.

8. Dispatch, Leboeuf to commanders of territorial divisions, 17 July 1870, SHAT, Vincennes, La 6.

9. Palat, *Histoire*, Part I: *La Guerre de 1870*, II, pp. 86-87, 179; Anatole Baratier, *L'Intendance militaire pendant la guerre de 1870-1871*, (Paris: J. Dumaine, 1871), p. 17.

10. Telegram, 8 August 1870, SHAT, Vincennes, La 7.

11. Quoted in Palat, *Histoire*, Part I: *La Guerre de 1870*, II, p. 177.

12. Baratier, *L'Intendance militaire pendant la guerre de 1870*, p. 13; Palat, *Histoire*, Part I: *La Guerre de 1870*, II, p. 87.

13. "Carnet de notes de Louis Lebeau, sous-lieutenant au 68e de ligne," SHAT, Vincennes, T 133, pp. 4-6. See also N. A., *Observations sur l'armée française à propos de la campagne de 1870* (Lyons: Charles Méra, 1871), pp. 58-59; G.C. Shaw, *Supply in Modern War* (London: Faber and Faber, 1938), p. 57.

14. General Frossard to the Intendant of the 2nd Corps, 24 July 1870, "Registre: 2e corps-correspondance générale," SHAT, Vincennes, Lb 50. Civil and military authorities intervened to put a stop to this sort of traffic.

15. Michael Howard, *The Franco-Prussian War*, (London: Rupert Hart-Davis, 1961), p. 65. The text of the memorandum may be found in Guerre, *Préparations à la guerre*, fn. 2, pp. 47-49.

16. General Coche, "L'Evolution du train depuis 1807," *Revue Historique de l'Armée*, I (February, 1959), p. 82; see also Le Comte de La Chapelle, *Les Forces militaires de la France en 1870* (Paris: Amyot, 1872), pp. 68-69 and Napoleon III, *Oeuvres posthumes et autographes inédits de Napoléon III en exil*, ed. by the comte de La Chapelle (Paris: Lachaud, 1873), p. 148.

17. Aristide Martinien, *La Guerre de 1870-71. La Mobilisation de l'armée: mouvements des dépôts (armée active) du 15 juillet au 1er mars, 1871* (Paris: L. Fournier, 1912), pp. 387-395.

18. Telegrams, Frossard to Bazaine, 23 July 1870, SHAT, Vincennes, La 6, and Frossard to General Vergé (Commander of first division, 2nd Corps), 23 July 1870, SHAT, Vincennes, Lo 4 and 5.

19. Message, Ministry of War, 3rd Direction, to Intendants of Territorial Divisions, 17 July 1870, SHAT, Vincennes, La 13.

20. Telegrams, AN, Paris, 15, 16, and 17 July 1870, and 25 July 1870, AB, XIX 1713.

21. N. A. *Observations sur l'armée française*, p. 15; Charles Fay, *Journal d'un officier de l'Armée du Rhin*, (Brussels: Muquardt, 1871), pp. 26-27; Louis Le Gillou, *La Campagne d'été de 1870*, (Paris: Charles-Lavauzelle, 1938), p. 90.

22. "Registre génie," SHAT, Vincennes, La 55; Telegram, 28 July 1870, AN, Paris, AB XIX 1713.

23. Telegram to Ministry of War, 26 July 1870, AN, Paris, AB XIX 1713; Message, Compagnie de l'Est to Ministry of War, AN, Paris, 13 AQ 667, p. 1275.

24. AN, Paris, 13 AQ 667, pp. 1314 and 1320.

25. Le Gillou, *La Campagne d'été de 1870*, p. 90; Palat, *Histoire*, Part I: *La Guerre de 1870*, II, p. 88; Emile-Alexandre Gavoy, *Le Service de Santé en 1870* (Paris: Charles-Lavauzelle, 1894), pp. 13, 21; Barthélemy Louis Joseph Lebrun, *Souvenirs militaires, 1866-1870. Préliminaires de la Guerre. Missions en Belgique et à Vienne* (Paris: E. Dentu, 1895), pp. 208-209.

26. AN, Paris, 13 AQ 667, p. 1252.

27. Letters, Dejean to Vice President of the International Red Cross, 25 July 1870, SHAT Vincennes, La 6. For the impatient response of a commander, see Marshal MacMahon's note of 28 July to Leboeuf, SHAT, Vincennes, Lb 2. See also, Palat, *Histoire*, Part I: *La guerre de 1870*, II, p. 88.

28. Information on the organization of the railroad *corps franc* may be found in the *registres* of the Compagnie de l'Est, AN, Paris, 13 AQ 365, pp. 299-300 and 13 AQ 667, pp. 1248, 1254, 1261, 1264, 1341-1346.

29. Memorandum, Ministry of War: 3rd Direction: Remount Service, 20 July 1870, SHAT, Vincennes La 6.

30. See, for example, the "Registre de correspondance du Maréchal Canrobert," 1 August 1870, SHAT, Vincennes, Lb 55. The problem is also noted in General Devauraix, *Souvenirs et observations sur la campagne de 1870* (Paris: Charles-Lavauzelle, n.d.), p. 29.

31. Telegram, 26 July 1870, AN, Paris, AB XIX 1713.

32. Telegram, Leboeuf to Dejean, 29 July 1870, SHAT Vincennes, Lb 5 and Lr 5.

33. François Jacqmin, *Les Chemins de fer français pendant la guerre de 1870-71* (Paris: Hachette, 1872), pp. 120-122; Edwin A. Pratt, *The Rise of Rail Power in War and Conquest, 1833-1914* (Philadelphia: Lippincott, 1916), p. 145; Palat, *Histoire*, Part I: *La Guerre de 1870*, II, p. 161.

34. Pratt, *The Rise of Rail Power in War and Conquest*, p. 161.

35. Instructions, Minister of War to Commanders of Territorial Divisions, 17 July 1870, SHAT, Vincennes, La 6.

36. Intendant General Wolff to the Director of Administration in the Ministry of War, 31 July 1870, SHAT, Vincennes, Lb 3.

37. Pratt, *The Rise of Rail Power in War and Conquest*, pp. 144-145; Palat, *Histoire*, Part I: *La Guerre de 1870*, II, p. 161.

38. Intendant General Wolff to the Director of Administration in the Ministry of War, 31 July 1870, SHAT, Vincennes, Lb 3.

39. Letter, Bazaine to Leboeuf, 18 July 1870, SHAT, Vincennes, La 6.

40. Telegram, General Manèque (Chief of Staff of 3rd Corps) to General Castagny (commander of second division, 3rd Corps), 22 July 1870, SHAT, Vincennes, Lo 2 and 3.

41. Telegram, Ministry of War to General de Failly, 19 July 1870, SHAT, Vincennes, La 6.

42. Telegram, Colsen to Abel Douai, SHAT, Vincennes, Lr 8.

43. Adhémar de Chalus, *Guerre franco-allemande de 1870-71; Wissembourg, Froeschwiller, Retraite sur Chalôns* (Besançon: Marion, Morel, 1882), p. 193; Germain Bapst (ed.) *Le Maréchal Canrobert: Souvenirs d'un siècle*, 6 vols. (Paris, Plon, 1898-1913), IV, pp. 166-167.

44. Telegram, Ministry of War to Peacetime Territorial Command in Strasbourg, SHAT, Vincennes, Lr 8.

45. SHAT, Vincennes, Lb 4, folder August 1.

46. Telegram, 22 July 1870, AN, Paris, AB XIX 1712.

47. The plight of the 2nd Corps may be traced in its *registre* of general correspondence for July 1870: "Registre: 2e corps- correspondance générale," SHAT, Vincennes, Lb 50.

48. Bouteiller, "Journal tenu par M. Bouteiller adjoint à l'intendance du 2nd corps pendant la campagne de 1870," SHAT, Vincennes, Lb 62, pp. 53, 55. See also Le Gillou, *La Campagne d'été de 1870*, p. 91.

49. "Registre: 2e corps- correspondance générale," No. 154 and 156, SHAT, Vincennes, Lb 50.

50. All these predicaments are described in Bouteiller, "Journal tenu par M. Bouteiller;" see especially pp. 56-57, 62-63, 66-67, 144-147, 164, and 166.

51. *Le Temps*, 30 July 1870, pp. 1-2.

52. Ibid., 3 August 1870, p. 2.

53. These documents are stored in the archives of the Service historique of the French army: SHAT, Vincennes, cartons La 6 and 7, Lb 2, Lo 5 and 6, Lr 1, 5, 7, 8, and 9. Until his departure for Metz on 27 July 1870, Napoleon III received copies of these same messages at his summer residence, and these copies are now stored in the Archives Nationales: AN, Paris, cartons AB XIX 1710 through 1713.

54. Letter, Leboeuf to Dejean, 1 August 1870, SHAT, Vincennes, Lb 4.
55. SHAT, Vincennes, Lr 9, folder 7.

6

The Concentration of the Army of the Rhine

In the first chapter we noted that one of the most difficult operations in modern warfare is the movement of mass armies from their bases to the decisive sites of action in the field. These maneuvers, which are called concentration, link most of the combat and support units into an increasingly large and ever denser mass. The object commanders seek in concentrating their forces is to bring their army to bear on the points where they think an enemy is weakest and where they can strike the blows which will force the enemy to retreat or, better still, capitulate. The concentration of an army, however, involves considerable risks if it takes place with inadequate preparations, for, as has already been pointed out, a compact army can become a cumbersome, incoherent mass incapable of rapid and decisive operations.

By 1870 there were two essentials of effective concentration: one was adequate utilization of the railroad; the other, carefully arranged marching routes. Understanding these elements, the Prussians reached solutions which in 1870 proved to be sufficient, if not wholly satisfactory. Moltke's successes were due in no small measure to the painstaking work the Prussian General staff put into devising military railroad schedules and to selecting the routes over which the Prussian army made its way to the Saar valley and to northern Alsace. For France this situation did not obtain. The French railroad network was adequate for the task of concentrating the Army of the Rhine in northeastern France, but military officials had plans neither for the military use of the railroads nor for the deployment of troops from the railheads. Instead, they directed men and equipment haphazardly to the German frontier and there condemned this force to an inadequate concentration directed by an irresolute commander-in-chief, who created a very faulty chain of command, listened to unfounded information about the enemy, and permitted the army to march about in hopeless confusion.

MOVEMENT BY RAIL, 16 JULY-26 JULY 1870

French concentration began even before most reservists received notification to rejoin the colors. The first measures the army took were reasonable enough. On 15 July the Ministry of War issued instructions to the railroad companies: the three lines leading to Northeastern France were to place all their means of transport at the disposal of the army and to limit both civilian travel and ordinary commercial traffic; the remaining French companies were asked to provide military transport upon notification and to lend their rolling stock to the other three lines upon request.   Subsequent communications provided instructions about rates, the transport of the *Garde Nationale Mobile*, postal service, and rail service beyond the frontier.[1] On the other hand there was no attempt by the government, even at this late date, to nominate any official responsible to oversee and co-ordinate military transports; none was forthcoming until 11 August when the Ministry of Public Works nominated the Count de Bonville "to oversee to the greatest extent possible the military transport required by the present war."[2]

When the Ministry of War called upon the railroad companies for these purposes, they were able collectively to place an excellent railroad network at the disposal of the military.   In the opinion of historian Martin Van Creveld, France's capacity to transport and supply its armed force was superior to Prussia's. Its network was more unified, standardized, and double-tracked than the German; its trains were faster; its stations and loading facilities were larger; its rolling stock was more plentiful in supply. Furthermore, the layout of French railroad lines was more affected by strategic considerations than the German.[3]

The French railroad system lived up to the advantages it produced. French railroad companies complied with the demands made upon them, and on the whole they executed their services very satisfactorily. Because it was in charge of the main connections from Paris to Metz and Strasbourg, the Compagnie de l'Est had the largest task to accomplish. According to one of its directors, the Hohenzollern crisis already put the company on its guard. When it received orders from the War Ministry on 15 July, it was immediately able to stop all but the necessary peacetime traffic, clear its cars and loading docks of freight, and prepare to transport men and supplies as demanded. The first troop train departed the next day, and from then until 26 July, the company dispatched an average of twenty-four trains a day on its main line to Metz and Strasbourg and eighteen a day on each of its two branch lines. Between 16 and 27 July the Compagnie de l'Est ran 594 trains carrying 186,620 men, 32,410 horses, 3,162 cannon and transport wagons and 995 caissons.[4] Between 26 July and 6 August, nearly six hundred more trains traveled along the company's tracks, and besides carrying 130,000 more men, they transported as many horses, cannon, vehicles, and caissons as they had prior to 26 July.[5]

The Compagnie du Nord and the Compagnie du Chemin de fer de Paris à Lyon et à la Méditerranée (the PLM), the two other lines mainly involved with the mobilization and concentration procedures, reported equally impressive results. Between 15 July and 15 August the Compagnie du Nord dispatched 201 special trains transporting 109,357 men, 12,137 horses and 593 transport vehicles, all this "without stopping ordinary passenger or freight service at any point."[6] Records of the PLM show that it sent three hundred thirty-two trains covering a distance of 85,467 kilometers between 16 and 25 July. These trains delivered 208,275 men, 14,871 horses and 437 wagons to their destinations.[7] Furthermore all three lines performed these services with few mishaps. The only accidental deaths reported appear in the records of the PLM. On the nights of 23 and 24 July in three separate places, three soldiers lost their lives after falling out of the troop trains.[8] In terms of the services provided and the utter lack of planning involved the performance of these three companies appears to have been remarkable. There were no complaints about the services provided by any of the railway companies during the concentration of the French army in 1870.

No complaints did not mean no recriminations. So unplanned was military transportation in 1870 that even questions regarding rates for military transport had not been fully settled between the state and the railroad companies. The result was nearly twenty-five years of litigation over the amount due. In August 1870 alone the Compagnie de l'Est estimated the state owed them 6,860,000 francs.[9] This figure grew. In 1872 all companies together submitted a bill of 59,344,000 francs; the National Assembly awarded them 50,000,000. In ensuing years state commissions reduced this sum and demanded restitution of the difference. The amount to be returned was fixed in 1879 at 1,521,019 francs, but not even this amount was considered final until so determined by a decision of the *Conseil d'Etat* in 1893. There the matter ended.[10]

The layout of French railroad lines determined the zones of concentration in 1870. There were two principal lines and one minor line serving Northeastern France. The most important of these belonged to the Compagnie de l'Est. This line ran east from Paris along the banks of the Marne River to Frouard where a branch took trains north to Metz and on to Germany while the main track continued   eastward   to   Strasbourg.   The   second   line,   the Paris-Lyon-Méditerranée, brought trains along the Rhone to Dijon and Chalon-sur-Saône, where connections led from these two points through southern Alsace to Strasbourg. The third line available to the army belonged to the Compagnie du Nord. It ran across northern France from Calais on the English Channel to Thionville, a minor railroad center fifteen miles north of Metz. Along these lines the Army of the Rhine reached its bases of operations: Metz and Strasbourg, the principal centers, and Thionville, Nancy, Saint-Avold,

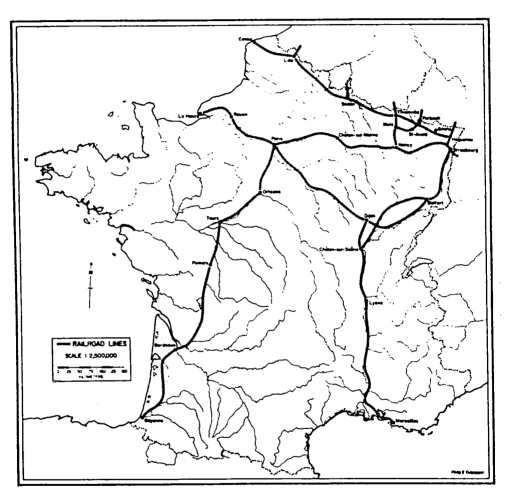

Map 1. Principal French Railroad Lines Serving the French Army in the Franco-Prussian War, 1870-1871

Bitche, and Belfort, the other important railheads where men and matériel were detrained in 1870.

In one respect the French army made good use of these lines. Each corps of the Army of the Rhine was composed of infantry and cavalry regiments stationed in the same region of France. Thus most parts of an entire corps utilized the same rail line to reach the zone of concentration. Although there was only one "Army of the Rhine", it was divided by the Vosges Mountains into two wings. The left and larger wing was based on Metz in Lorraine. The 2nd Corps, composed of troops on summer maneuvers at the Camp of Châlons occupied the forward position of this wing. It was transported along the main line of the Compagnie de l'Est to its assembly point at Saint-Avold, twenty miles beyond Metz. Behind and to its left, was the 4th Corps, composed of units transported along the northern line to Thionville from their bases in Northern France. In the center was the 3rd Corps, which assembled around Metz and which was composed of units from Paris. On the right was the 5th Corps, initially located in Bitche. The 5th Corps was composed of units stationed in Lyons and Southeastern France.

Two army corps composed the right wing of the Army of the Rhine. The 1st Corps, made up principally of units transported to Marseilles from Algeria, was located near Strasbourg. The 7th Corps, whose units came from Southeastern France, was to assemble at Belfort and was thus located to the right of the 1st Corps. Both these corps reached Alsace via the rail connections along the Rhone River. Of the remaining units of the Army of the Rhine, the Imperial guard, the elite corps of the French army, was transported from its garrisons near Paris to Nancy where it served as a first line reserve force. The 6th Corps, composed of regiments from West-Central France was assembled at the Camp of Châlons and was intended as a second line reserve force.[11]

In spite of the excellent services provided by the railroad companies and in spite, too, of the army's rational distribution of labor among the three lines reaching Northeastern France, responsible French military officials for the most part failed to make good use of the rail services available to them. In the first place, they acted rashly, sending troops forward without first allowing reservists to join their comrades. Driven by a strong desire to beat the Prussians to the draw, the French army dispatched its first troop trains too early. On 16 July two regiments departed from Paris for Metz. At the same time, regiments undergoing summer training at the Camp of Châlons prepared to advance to Saint-Avold in Lorraine, and units in Algeria began to embark for the two day crossing to Marseilles.[12] During the next ten days almost every infantry and cavalry regiment assigned to the Army of the Rhine had arrived at the point of assembly from which it was supposed to undertake operations against the Prussians. Not all who got there knew where they belonged. "The fifth battery of the 5th Artillery Regiment arrived yesterday in Lutzelbourg without knowing where they are supposed to be," wrote the general in command of the territorial division in Strasbourg to the Ministry of War. "What corps do they belong to?"[13] In the meantime, the reserves whose strength these active units badly needed, lingered in the regimental depots and made their slow way to the Army of the Rhine by that process which, as we have seen, defied common sense.

The French army committed other serious mistakes as well. Officers failed to maintain discipline among troops entraining for the zones of assembly. The most noted disorder occurred in Paris. On 16 July Marshal Canrobert, at that time in command of the troops in Paris, received a schedule of departure for the units stationed in or near the city. The orders clearly stated that infantry units scheduled to depart from the Gare de l'Est or from the station at La Villette were to assemble one and one-half hours before departure.[14] The first regiment scheduled to leave was expected to arrive at the station at 4:15 P.M. on 16 July. It got there at 2:00 P.M. in a condition vividly described in *Le National* the following day. The streets and cafés were full of a boisterous crowd of citizens. Soldiers broke ranks and joined them in nearby drinking houses. Soon another unit--one, in fact, supposed to be embarked at La Villette--arrived on the scene, and the charivari repeated itself. As departure time neared, civilians bore soldiers on their shoulders while others carried their effects, and this sprawling mass was dumped in the station and left for officers to sort out. It took several hours to round up drunken soldiers and salvage as many of their lost effects as they could locate. Thus the first trains departed late, and even then a few men were left behind.[15] The following day a notice posted by the Prefect of Police urged citizens to regain their "customary" composure and asked them to abstain from further "demonstrations which cannot be prolonged without causing inconveniences."[16]

Outside of Paris the entraining of troops took place in better order. Even there, however, there were troublesome incidents. On 22 July the prefect in Lyons reported a "good patriotic demonstration" but warned that a "negative one might occur later in the day." When it did--an enthusiastic crowd invaded the railroad station--cavalry units were called out to disperse the demonstrators.[17] A day later the prefect of Nîmes reported a noisy crowd disrupting a "patriotic circle" as it offered a round of drinks to officers of the 56th Line Infantry Regiment shortly before their departure for the front.[18] In Besançon there were no unruly people to stop the embarkation of three batteries of the 9th Artillery Regiment and two others of the 12th. Instead it was local officials of the PLM Line who refused to take them even though the military had received orders to dispatch these units to Strasbourg.[19]

The cause of most of these incidents lay in the fact that French officers ignored or had forgotten existing military railroad regulations. These had been written in 1855 and had never been revised. Although they clearly stated that officers were "responsible for prescribed movements in connection with the entraining, . . ."[20] officers at first left the task of putting men on the trains to railway officials who had no authority over the troops. As a result, soldiers missed trains and milled about stations, adding to the disorder.   The War Ministry, soon aware of what was happening, took immediate action. It ordered staff officers to railroad stations where they were to serve as intermediaries between troops and railway officials.[21] It also reminded officers of the 1855 regulations.   Furthermore, army officials reduced the opportunity for acts of indiscipline by assembling these men at stations only shortly before the hour of departure, and in Paris they discreetly embarked men at suburban stations. As a result of these measures, the entraining of the remaining regular soldiers took place calmly. Reservists and members of the *Garde Mobile*, however, continued to cause difficulties for railway officials.[22]

The army committed even greater mistakes when it began to use rolling stock. When it called upon railroad companies to carry men to Alsace and Lorraine, it failed to inform railway officials how many men to expect. Consequently, these officials believed each unit would be at full wartime strength and set up trains accordingly.   They thought, for example, that an infantry regiment mustered 70 officers and 2,890 men, who, along with regimental horses and vehicles, could be transported on three trains. Not once did an infantry regiment produce this number of passengers; generally they sent about 58 officers and 1,332 men.[23] Thus half-empty troop trains traveled to the railheads,. where in the second and third weeks of concentration, they became entangled with military freight traffic.   This congestion was dealt with only with great difficulty by the Compagnie de l'Est, and by the second week of August it was barely able to assure railroad service in the Metz, Frouard, Nancy region.[24]

Railroad personnel found no satisfactory way to eliminate the use of unnecessary passenger cars. Presumably extra cars could have been removed from a troop train, but at some stations sidings were too small to hold these extra cars.   In these circumstances, railroad officials kept the main lines clear by dispatching the trains, empty cars included. Then, after the second week of the concentration, they found that they could fill extra space with reservists, stragglers, and miscellaneous collections of horses, supplies and munitions.[25] Although soldiers were able to find their way to their units and the army obtained supplies, this method created confusion.   The trains, after all, were expected to transport a regiment to a specified destination; they were of marginal help to reservists and stragglers, most of whom had different destinations, and of no help at all to intendants waiting at still other locations for the supplies.

THE CONCENTRATION OF THE ARMY, 28 JULY-6 AUGUST 1870

On 28 July, 1870, two days after the last regiment of the Army of the Rhine was supposed to have been transported to the frontier, Napoleon III arrived in Metz to take command of the Army of the Rhine.   July 28 was the date he wished to launch an offensive against the enemy.   The emperor's appearance hardly aroused confidence. His gall stone caused him such extreme pain that he could barely mount a horse, and he had to touch his face with rouge to replace the color that had drained away in the past few weeks. His official proclamation to the army betrayed his gloom. Although it spoke of coming glory and praised the army for its past campaigns, it reminded the soldiers that the war "will be long and arduous, because the theater [of war] will consist of places bristling with obstacles and fortresses."[26] "Visibly," as historian Barthélemy Palat cogently suggested, Napoleon III "had entered into the period of uncertainty, hesitation, irresolution, which was to cease only with the end of the Empire."[27]

Well might the emperor's words betray uncertainty. If he had expected to begin military operations on 28 July, a conference he held with his major advisors on the evening of 28 July quickly informed him of the impossibility of executing his plan.[28] By this date the army was not yet concentrated; its position resembled a thin cordon stretching from Thionville close to the Franco-Luxemburger border to Belfort, near the Swiss frontier, a distance of two hundred miles covered by less than 280,000 men. The only units even close to actual concentration were the 2nd and 3rd Corps. One division of the 2nd Corps had already occupied Forbach on the Franco-Prussian frontier five miles south of Saarbrücken. Its other infantry and cavalry units were marching toward it from Saint-Avold, ten miles to the left and rear. The 3rd Corps was advancing to the left of the 2nd Corps, its forward units close to Saint-Avold. One division of the 3rd Corps, however, was still in Metz, twenty miles by rail from Saint-Avold. Otherwise, the remaining units were in position too far from one another to offer support in any offensive operations.   The 4th Corps, for example, was still assembling at Thionville, thirty miles to the west of Saint-Avold, and the 5th Corps, which occupied positions to the right of the 2nd Corps, was stretched from Sarreguemines eastward toward Niederbronn, a distance of about thirty miles. Both the 4th and 5th Corps were woefully lacking in reserve strength and auxiliary services, especially transport.[29]

In Alsace, the 1st Corps was still assembling around Strasbourg; Turco and Zouave regiments from Algeria were only then disembarked at Marseilles for the trip to Strasbourg.[30] The units of the 7th Corps were scattered from Colmar in southern Alsace to Lyons. Meanwhile, the Imperial Guard, recently arrived in Metz, lacked most of its auxiliary services; and only two of the four divisions of the 6th Corps had yet reached the army camp at Châlons.[31] The 6th Corps entirely lacked the mobility to become a concentrated force.   A message to

Leboeuf on 29 July informed him that the 6th Corps lacked *Train* personnel, transport, food supplies, and auxiliary services.   Subsequent correspondence revealed the shortage of manpower due to reservists who were not sent forward from their depots or who got misdirected on the way.[32] As a consequence units of the 6th Corps remained scattered for several days between Nancy and Paris unable to lend support to the forces on the frontier.[33] Even as late as 12 August, by which time the entire corps was joined with the Army of the Rhine under the guns of Metz, Canrobert was still complaining about the shortage of troops and about the difficulty of feeding the men he had.[34]   Long before that date, however, it had become obvious to the emperor that his hoped-for offensive would have to be postponed until the army could complete its mobilization and concentrate all its strength along the main routes to Strasbourg and Metz.[35]

As of 28 July the French had another week to accomplish these tasks. The Prussians were only beginning their movement from the Rhine railheads into Prussia's Rhenish provinces and the Bavarian Palatinate. Given the French army's overall numerical inferiority, the French needed to calculate where they might best place their troops so as to enjoy local superiority against dispersed Prussian columns or to be at full strength on a well-selected and well-protected defensive position. It is reasonable to argue that the army could have increased its chances of meeting the Prussian challenge by dividing its forces into two groups and by assigning three army corps to the defense of Alsace and the rest to the defense of the main route to Metz. By positioning MacMahon's 1st Corps on the heights around Froeschwiller in northern Alsace and by giving it the support of both the 5th and the 7th Corps, the French army would have had a force of 90,000 to block the main road to Strasbourg. Concentrating the 4th Corps, the Imperial Guard, and the 3rd Corps from left to right respectively behind the 2nd Corps near Forbach and placing 6th Corps in reserve at Saint-Avold would have allowed the French an army of at least 150,000 men to guard Lorraine. This kind of concentration would not have offset France's total numerical inferiority, but, given the difficulties Moltke encountered in moving his men from the Rhine bridgeheads to the Saar Valley and the alarming results produced by Steinmetz' disobedience, a French concentration like the above would have given the French the opportunity to destroy Steinmetz' army in Lorraine and halt the Prussian invasion of Alsace, thus ruining Moltke's chances of enveloping the Army of the Rhine's flanks.[36]

To execute this kind of concentration would have been too much to ask of the French army in the last days of July 1870. All the faults of the mobilization contributed to its inadequacy. Generals hesitated to risk an encounter with the enemy without the reserves which had not yet filled the ranks of the Army of the Rhine. Furthermore, they were reluctant to abandon the places where they had been collecting supplies because they had neither enough vehicles to transport these supplies nor any guarantee that they would obtain what they lacked some place else. But there were also problems which were specifically related to the execution of military operations; the French failure to overcome these difficulties counted heavily in their failure to concentrate their forces against the Prussians.

The first, and most serious of these problems was the commander-in-chief. Napoleon III, in assuming personal command of the Army of the Rhine, had undertaken more than he was capable of accomplishing. He had no clear plan of operations, and he lacked the will and insight to conceive of a workable one. The orders which emanated from Imperial Headquarters between 28 July and 5 August implemented the emperor's vacillating projects and condemned the Army of the Rhine to a series of maneuvers that failed to concentrate it either for an offensive blow against the Prussians or defensive operations designed to counter the threat posed by Moltke's increasingly massed forces.

When, on 28 July, Napoleon decided to postpone an invasion of Germany, he did not abandon his hopes for an eventual offensive. At a meeting the following day with Leboeuf, Bazaine, and Frossard, he accepted the latter's recommendation that Saarbrücken be occupied.[37] There was no particular reason for adopting this plan except that no other plan was put forth. The project did not convince Bazaine: "No decision has yet been made on the operation the army is to undertake," he grumbled in a telegram to Ladmirault (4th Corps).[38] On 30 July Napoleon III sought to justify the Saarbrücken expedition on the grounds that it would be more difficult later and that, at any rate, it would soothe both the country and the army.[39] The date for the attack was set for 2 August, but due to Bazaine's objections, occupation was limited to the left bank of the Saar. To cross the river, noted Leboeuf, was too audacious a project. "This will only be a preliminary move after which a new pause undoubtedly will ensue."[40] The attack was carried out successfully, but it exerted an undesirable effect on the concentration of the army. The divisions involved in the operation came from the 2nd, 3rd, and 5th Corps. If the expedition brought the 3rd Corps into closer contact with the 2nd Corps, it also extended the left wing of the 5th Corps so that this undermanned unit was stretched over a wider front than before. In the meantime, units of the 4th Corps, far to the left of this purposeless enterprise, were ordered to undertake a "reconnaissance offensive," but because these units were forbidden to cross the frontier, they neither obtained information about the enemy nor made a move to concentrate themselves closer to the left wing of the 3rd Corps.

No clear plan emerged from Imperial Headquarters following the attack on Saarbrücken. On 3 August, Napoleon III thought of nothing more than another "reconnaissance offensive" to be executed by the 4th Corps. The idea was dropped.[41] The next day, the high command learned of the defeat of a division of the 1st Corps at Wissembourg. Sensing that the Prussians were now closing in on the frontier, Napoleon III issued orders that in effect demanded a retreat of the 3rd Corps and the Imperial Guard. Afterwards, however, he changed his mind; he thought he had a better idea. The army could undertake operations about ten miles east of Saarbrücken; it would seize Zweibrücken, thereby obtaining control of the railroads from Mainz and Mannheim and retarding the German concentration. On the advice of the *Intendant-Général* Wolff, the project was not adopted.[42] There were no new plans on 5 August; instead Napoleon III delegated part of his authority to Bazaine and MacMahon. Thus followed, one upon the other, the projects and schemes that the commander-in-chief adopted and discarded between 28 July and 5 August. None of them held much promise. They were worthy of the kind of mind Napoleon III possessed--one rich in intrigue and plots but rarely capable of conceiving and carrying out a long-range objective. For the men of the 2nd, 3rd, 4th, and 5th Corps, these projects had done little more than force them to march and counter-march. As a result, they were in hardly a better position to support one another on 6 August than they had been on 28 July.

Then, on 5 August, Napoleon III surrendered part of his command to MacMahon and Bazaine. In doing so, he was returning to the paper plans he had inspired before the outbreak of war. It will be recalled that some French military projects called for two distinct armies of Alsace and Lorraine but that the emperor's decision to take command of a single Army of the Rhine had altered these plans. On 5 August he gave direction of the 2nd, 3rd, and 4th Corps to Marshal Bazaine and of the 1st, 5th, and 7th to Marshal MacMahon. These measures were too partial and came too late; the chain of authority was blurred. No new staffs were created to aid the marshals, who simultaneously retained command of their respective corps. Furthermore, their duties and responsibilities remained vague: their authority was limited to "military operations", and Napoleon continued to issue orders directly to subordinate corps commanders.[43] Bazaine ignored his newly gained authority, and so did his subordinates. MacMahon had little chance to exercise his; he was unable to concentrate the 5th and 7th Corps onto the position occupied by the 1st Corps before a German attack drove him from Alsace.

Incompetent as the French high command was to establish a plan of action or to create a clearly organized chain of command, it was even less equipped to gather information about the movements of the enemy. Since the army had no organized information services, Imperial Headquarters had to rely on deserters and spies. It accordingly received very inadequate intelligence. "Espionage is not well-practiced among Frenchmen," was Leboeuf's lame excuse.[44] Moreover, the French did not have the proper trained personnel to evaluate or corroborate the information they obtained. The French cavalry, potentially an information gathering branch of the armed forces, did nothing to fill the void. While Prussian cavalrymen conducted reconnaissance raids into Alsace, French cavalrymen remained inactive, many bogged down, so asserted General DuBarail, by useless baggage, "as if they were going to maneuver in the desert

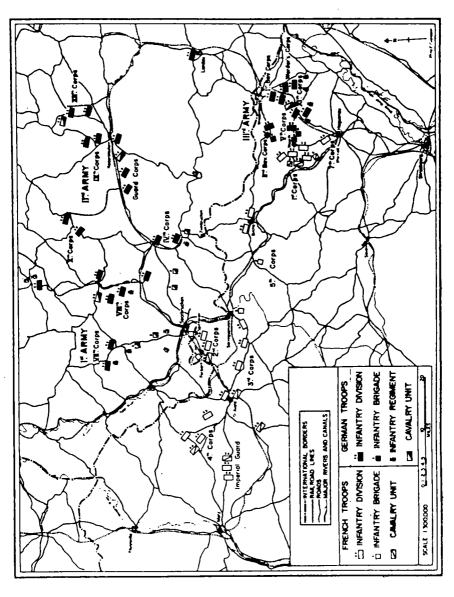

Map 2. Positions of the French and German Armies on the evening of
5 August, 1870

where they had to bring everything along, unable to procure anything once there."[45]   This inability to acquire accurate information led to two illusions which adversely affected French concentration. Vague and contradictory reports of heavy German concentrations in the Saar valley made commanders fearful of invasion and encouraged them to seek to plug every possible route into France. This reaction was most pronounced in General de Failly whose 5th Corps straddled the Vosges and guarded routes of little or no strategic importance. Failly parcelled out battalions to cover each road he believed to be vital, fretted when these detachments were told to rejoin their regiments, and disobeyed orders to march his corps toward the 1st Corps on 5 August because he was afraid to abandon the positions he was protecting.[46] Until 3 August, the belief in heavy concentration north of the Saar was unfounded; in fact, only weak garrisons covered the region.[47]

Of more serious consequence was the idea that Germans were concentrating in the Black Forest, preparing to attack Belfort in southern Alsace and to menace the railroad from Lyons to Strasbourg. This fear was combined with another concern. Just before the outbreak of the war a prolonged strike by textile workers in Southern Alsace, especially in Mulhouse, led to violence and the calling in of troops to restore order. Although the strike was settled on 17 July, some wildcat walkouts took place afterward, thus adding the spectre of civil unrest to the supposed menace of foreign invasion.[48] Since the *Garde Nationale Mobile* could not be trusted to keep domestic order and more especially since it was unprepared to counter the supposed threat from the Black Forest, the task was assigned to the 7th Corps.[49] The Germans did not attack Belfort; they did not even intend to do so, but in the meantime, the 7th Corps remained isolated, too far distant to draw up rapidly on the right flank of the 1st Corps when finally it was ordered to do so. Only one of its divisions was available to MacMahon at the Battle of Froeschwiller on 6 August.

Another difficulty confronting the French during the concentration of 1870 was that of executing marches. French officers often proved to be incapable of planning a single day's itinerary of an army corps. Without detailed maps, without trained staff officers to aid them, officers dispatched columns along roads that were being used simultaneously by units of other corps. It was more a result of luck than of foresight if a column was not halted to allow another to cross its path. It might even happen that a column was cut in half by such maneuvers.[50] Even without such mistakes, the army's camping habits retarded efficient movement. Following the custom acquired in Algeria, units on the march closed in on the head of the column at night instead of bedding down alongside the road. In the morning the vanguard broke camp several hours before the tail of the column departed. As a result the column was limited to distances that the rear guard could cover before nightfall. In 1870, a French army corps did well to cover seven or eight miles a day on foot.[51]

Faced with these problems which proved to be insoluble at the time, the French failed to execute a concentration of its armed forces in time to resist the first Prussian attacks in 1870. On 6 August, the French were too weak at the points where the Prussians mounted an attack. In Alsace only five of the ten infantry divisions under Marshal MacMahon's command saw action at the battle of Froeschwiller; another was able to reach the battlefield only in time to cover the retreat of the 1st Corps. The remaining four were too far distant from the action to offer assistance. In Lorraine the four divisions of the 3rd Corps were in position to help the 2nd Corps, which was attacked on the Spicheren heights south of Saarbrücken on the morning of 6 August.[52] One division of the 4th Corps had been marching east since Napoleon's decision to attack Saarbrücken, but it was still further than one day's march from the 2nd Corps. Furthermore, the 4th Corps still covered a front of nineteen miles.[53] The leading column of the Imperial Guard had not yet reached Boulay, twenty miles west of the Spicheren heights. Not until the middle of August did the French forces in Lorraine effect their concentration, but by then they had tasted defeat, abandoned an excellent defensive position, and lost many of the supplies which they had collected with great difficulty during the period of mobilization and concentration. The French forces assigned to Marshal MacMahon on 5 August were never concentrated. After the loss of the Froeschwiller heights, the debris of these units retreated to the Camp of Châlons where they formed the army that surrendered to the Prussians at Sedan on 1 September.

In sum, the concentration of the French army in 1870 was as unsatisfactory as its mobilization. In spite of the services provided by French railroad companies, the French army was not prepared rapidly to transport its manpower and supplies to the theater of operations. Given the irresolution of the commander-in-chief, the faults in the command structure, and the armed force's inability to obtain reliable information about the enemy as well as to maneuver efficiently, the Army of the Rhine could not bring the strength it had mustered to bear in the crucial places and at the proper time. Before the French command could remedy this situation, the Germans delivered the first and in many ways the most decisive blows of the war.

NOTES

1. Circular, Ministry of War to Minister of Public Health, 15 July 1870, SHAT, Vincennes, Lo 2 and 3; Minutes, Meeting of 21 July 1870, Compagnie de l'Est, AN, Paris, 13 AQ 54, pp. 54, 195-197; Circulars, 16 through 21 July 1870, Compagnie du Nord, 48 AQ 3190; Copies of orders to railroad companies, SHAT, Vincennes, Lo 42. See also Edwin A. Pratt, *The Rise of Rail Power in War and Conquest, 1833-1914* (Philadelphia: Lippincott, 1916), p. 139 and François Jacqmin, *Les Chemins de fer français pendant la guerre de 1870-1871* (Paris: Hachette, 1872), p. 111.

2. Letter of acknowledgment from the Compagnie de l'Est to the Ministry of Public Works, 11 August 1870, AN, Paris, 13 AQ 667, p. 1372.

3. Martin Van Creveld, *Supplying War: Logistics from Wallenstein to Patton* (New York: Cambridge University Press, 1977), p. 86.

4. Jacqmin, *Les Chemins de fer français pendant la guerre de 1870-1871*, pp. 112-113, 118-119. The author does not break down figures to allow us to distinguish between the number of cannon and the number of transport vehicles shipped.

5. France, Assemblée Nationale, *Enquête parlementaire sur les actes du Gouvernement de la Défense Nationale: dépositions des témoins*, 5 vols. (Paris: Germer-Baillière, 1872-1875), I, p. 52, (cited hereafter as D.T.).

6. "Registre," Compagnie du Nord, 19 August 1870, AN Paris, 48 AQ 17.

7. "Registre," Compagnie du Chemin de fer de Paris à Lyon et à la Méditerranée, AN, Paris, 77 AQ 183, p. 276.

8. Ibid., p. 271. While the absence of information regarding accidental deaths of soldiers in the *registres* of the other two companies is not conclusive proof that no such mishaps occurred, it is worth noting that no other source refers to any accidents. Furthermore records of all three companies generally noted accidental deaths along their lines in peacetime, so one is entitled to think that they would have reported any similar incidents had they occurred during the mobilization.

9. "Registre," Compagnie de l'Est, 19 August 1870, AN, Paris, 13 AQ 667. p. 1403.

10. "Transports militaires en 1870-1871," AN, Paris, F^{14} 12844.

11. France, Armée, Etat-major, Service historique, *Préparation à la guerre* in *La Guerre de 1870-71*, 35 vols. (Paris: Chapelot, 1901-1903), p. 34. (cited hereafter as Guerre followed by the title of the particular volume to which reference is made).

12. Ibid., p. 43.

13. Telegram, 22 July 1870, AN, Paris, AB XIX 1712.

14. Instructions, Compagnie de l'Est to Canrobert, 16 July 1870, AN, Paris, 13 AQ 667, p. 1249.

15. "Le départ des troupes," *Le National*, 17 July 1870, pp. 1-2, and 18 July 1870, p. 2. See also Jacqmin, *Les Chemins de fer français pendant la guerre de 1870-1871*, pp. 114-115; Alfred Ernouf, *Histoire des chemins de fer français pendant la guerre franco-prussienne* (Paris: Librairie Générale, 1874), pp. 4-5.

16. J.O., 18 July 1870, p. 1276.

17. Telegram, Prefect of Rhône to Minister of the Interior, 22 July 1870, AN, Paris, AB XIX 1712.

18. Telegram, Prefect of Gard to Minister of the Interior, 22 July 1870, AN, Paris, AB XIX 1712.

19. Director of Artillery (Besançon) to Minister of War, 26 July 1870, SHAT, Vincennes, Lb 1.

20. Ibid., p. 5; Pratt, *The Rise of Rail Power in War and Conquest*, pp. 141-142.

21. Circular of General Leboeuf, 16 July 1870, SHAT Vincennes, Carton La 6.

22. Barthélemy Edmond Palat, *Histoire de la guerre de 1870-1871*, Part I: *La Guerre de 1870*, 6 vols. (Paris: Berger-Levrault, 1903-1908), II, pp. 158-160; Ernouf, *Histoire des chemins de fer français pendant la guerre franco-prussienne*, pp. 4-5.

23. Jacqmin, *Les Chemins de fer français pendant la guerre de 1870-1871*, p. 116.

24. Telegram, Compagnie de l'Est to Minister of War, 9 August 1870, AN, Paris, 13 AQ 667, pp. 1364-1365.

25. Pratt, *The Rise of Rail Power in War and Conquest*, pp. 140-141.

26. J.O., 29 July 1870, P. 1343. The text is reproduced in Guerre, *Les Opérations en Alsace et sur la Sarre, 28 juillet au 2 août*, p. 1.

27. Palat, *Histoire, Part I: La Guerre de 1870*, II, p. 299.

28. Marshal Bazaine and Generals Leboeuf, Lebrun, and Jarras were present. Guerre, *Les Opérations en Alsace et sur la Sarre, 28 juillet au 2 août*, pp. 2-3.

29. Palat, *Histoire*, Part I: *La Guerre de 1870*, II, p. 300; Victor Dérrécagaix, *La Guerre moderne*, 2 vols. (Paris: L. Baudoin, 1885), I, pp. 420-422.

30. Telegrams to Imperial Headquarters, 25, 26, and 27 July 1870, AN, Paris, AB XIX 1713.

31. Palat, *Histoire*, Part I: *La Guerre de 1870*, II, pp. 300-301.

32. "Registre Canrobert," 29 July and 2, 3, 4, and 12 August 1870, SHAT, Vincennes, Lb 55; "Registre: 6e corps, 4e division- correspondance," entries for July and August 1870, SHAT, Vincennes, Lb 55; "Journal de marche- 6e corps, 3e division," entries for July and August 1870, SHAT, Vincennes, Lb 55.

33. "Journal de marche du 6e corps," SHAT, Vincennes, Lb 64, pp. 6-7.

34. Message to Leboeuf, 12 August 1870, "Registre Canrobert," SHAT, Vincennes, Lb 55.

35. Guerre, *Les Opérations en Alsace et sur la Sarre, 28 Juillet au 2 août*, pp. 2-3.

36. See Michael Howard, *The Franco-Prussian War* (London: Rupert Hart-Davis, 1961), pp. 83-85, 88-89.

37. Barthélemy Lebrun, *Souvenirs militaires, 1866-1870; préliminaires de la guerre; missions en Belgique et à Vienne* (Paris: E. Dentu, 1895), p. 215.

38. Palat, *Histoire*, Part I: *La Guerre de 1870*, II, p. 325.

39. Guerre, *Les Opérations en Alsace et sur la Sarre, 28 juillet au 2 août*, pp. 23-24; Charles Auguste Frossard, *2 Rapport sur les opérations du deuxième corps de l'Armée du Rhin dans la campagne de 1870* (Paris: Dumaine, 1872), p. 15; André Guérin, *La folle de guerre de 1870* (Paris: Hachette, 1970), p. 77.

40. Letter, Leboeuf to Dejean, 1 August 1870, SHAT, Vincennes, Lb 4.

41. Palat, *Histoire*, Part I: *La Guerre de 1870*, III, pp. 4-5.

42. Ibid., III, pp. 83-87.

43. Ibid., pp. 113-114.

44. D.T., I, p. 58.

45. François-Charles DuBarail, *Mes Souvenirs, 1820-1879*, 3 vols. (Paris: Plon, 1913), III, p. 151; W. D. Bird, *Lectures on the Strategy of the Franco-German War, 1870, up to the Battle of Sedan* (London: Hugh Rees, 1909), pp. 12-13.

46. Palat, *Histoire*, Part I: *La Guerre de 1870*, II, pp. 279 and 307, and III, pp. 150, 152-153.

47. Germany, Army, Generalstab, Kriegsgeschichtliche Abteilung, *The Franco-German War, 1870-1871*, Translated by F. C. H. Clarke, 5 vols. (London: Her Majesty's Stationery Office, 1874-1884), I, i, p. 27.

48. Telegrams, 7 to 17 July 1870, AN, Paris, AB XIX 1709 and 1710.

49. Guerre, *Préparations à la guerre*, pp. 58-59; D.T., I, p. 52.

50. See, for example, the humorous description of a division on the march in Alexandre Meissas, *Journal d'un aumônier militaire* (Paris: C. Duniel, 1872), p. 44.

51. Even the rear guard frequently arrived at camp long after dark. Louis Le Gillou, *La Campagne d'été de 1870* (Paris: Charles-Lavauzelle, 1938), pp. 41-42; Anatole Baratier, *L'Intendance militaire pendant la guerre de 1870-1871* (Paris: J. Dumaine, 1871), pp. 33-34.

52. Due mainly to bad communications, not one of these divisions aided the 2nd Corps.

53. Palat, *Histoire*, Part I: *La Guerre de 1870*, III, pp. 93 and 105.

7

The Destruction of the Army of the Rhine

In four weeks, beginning on 6 August 1870, the Army of the Rhine suffered a humiliating defeat. In spite of the tactical successes in which skilled French troops held ground while Prussian casualties mounted, the Army of the Rhine was put out of action by 1 September. At the end of that day five of the eight corps of the Army of the Rhine were hopelessly besieged in Metz, and the rest had just been surrendered by Napoleon III at Sedan. For the Prussian General Staff this was an accomplishment which overshadowed the defeat of Austria in 1866, for this time their forces had prevailed over the greatest military power in Europe.

If the campaign resembles a *Blitzkrieg*, it was not an easy, inexpensive, and foreordained one. No veteran of fields swept by the fire of *chassepots*, no overburdened *Intendantur* official could ever have remembered the war that way. Neither the battle of Sedan nor the siege of Metz were foreseen by anybody. They are as much the product of Prussian mistakes as they are of Prussian planning. The outcome, however, indicates how unprepared the French army was to meet the Prussian challenge or exploit Prussian mistakes. The French paid dearly for not having mobilized their army rapidly and for not having concentrated their strength where its effect might have been felt. As a result they were overwhelmed by superior numbers, and as they retreated they abandoned the supplies they had collected with such great difficulty. France's defeat stemmed in large measure from its faulty mobilization and its equally badly executed concentration.

WISSEMBOURG AND FROESCHWILLER

The serious predicament with which the French were confronted was first revealed by two defeats suffered by Marshal MacMahon's 1st Corps. The 1st Corps was comprised of some of the most highly regarded units in the French army, and Napoleon III had expected it to spearhead the drive into south Germany. Instead it suffered France's first defeats of the war. On 4 August its second division was crushed by the II Bavarian Corps at Wissembourg, and on 6 August, the entire corps was defeated by the German Third Army at Froeschwiller.

The faulty mobilization and concentration of the French army is central to the explanation of the fate of the 1st Corps. Rapidly assembled in the vicinity of Strasbourg by 28 July, the 1st Corps was thereafter doomed to inaction by sheer inability to maneuver. A leading cause of its trouble was its lack of transportation. On 28 July the chief intendant of the 1st Corps asked for his transport and adminstrative soldiers, none of whom, he said, were yet available. The War Ministry assured him that men and equipment of the *Train* had just set out for Strasbourg and furthermore that a ministry official would soon be prepared to answer to the needs of the 1st Corps. Tables in Martinien's study of the mobilization of 1870 show, however, that too few of these workers ever reached the 1st Corps in time to rescue it from the plight in which it found itself.[1]

Until the services of the *Train* could be made available, the 1st Corps had no convenient contact with its rail depots. The immediate result was a food crisis. As soon as troops rapidly consumed their rations of *biscuit*--those, that is, who had not already thrown them away to lighten their load--stores of food in and around Strasbourg were rapidly consumed. Then the *"Système D"* took effect. Some troops tried to solve the problem by an age old method; on 5 August one division resorted to marauding.

General Abel Douay, commander of the second division, sought a different solution. He requested permission to extend his lines to Wissembourg, an old town on the frontier of the Bavarian Palatinate. Wissembourg offered Douay only one advantage: he could find food there for his men. Their indiscipline in the previous week had become a matter of concern to civil authorities in nearby Haguenau.[2] He occupied Wissembourg on 3 August, but although he found temporary relief from the food shortages, his solution caused him to commit a tactical blunder. His maneuver severed him from contact with the rest of the 1st Corps. On the following day, Bavarian and Prussian units crossed the frontier, routed his division, caused 1,000 French casualties including General Douay, who was killed by a German shell, and took 1,000 prisoners.

The defeat at Wissembourg was by no means a significant setback to the French. The army looked upon it as an unfortunate mistake. Still the battle specifically illustrates the dangers the French army risked by not preparing the mobilization of its supplies and services long in advance. Two days later similar problems combined with several others were brought to bear in a battle between the entire 1st Corps and the German Third Army, and this time the result was strategically significant.

On 5 August, MacMahon drew the 1st Corps up along the Froeschwiller Heights to the southwest of Wissembourg. On the same day, as has been noted in the preceding chapter, MacMahon was assigned temporary and vaguely defined command over the 5th and 7th Corps. Potentially this placed six new divisions at his disposal, giving him on paper 90,000 men, a considerable force with which to prevent the German Third Army, now concentrating close by the Froeschwiller Heights, from entering Alsace. MacMahon needed all the aid he could obtain from the 5th and 7th Corps, but all he had at his disposal during the Battle of Froeschwiller the next day was one division of the 7th corps. That there were no more is largely to be explained by all the organizational and conceptual faults of the French mobilization and concentration.

MacMahon had no hope of rapidly assembling the remaining two divisions of the 7th Corps. They lay sixty to one hundred miles distant to the south in Mulhouse, Belfort, and Lyons, plugging openings threatened by nonexistent forces, and they were, as we have seen, so woefully short of men, supplies, and transport that they were unable to respond to any orders even if they had received them. The 5th Corps under General de Failly lay closer by to MacMahon's left, but from this source too there was little possibility of immediate aid. De Failly's front was stretched thinly along a front of thirty miles, the result both of Napoleon's senseless marching and countermarching and of de Failly's insistence upon 'covering' every frontier post near his command.[3] He likewise was short of *Intendance* officials and *Train* soldiers, so an order to concentrate on MacMahon's left would have been difficult to carry out, even if de Failly were inclined to obey MacMahon's instructions. He was not. Told to draw his men into closer contact with the 1st Corps, he first delayed until MacMahon's authority over him was confirmed, and then he dispatched only one division to Froeschwiller.

The progress made by this division was painfully slow. Second Lieutenant Louis Lebeau, who served in the 68th Line Infantry Regiment in 1870, participated in this maneuver. He noted in his diary how his battalion was awakened at 4:00 A.M. on 6 August and stood ready soon after. Yet except for a three kilometer advance from their bivouac to Bitche at 6:30 A.M., they did not set out for Froeschwiller until 9:30 A.M. The pace was slow, and there were frequent halts. His unit did not reach Niederbronn, a village close by Froeschwiller, until 4:30 P.M., but by then they were too late. They were caught up in the retreat of the 1st Corps, came under the fire of pursuing Prussian guns, and continued in considerable disorder another ten and a half hours before they thought they could safely halt.[4]

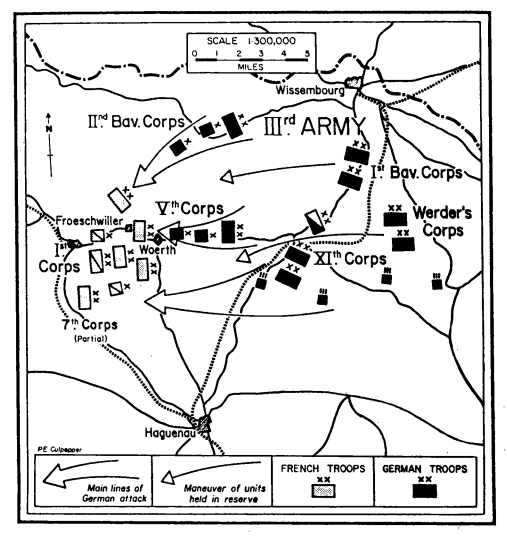

Map 3. The Battle of Froeschwiller (Woerth) on 6 August, 1870

MacMahon thus had only five divisions available when he was attacked on the Froeschwiller Heights on 6 August. Even so the position he held offered him a number of strategic and tactical advantages. Since the four and a half mile long heights face toward the Rhine, they allowed him both control of communications to the rear through defiles in the Vosges to the army in Lorraine and domination of the countryside to the east including the route to Strasbourg. The Germans were thus at a risk. They could attack the position only with great difficulty. Their frontal attack would take troops through an open valley, across a stream, and up steep slopes covered by French rifle fire. If they attacked the French left, they had to go through thickly wooded ground. Much of the heights gave MacMahon good cover because they were criss-crossed by roads bordered with hedgerows, dotted with villages, and planted with vineyards. Only the French right, where the woods were less thick and the ground rises more gently, supplied the Germans a greater opportunity to turn the French flank. Here there were man-made barriers on which the French could anchor their line. Here in particular MacMahon needed the manpower of the 5th and 7th Corps. Even without them, the Froeschwiller Heights are imposing enough to have given MacMahon good reason to expect to hold the Prussians there.[5]

In all there were about 45,000 men in position on the Froeschwiller Heights on the morning of 6 August.[6] To the left General Ducrot's Algerian veterans guarded the wooded defiles which approached the village of Froeschwiller. In the center looking down the slopes to the valley beyond were the two divisions of Generals Raoult and Conseil-Dumesnil, the latter that one division of the 7th Corps which MacMahon did obtain. It, however, lacked its artillery. To the right, at that weakest point in the French line, stood the division of General Lartigue. In reserve MacMahon placed both General Pellé's infantry division, now exhausted veterans of the engagement at Wissembourg, and the cavalry division of the 1st Corps.

MacMahon expected to use 6 August to strengthen his positions, particularly by bringing up as much of de Failly's 5th Corps as he could. His opponents had similar expectations. The positions of the German Third Army on the evening of 5 August suggested, as was noted above in the third chapter, that the Prussians had not located the main body of French troops in Alsace. For Moltke the problem was time. His attention was focused on the Saar Valley where he needed to extricate Steinmetz from the position he had occupied in Saarbrücken. For Crown Prince Frederick, commander of the Third Army, the objective was to continue along the road to Strasbourg and locate MacMahon somewhere along the way. His chief of staff, Blumenthal, thought that 6 August should be a day of rest and reorganization.[7] It was none of these.

The Battle of Froeschwiller was in many ways the Franco-Prussian War in miniature. It was begun on the initiative of Prussian officers whose imprudence led them to disobey instructions and upset the plans of their superiors. The

Battle erupted about 8:00 A.M. when patrols of the V Prussian Corps sighted the French on the heights above and, mistaking their activity for a retreat, entered the village of Woerth below. French fire forced them to withdraw, but the sound of the cannon alerted the II Bavarian Corps on their right. They attacked the Ducrot division, and this action encouraged the commander of the V Prussian Corps to return to the fray. Shortly thereafter a brigade of the XI Prussian Corps appeared on their left. By this means the Prussians were drawn piecemeal into the battle, but they failed to dislodge the French. In fact they exposed themselves to a counterattack. None was forthcoming, however, even though the French still enjoyed a temporary local superiority in numbers.

The French failure to sieze the initiative opened the way to defeat. About noon, Crown Prince Frederick, now realizing he was engaged in a major battle, acceded to the request of his subordinates for reinforcements and ordered the I Bavarian Corps and the XI Prussian Corps to deploy against the French. The latter, which in fact was already marching toward the battlefield, soon brought four divisions and seventy-two guns to bear against Lartigue's division holding the weak position on the French right. Here a Prussian division crossed the Sauer well to the south of Lartigue and occupied the village of Morsbronn. Having thus turned the French right, the Prussians were then able to force Lartigue's men to retreat. This was the decisive maneuver of the battle, for MacMahon lacked sufficient reserves to counter this threat.   French counterattacks failed to drive the Prussians from their newly conquered ground, and later in the afternoon, when the French left also began to crumble, MacMahon ordered retreat.   The French abandoned the heights in great disorder, having lost 630 officers and 19,000 men. Prussian casualties were 10,500, a tribute to the *chassepot* and to the well-sited French defense.[8]

The French defeat at Froeschwiller underscored most of the faults of the French army in 1870. The range and accuracy of Prussian artillery appalled the French whose guns were unable to answer their murderous fire. Inadequacies of the commanders, particularly MacMahon's inflexibility, unimaginativeness, and lack of initiative, condemned the French to a static defense. But since the French, although outnumbered two to one, were able to hold ground until late in the afternoon, it is clear that their defeat was not merely a consequence of inferior guns or unenterprising commanders. The loss of the battle stemmed mainly from the faults of mobilization and concentration. The French were mostly short of manpower, and this deficiency need not have existed. With a more efficient incorporation of the reserves and the well-planned concentration of the 1st, 5th and 7th Army Corps on the Froeschwiller Heights, MacMahon would have had numbers more nearly equal to those with which the Germans confronted him on 6 August. The reasons why these numbers were never forthcoming has been the principal subject of this study.

SPICHEREN

On the same day the French suffered a second defeat when an unplanned Prussian attack forced General Frossard's 2nd Corps to abandon its positions on the Spicheren Heights in Lorraine. As in the Battle of Froeschwiller, Prussian officers disregarded the commands of their superiors and risked defeat by ordering an assault on well-sited French positions. The French once again fought well and held their ground while inflicting heavy casualties on the enemy, and as at Froeschwiller they did not seek to maneuver around the Germans. Furthermore they failed to call in time for reinforcements from the 3rd Corps, some units of which were encamped less than a day's marching distance from Spicheren. As a result, the Prussians were able to increase their strength as more and more units of both the First and Second Armies marched to the guns, and when they mounted a threat to the French left and rear, Frossard was forced to order a retreat.

The ground on which the battle was waged was as favorable to the defense as the position at Froeschwiller. The Spicheren Heights are a U-shaped bluff pointing directly at Saarbrücken three miles to the north. The bluff is difficult to assault directly because the slope is steep and rocky and leads to open land covered by French fire. Its eastern slope is, furthermore, wooded and cut by deep ravines. The western slopes protect a narrow valley through which runs the main highway and railroad from Metz to the Rhineland and in which are located the iron foundry towns of Forbach and Stiring. Here in the rail yards were the 2nd Corps' supply depots which Frossard had put together with great difficulty.

Frossard had skillfully placed his men for the defense of his location. One division occupied the heights, a second held the valley, and the third stood in reserve south of Forbach. His cavalry kept a wary eye on the road to the west of Forbach, which, Frossard correctly thought, was where he was most vulnerable.

The French also enjoyed a further advantage in that they had more men within a day's marching distance than did the enemy. There is some irony in the fact that although the French were dangerously dispersed on 6 August, the Prussians stumbled into them at the one point where they had seven infantry divisions within supporting distance of one another. Besides the three divisions of the 2nd Corps, all four divisions of the 3rd Corps lay within 15 miles distance of Frossard. Altogether there were 54,900 Frenchmen available against 42,900 Prussians.

In spite of these advantages the French were forced, after a seven hour battle, to abandon the Spicheren Heights. This battle was no more intended than the one at Froeschwiller. It was begun as another result of Steinmetz' insubordination. Told to get out of the way of the oncoming Second Army, Steinmetz, instead of ordering his men to sidestep to their right where they

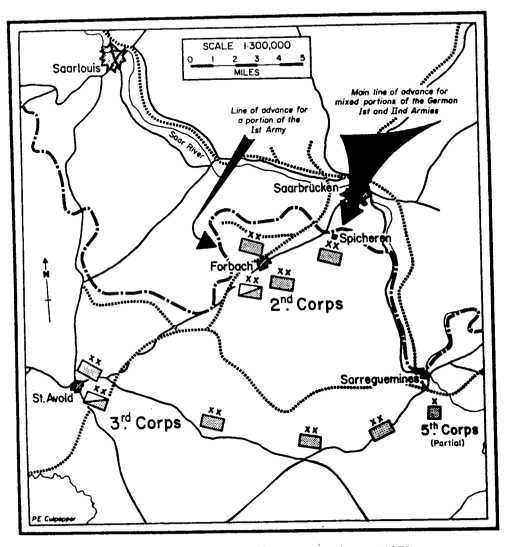

Map 4. The Battle of Spicheren on 6 August, 1870

belonged, commanded the 14th Division of VII Prussian Corps (the offending unit in this situation) to move *forward* to reach but not cross the Saar.

The Commander of the 14th division, General von Kameke, ignored these instructions. His cavalry, noting that the French had abandoned the hills which they had occupied four days earlier in the "invasion" of Saarbrücken, reported that the French were in retreat. The men he saw on the Spicheren Heights, thought Kameke, must be a rear guard, and he ordered the position to be cleared and occupied. About noon six battalions and four batteries crossed the Saar and launched the assault, but they were held in check by the French. The sound of guns alerted all available units of the Prussian Army in the vicinity, and soon much of the First Army and the advanced guard of the Second became involved in the attack. These reinforcements drew the entire 2nd Corps into a defense of both the heights and of the Forbach valley to their left, and this action in turn uncovered the French rear. In the meantime the 13th Prussian division crossed the Saar below Saarbrücken and advanced upon Forbach which it approached at seven in the evening. This was precisely the direction from which Frossard believed he was most vulnerable, but since he had already committed his reserves and obtained no reinforcements from the 3rd Corps, he was forced to withdraw from his position before his entire corps was taken.

The failure of the 3rd Corps to support Frossard contrasts unfavorably with the speed the Prussians displayed in reinforcing Kameke. To be sure the battle developed slowly, and because the 2nd Corps was able to hold its own for most of the afternoon, Frossard did not sense the real danger he faced until 5:00 P.M. Even so, while Prussian major-generals and brigadiers had taken the initiative at the sound of the guns, their French counterparts generally awaited orders from above. Only General Castagny, in command of the third division of the 3rd Corps, took it upon himself to offer Frossard help, but his activity was limited. His division set out for Forbach but returned to its bivouacs when the noise of battle died away early in the afternoon. Two other divisions set out also, but not until late in the afternoon and only after receiving belated orders from Bazaine. One general, Metman, received his first from Frossard, but since nobody had told him that Bazaine had already placed him temporarily under the command of Frossard, he delayed his advance until he verified the situation. The process took two and a half hours. General Montaudon, the other divisional commander, had received his orders directly from Bazaine, but they had arrived too late. It had taken a messenger two hours to deliver them. As a result there was no army to protect Forbach when the Prussian 13th division approached from the west. Having yielded little ground, Frossard still had little choice but to retreat. The withdrawal was costly; he abandoned both his wounded men and most of the supplies he had been collecting with great difficulty over the past two weeks.[9]

THE RETREAT INTO METZ

The battles of Froeschwiller and Spicheren opened France to invasion. They also destroyed any hopes of a timely Austrian alliance. Already the defeat at Wissembourg had prompted French ambassador La Tour d'Auvergne to warn Paris of uncertainties and anxieties in Viennese opinion "which only more favorable news can dissipate."[10] On 7 August he informed his government that the news of the events of the previous day had deeply discouraged Austrian officials. "Unfortunately," he wrote, "nobody here displays resolution and energy enough to let us count immediately on the co-operation which we shall greatly need in time."[11]

In the field the twin battles of 6 August 1870 paralyzed the French command. In spite of the impressive number of troops now concentrating in Lorraine, Napoleon III could think of no better a plan than to withdraw the left wing of the Army of the Rhine into Metz. Common sense called for either a defense of the region concentrating on Frossard's beloved Cadenbronn Line or a withdrawal to the upper Marne, a maneuver affording the two wings of the Army of the Rhine the opportunity to join forces and threaten the left wing of the invading German troops. The Prussians, furthermore, gave the French three days to adopt either one of these options. Moltke called a halt on 7 August: he still needed to extricate the First Army from the route of the Second, and he wanted to give the Third Army brief respite after its well-earned victory at Froeschwiller. But the French took no advantage of this time. Frossard, shaken by his defeat, recommended a retreat into Metz, and Napoleon, having tried but failed to devise any more meaningful strategy, finally agreed.[12]

The retreat took place under the same conditions and for the same reasons as did the maneuvers of the army prior to 6 August. Because of an incessant downpour, troops slogged along muddy roads to uncomfortable water-logged bivouacs. As usual, nobody assigned marching routes, and elements of two or three corps became entangled along the same road. Baggage trains and food convoys followed with exasperating irregularity. Unless intendants were able to obtain food by local requisition, soldiers went hungry. Even when food was obtained, many men were unable to prepare it, because they had thrown their cooking gear away. Under these circumstances, officers and men began to neglect even elementary procedures: some officers failed to maintain discipline when troops approached villages, and troops sometimes robbed local inhabitants of food, wood, and bedding. In bivouac officers did not bother to post sentries.[13]

For the men of the 5th Corps the retreat was a long, difficult, and exhausting task made all the more exasperating by the faults of the mobilization. Lieutenant Lebeau's diary supplies us with telling details about the plight of his regiment. He shows vividly how harshly his men suffered due to long marches and inadequate supplies. Between 6 and 8 August they covered eighty kilometers in less than 48 hours. Because they had been awake longer than that, they quickly fell asleep on short halts. His unit received no distribution of rations during those three days and no adequate amount until 10 August. As the 68th became mixed in with stragglers of the 1st Corps, disorder, looting, and indiscipline increased; officers too, he noted, abused the hospitality of inhabitants of the region. Heavy rain burdened everybody for five straight days. Not until 15 August was the 68th assured regular distribution of supplies. It obtained rail transport only on 16 and 17 August. Three days later Lebeau and his men were camped in relative comfort in the Camp of Châlons.[14]

The retreat was equally burdensome to the 1st Corps. Believing the Prussians close on his heels, MacMahon begged for both artillery shells and cartridges for the infantry. He had, he said, consumed all he had on 6 August, and he never did have a sufficient reserve park set up.[15] His colleagues had little to spare. He also required food, and Canrobert dispatched bread, sugar, coffee, and *biscuit*.[16] Eventually his men received enough rations. Despite this, other supplies went lacking, and indiscipline remained a problem until the 1st Corps reached Châlons. Like the 5th Corps the 1st did not find rail transportation until 16 August. The reason is clear: both MacMahon and de Failly thought the Germans had seized rail junctions. They had not bothered to scout the territory.[17] In fact the Germans were two to three days behind them, and the French could readily have obtained rail services. Failing to do so they prolonged the retreat and further exhausted their depleted manpower resources.

There was no direction from above to rectify this situation and impose order upon the operations of the army. In Paris, the Ollivier ministry fell on 9 August; its place was taken by a cabinet headed by the Count of Palikao, who served as both Prime Minister and Minister of War. Palikao, a military hero, reassured an agitated Parisian public that the government could take measures to rescue the French army from its predicament. He failed, however, to take Empress Eugénie into consideration. The empress, fearful that a defeat would result in the downfall of the regime, tried to influence the direction of military operations, but eventually her meddling helped produce the consequence she wished to avoid. From Imperial Headquarters in the meantime there was no direction at all. Napoleon III frequently changed his mind about military objectives. In the end all he could do was retreat into Metz and, on 12 August, relinquish command of the Army of the Rhine to Bazaine.

Bazaine, likewise, had no consistent plan of action. Nor did he appear willing to accept the responsibilities placed on his shoulders. He had not obtained the services of the staff he wanted, and he was uncertain of the extent of his authority. Napoleon III continued to issue orders directly to corps commanders, and Bazaine's command did not extend to the Imperial Guard.[18]

In these circumstances Bazaine abdicated all responsibility and failed to offer the army in Lorraine any direction.

Meanwhile the Prussians were bearing down upon the French.   After Moltke had put his armies in order, he advanced them along three parallel routes, the first two armies upon Metz, the third to their left upon Nancy. They proceeded with difficulty.   Their cavalry had lost contact with the French, so their objective was uncertain.   The rain made life as unpleasant for them as it did for the French.   There were too few good roads to allow for efficient maneuver.   And they had long since outrun their lumbering supply columns.[19]

Yet the Prussians possessed both the experience and the staff to cope with these problems. The hours the Prussian officials spent planning marching routes, directing convoys, and clearing roads of unnecessary traffic were well rewarded; while the French retreated in confusion, the Prussians remained a relatively cohesive mass capable of accomplishing Moltke's objectives.   By the middle of August the First and Second Prussian Armies had regained contact with Bazaine's army.   At the same time the Third Army had occupied Nancy, and all three armies were preparing to seize crossings over the Moselle and trap Bazaine.

It was the contact made by the First and Second Armies to the east of Metz that prompted both Bazaine and Napoleon III to decide to retreat west of Metz. Nothing illustrated the difference between the mobility of the two armies in 1870 than the attempted evacuation of Metz.   Even when marching as a concentrated force and when confronted by vexing supply problems, the Prussians remained dispersed enough to allow for greater articulation and more rapid advance than did the French. By contrast, Bazaine, as he withdrew from Metz between 14 and 16 August, attempted to pass 170,000 men through the narrow, twisting streets of an aged city, cross seven bridges, and then somehow mount a rise along one single road.

During the retreat Bazaine committed innumerable errors.   He failed to consult his chief of staff on major questions of organization.   He ignored the existence of another bridge shortly upstream from the city; he knew little about the roads available to the army west of Metz; he set no destination for the army to reach and no military objective for it to achieve.   The army was told to prepare its departure for the morning of 14 August, and many units stood ready. There was no schedule for the advance of these units.   When they set off they were allowed to find their way on their own through the city.   Two corps learned that they were expected to cover the same route simultaneously.   As a result the departure did not begin until late in the afternoon of 14 August, and the French lost valuable time.

Five days later these same troops streamed back into Metz in defeat, and shortly afterward they were besieged by the Prussians.   The ponderous, inarticulate, ill-organized French had surrendered all the advantages to the better mobilized and more enterprising Prussians. In three engagements on 14, 16, and 18 August the Prussians halted the French retreat. On 14 August the Prussian First Army drew outposts of the 3rd French Corps into a tactical defense of their positions at Borny, east of Metz. The French held their ground but suffered a strategic defeat by delaying the retreat of the 3rd Corps and depriving the French of even more time. Borny also gave the Prussians time to sieze bridgeheads and cross the Moselle upstream of Metz. Thus as the French withdrew from Metz, the Prussians were already outdistancing them to the south.

The subsequent battles of 16 and 18 August sealed the fate of Bazaine's army. By 16 August Napoleon III had departed for Châlons leaving the forces in Lorraine now entirely on the care of Marshal Bazaine. His task was to direct a retreat to the Meuse at Verdun. He would have preferred an attack on those German forces which had already crossed the Moselle, but he was unable to concentrate sufficient forces against them.[20] He knew the retreat had to proceed with utmost speed to avoid an attack upon his flank. On 15 August, however, the retreat proceeded with the same disorder as on the previous day. Until they reached Gravelotte, five miles west of Metz, the French advanced along a single road. At Gravelotte the route forked. There the 3rd Corps took the northern branch but progressed so slowly that the 4th Corps behind it still stood on the banks of the Moselle the following morning. The 2nd and 6th Corps and the Imperial Guard took the southern route. On the morning of 16 August, they were preparing to continue on to Verdun when they were attacked at the villages of Vionville and Mars-la-Tour by two corps of the Prussian Second Army.

The Prussians approaching cautiously from the south thought the forces they had encountered were a French rear guard; instead they assaulted the entire French army in Lorraine. Once again the French enjoyed local superiority. They did not press the advantage, however, partly because they mistook two Prussian corps for all of the Prussian Second Army and partly because of Bazaine's perceptions of the nature of the engagement. He sent reinforcements to the wrong place in the line of battle and thereby missed the opportunity to overwhelm the attackers. The results were correspondingly harmful to the French. Their retreat was halted, and by the end of the day they had allowed the Prussians to cut the main road to Verdun.

The loss of this road was not the only problem to beset Bazaine in the aftermath of this encounter. If he was to escape from Metz at all, he needed time to regroup his forces. He had to sort out the various corps which had become entangled during the battle. There was also the problem of supplies. His army had advanced no further than ten miles from Metz in three days, but transport soldiers were already unable to reach the men. The army consumed large stores of ammunition on 16 August, and the nearest arsenals were in Metz. There it could replenish its dwindling supplies of food and ammunition and prepare itself either to renew its march to the Meuse or to ward off still another attack. On 17 August the French turned back towards Metz. On the following day, the Germans located them, gave battle, and drove them into the city.

The battle of Gravelotte-Saint Privat (18 August 1870) was the largest and bloodiest encounter of the War of 1870. It also ranks with Sedan as one of the most decisive. Altogether 300,000 men were engaged, and at its conclusion, the Prussians listed 20,000 casualties; the French, 12,273.[21] For the Prussians the price was high, but they were well rewarded for their efforts. On 19 August they began to shut Bazaine into Metz where they besieged him until he surrendered in October.

On the whole the outlines of the battle are simple. The French faced west along a seven mile front. Their left flank, anchored on woods and sited above deep ravines, was impregnable. Their right flank, however, was weak. The 6th Corps which occupied the position on the extreme right of the French line had been unable to obtain their artillery from Châlons before the Prussians seized the railroad lines south of Metz. Furthermore the ground it occupied was open and therefore vulnerable to a turning movement to the north. In the battle the Prussians approached from the south and advanced boldly across the French front engaging them corps by corps in turn from south to north. Finally, after drawing the 6th Corps into the encounter, the Prussian XII Corps maneuvered around the open French flank and forced the 6th Corps to fall back. With its right wing broken, the French were forced to abandon the battlefield.

Strategically the battle of Gravelotte-Saint Privat was a masterpiece of Prussian leadership. It was unintended, however. The bold march across the French front was not bravado; the Prussians had blundered into the French not realizing yet that they had located Bazaine's entire army. And, tactically, the casualty figures show that the battle was nearly a disaster for them. The battle unfolded bit by bit as the Prussians found more French units whom they attacked in dense columns. Where the French had dug into good ground or where their *chassepots* and *mitrailleuses* swept open, sloping fields, they brought Prussian attacks to a halt and caused them heavy casualties.

Never once, however, did the French launch a counterattack even though the Prussians gave them opportunities to do so. Instead the French passively awaited each German attack. With the initiative entirely in Prussian hands, the French allowed the Prussian XII Corps to find, turn, and assault the undefended flank of the 6th Corps. As at Froeschwiller and at Spicheren, French troops who had fiercely--and on the whole successfully--defended their ground, were forced to fall back. This time they gained no opportunity to regroup for maneuvers against the enemy. Within a week Moltke had drawn a ring around Metz, and the French forces in Lorraine never broke out of it. They had ceased to play an active role in the War of 1870.

LA DEBACLE

Gravelotte put a large part, but not all, of the Army of the Rhine out of action. There remained a considerable number of soldiers gathering at the Camp of Châlons. These included the 1st Corps which had retreated over 150 miles since its defeat at Froeschwiller; it was joined by the 7th Corps and two divisions of the 5th. There were other forces there as well. The Paris *Garde Mobile* was still encamped there, and the army had also been collecting regular army units previously assigned to cover the Spanish frontier.   There were furthermore several temporary regiments (called *régiments de marche*) forged out of soldiers who had remained in regimental depots after the regulars and contingents of reservists had departed for the frontier in July. Because most of the men in these *régiments de marche* were untrained conscripts of the second portion of the annual contingent, they were of doubtful military value.   On 19 August Napoleon III named this varied collection the Army of Châlons and placed MacMahon in command.

Napoleon had to decide what use to make of this force.   There were two possible answers. One was to fall back on Paris, where, under the guns of its fortresses, the Army of Châlons could maneuver and build the strength needed to assault the German Third Army.   The other was to bring aid directly to Bazaine either by drawing Prussian strength away from Metz or by joining hands with him on the Meuse in order to crush the First and Second Prussian Armies.

Neither of these alternatives appealed to the emperor. If he allowed the Army of Châlons to attempt a junction with Bazaine, he would be asking a poorly supplied and partly untrained armed force to maneuver across the front of the oncoming Germans.   But a return to the fortress system of Paris was equally unacceptable. It would have been an admission of defeat, and both the empress and the cabinet warned him of the consequences.   Empress Eugénie wrote a letter to Napoleon III begging him not to abandon Bazaine, who, she thought, was retreating to Verdun.[22] This intervention was implicitly political; advice from the government was more direct, and the reason is clear. It was "an imperative duty on us," said a government official later on, "to avoid any act which might bring on a revolutionary movement."[23] On 21 August for lack of anything better to do and with no mission in sight, the Army of Châlons set out for Rheims.

Its mission came to be defined by a message from Bazaine. On 21 August Napoleon III and MacMahon received a message Bazaine had dispatched two days earlier on the morrow of Gravelotte. It told the emperor that he intended to break out to the north-east toward Montmédy, thence to Ste. Ménéhoulde.

A final message of 20 August seemed to confirm this, although Bazaine added that he would do so if he could without compromising his army.[24] With the telegraph line to Metz now cut and with no later communication from Bazaine, Napoleon and MacMahon decided to attempt a linking of the Armies of the Rhine and of Châlons. The maneuver was complicated; it involved an arc-like movement to the north and east over inferior roads. But it was not a retreat. On 23 August the Army of Châlons set out from Rheims to meet Bazaine in Montmédy.

The campaign conducted by the Army of Châlons in August 1870 is one of the most tragic in the annals of French military history. MacMahon's force was expected to join Bazaine, maneuver in the open and deliver a crashing blow to the invader, but Bazaine never seriously tried to break out of Metz. Meanwhile, the Army of Châlons, which had plenty of men and weapons, somehow had to execute its mission with speed and efficiency.

These skills were even less qualities of the Army of Châlons than of any other French armed force in 1870. Because many of the men were untrained, the pace of the Army of Châlons was limited to what raw troops could bear. Furthermore, the entire force was short of essential supplies and services: haversacks, camping equipment, cooking utensils, munitions, forage, ambulances, transport vehicles, and maps. Members of the *Garde Nationale Mobile* were the worst equipped of all. Officials in Châlons noted that apart from rifles they had been issued no equipment at all. Many lacked shoes, and their uniforms were incomplete.[25] *Intendance* officials, overworked, understaffed, and poorly prepared for their duties, were unable to fill the army's needs.

In these conditions, the Army of Châlons could resort to one of two expedients. One was to live off the country, but this encouraged pillaging. The other was to advance from supply depot to supply depot, even though to do so was to draw the army away from its objective. Certainly the move from the Camp of Châlons to Rheims on 21 August was prompted by the promise of finding supplies there. Assured of a shipment of shirts and shoes by the Ministry of War, MacMahon was also told they "perhaps have arrived and are stored in Rheims. Certainly there are numerous pairs of shoes there."[26] As a result MacMahon chose the later alternative, and between 23 and 26 August, he pursued a zig-zag course--due east, due north, northeast--through a region endowed with poorer roads and less rail service than that being traversed by the Germans. As a result, when the advances guard of the Army of Châlons finally reached the Meuse on 29 August, they discovered that the Prussians had already crossed the river and were pressing upon the French right flank from the south.

By then MacMahon already doubted that he could link forces with Bazaine and had informed Paris that he was withdrawing to the north-west, beyond Sedan to Mézières. Palikao countered these orders and required MacMahon to advance to the Meuse.[27] MacMahon obeyed, but the march was an ordeal.

Lacking supplies, rations, and transport, the Army of Châlons was an immobile, incoherent, inarticulate force incapable of being rapidly deployed against a growing Prussian threat.   Some officers did not know how to organize a marching column and received instructions on how to do so on 21 August.[28] Even then contradictory orders delayed the advance. Columns lost their way for lack of maps or of civilian guides; lacking a clear objective commanders did not know where to direct their men. In these circumstances, exhausted reservists and *gardes* fell by the wayside, forming a growing mass of undisciplined stragglers.[29] The French frequently failed to post sentries, and by 27 August the Prussian vanguard began to harass these disorganized units.[30]   They also blocked MacMahon's route across the Meuse, forcing him to veer his course northward in hopes of finding an unoccupied bridgehead. The search was unsuccessful, and when, on 30 August, the Prussians, whose patrols had now located the Army of Châlons, routed the southernmost of MacMahon's corps (it was the 5th) from positions it held on the Meuse, MacMahon gave up all hope of aiding Bazaine and ordered his troops to retreat into Sedan.

Sedan, an old fortress city, lies astride the Meuse seven miles south of the Belgian frontier. It is dominated from the northeast and from the south by heights which make excellent gun sites. As the French retreated into Sedan on 31 August, they failed to occupy these positions; the Prussians, who followed in close pursuit, did. Therein lay the key to the crushing defeat the French suffered the following day. On 1 September the Prussians poured shells onto the French positions below, and the French artillery, too far out of range, was unable to respond. All French attempts to break out of the trap failed; the Prussian infantry had blocked all of the exits the French could take. Aware that further resistance was futile, Napoleon III, who had accompanied the Army of Châlons on its disastrous campaign, took responsibility for the defeat. At eleven the following morning he signed the surrender of 83,000 men to the Germans. With this capitulation the armed force which seven weeks earlier had been assigned to destroy the armies of the North German Confederation and its allies has ceased to exist.

The war lasted four more months.   A bloodless coup in Paris on 4 September brought to power a cabinet composed of the republican deputies in the *Corps Législatif.* The new government declared the dissolution of the Second Empire and sought to open negotiations with Bismarck. Bismarck's terms, however, were too onerous: Prussia needed a frontier to protect herself from further French attacks, and this frontier meant Alsace and Lorraine. Determined to resist these demands, the government constituted itself as the Government of National Defense and attempted to raise new armies to drive the Germans out. Their efforts were futile, and on 28 January 1871 Jules Favre, representing France as provisional foreign minister, signed an armistice.

On 10 May, 1871 the French signed the Treaty of Frankfurt. By its terms, France ceded Alsace and part of Lorraine to the newly formed German Empire. The French also agreed to pay Germany an indemnity of 1,500,000 francs, and until France paid this amount, the Germans were allowed to maintain 50,000 troops in six northeastern departments of France. Germany's terms constituted a high price for France to pay for peace, but every mistake the French Army committed during the first three weeks of the war made so great a sum more and more inevitable.

NOTES

1. Telegram, Intendant of the 1st Corps to Minister of War, 28 July 1870, SHAT, Vincennes Lb 2; Telegram, Ministry of War to MacMahon, 29 July 1870, SHAT, Vincennes La 6; Aristide Martinien, *La Guerre de 1870-71. La Mobilisation de l'armée: mouvements des dépôts (armée active) du 15 juillet au 1er mars, 1871* (Paris: L. Fournier, 1912), pp. 387-395.

2. For accounts of this situation see Anatole Baratier, *L'Intendance militaire pendant la guerre de 1870-71* (Paris: J. Dumaine, 1871), pp. 23-25; Louis Le Gillou, *La Campagne d'été de 1870* (Paris: Charles-Lavauzelle, 1938), p. 91; Michael Howard, *The Franco-Prussian War* (London: Rupert Hart-Davis, 1961), p. 100. Correspondence regarding shortages of food and irregular distribution of rations is stored in SHAT, Vincennes, Lr 8, folder 5.

3. Although de Failly exaggerated the threat to his lines of communications, he must sincerely have thought the rail lines at Bitche, where his headquarters was located, could easily have been seized by the Germans, thus cutting the link between the troops in Alsace and those in Lorraine. De Failly's reputation was ruined by the Franco-Prussian War, and the hesitant leadership he displayed in the early days of the campaign is one of the reasons why. Even so his fretting about his lines of communication has its defender. See the letter deposited in the papers of Georges Chivot: MAE, Paris, Papiers Chivot.

4. "Carnets de route de Louis Lebeau, sous-lieutenant au 68eme régiment d'infanterie (campagne de 1870-1871)," SHAT, Vincennes, T 133, pp. 5-7.

5. Barthélemy Edmond Palat, *Histoire de la guerre de 1870-1871*. Part I: *La Guerre de 1870*, 6 vols. (Paris: Berger-Levrault, 1903-1908), III, pp. 142, 172.

6. See Appendix III. These figures are based on Martinien, *La Guerre de 1870-71. La Mobilisation de l'armée.*

7. Howard, *The Franco-Prussian War*, p. 108.

8. Palat, *Histoire*, Part I: *La Guerre de 1870*, III, p. 553; Germany, Army, Generalstab, Kriegsgeschichtliche Abteilung, *The Franco-German War*, Translated by F. C. H. Clarke, 5 vols. (London: Her Majesty's Stationery Office, 1874-1884), I, i, Appendix, p. 107, (cited hereafter as G. G. S.).

9. A useful account of the experiences of a battalion of *chasseurs à pied* corroborates this description; it is deposited among the small handful of papers left by Emile Ollivier to the Ministry of Foreign Affairs. Letter (undated), MAE, Paris, Papiers Emile Ollivier.

10. MAE, Paris, CP Autriche, 6 August 1870, p. 72.

11. MAE, Paris, CP Autriche, 7 August 1870, pp. 74-75.

12. Charles-Auguste Frossard, *Rapport sur les opérations du deuxième corps de l'armée du Rhin dans la campagne de 1870* (Paris: Dumaine, 1872), pp. 62-63, 142.

13. For a description of French troops on retreat see Palat, *Histoire*, Part I: *La Guerre de 1870*, IV, pp. 52-53, 90-92, 122-195; Jean-Baptiste-Alexandre Montaudon, *Souvenirs militaires*, 2 vols. (Paris: C. Delagrave, 1898-1900), II, p. 87.

14. "Carnets de route de Louis Lebeau, sous-lieutenant au 68eme régiment d'infanterie (campagne de 1870-1871)," SHAT, Vincennes, T 133, pp. 8-10.

15. Telegram, MacMahon to Ministry of War, 8 August 1870, SHAT, Vincennes, La 7.

16. These supplies were dispatched by Canrobert on 7 August, clearly indicating that MacMahon had addressed an appeal to him: Telegram, Canrobert to MacMahon, 7 August 1870, "Registre Canrobert," SHAT, Vincennes, Lb 55.

17. "Armée de Châlons: correspondance du 12 août au 2 Septembre 1870," folders 16 and 19 August, SHAT, Vincennes, Lc 1. Folders for 12 to 20 August document details of the retreat of the 1st Corps.

18. Palat, *Histoire*, Part I: *La Guerre de 1870*, IV, pp. 47, 75; Howard, *The Franco-Prussian War*, pp. 125, 134-135; Edmond Ruby and Jean Regnault, *Bazaine, coupable ou victime? A la lumière de documents nouveaux* (Paris: Peyronnet, 1960), pp. 110-117.

19. Howard, *The Franco-Prussian War*, pp. 127-128, 168-169; G. G. S., I, i, pp. 288-289.

20. Palat, *Histoire*, Part I: *La Guerre de 1870*, V, p. 42.

21. G. G. S., I, i, Appendix, p. 23; France, Armée, Etat-Major, Service historique, *Les Opérations autour de Metz*, III, in *La Guerre de 1870-71*, 35 vols. (Paris; Chapelot, 1901-1903), p. 79, (cited hereafter as Guerre followed by the title of the particular volume to which reference is made).

22. Copy of letter, Empress Eugénie to Napoleon III, 17 August 1870, SHAT, Vincennes, Lc 1.

23. France, Assemblée Nationale, *Enquête parlementaire sur les actes du Gouvernement de la Défense Nationale: déposition des témoins*, 5 vols. (Paris: Germer-Baillière, 1872-1875), I, p. 21.

24. Telegram, Bazaine to Napoleon III, 20 August 1870, "Armée de Châlons: Correspondance du 12 août au 2 Septembre 1870," folder 22 August, SHAT, Vincennes, Lc.

25. Telegram, Prefect of the Somme to Ministry of Interior, 28 August 1870, AN, Paris, F⁹ 1259.

26. Telegram, Ministry of War to MacMahon, 20 August 1870, "Armée de Châlons: Correspondance du 12 août au 2 Septembre 1870," folder 20 August, SHAT, Vincennes, Lc 1.

27. Guerre, *L'Armée de Châlons*, I. Documents annexes, p. 279.

28. "Ordre general du corps d'armée. Armée de Châlons: Correspondance du 12 août au 2 Septembre 1870," SHAT, Vincennes, Lc 1.

29. "Carnets de route de Louis Lebeau, sous-lieutenant au 68eme régiment d'infanterie (campagne de 1870-1871)," SHAT, Vincennes, T 133, pp. 8-11.

30. "Relation du Colonel en retraite Lespinasse concernant les marches, combats et batailles auxquels a participé le 3e bataillon de 88e," SHAT, Vincennes, Lq 2.

Conclusion

The Franco-Prussian War of 1870-71 is sometimes treated as a "watershed war." Insofar as this term implies that this conflict marks the transition from nineteenth century limited wars waged by unprofessional soldiers to twentieth century total wars directed by skilled technocrats trained in the efficient management of violence, the concept, though useful, is overdrawn. Helmuth von Moltke has more in common with General Leboeuf than with the Joint Chiefs of Staff of the 1960's. Likewise some of the "lessons" the Franco-Prussian War had to teach were misleading. The American Civil War had as much, if not more, to tell about war in the future than did the campaign of August 1870. Yet in terms of the organization and management of armed forces, 1870 does represent a significant transition. No modern war so dramatically contrasts procedures of mobilization and concentration as does this one. None illustrates more vividly how a military defeat can stem from a failure to modernize an army as does the debacle France endured in the *année terrible* of 1870.

Central to France's defeat in 1870 was the failure of the French army to learn and adapt to military uses the technological developments of the era. These developments, particularly the ones relating to transportation, permitted resourceful military leaders to shift armed forces rapidly from peacetime to wartime organization and then deploy these against opponents soon enough to fulfill their military objectives. By 1870 the Prussians had clearly identified these phases of military operations, named them, and prepared their army to execute them. The French, on the other hand, confounded mobilization and concentration and put both in operation simultaneously.

This mistake derived partly from the military institutions France maintained in 1870. Recruitment laws and practices supplied the French army with a cadre of long service troops who made it theoretically possible to deploy peacetime effectives without a transitional mobilization period. In fact the army was not prepared for a rapid deployment of its forces. There was a small reserve system. The army depended upon these men to flesh out its battalions in wartime but had not drawn up any schedule to reincorporate them efficiently. Likewise its officers, some the products of a second-rate military academy, others recruited from the ranks, lacked training for the tasks they had to fulfill and generally could not cope with the problems confronting them in 1870. Meanwhile the army's peacetime structure was unsuited for the conduct of a rapid mobilization. Since its largest peacetime unit was the regiment, all larger formations and their respective commands and staffs had to be created on an *ad hoc* basis after war was declared. Even the few and inadequate reforms adopted by Napoleon III's government following Prussia's surprising defeat of Austria in 1866 served the army poorly. They produced a misleading impression on army officials. Many, General Leboeuf most notably, thought reform had prepared the army for war with Prussia. In fact it had not.

Prussia entered that conflict with a military system the French did not match. The Prussians had a larger reserve of trained soldiers, endowed their army with a peacetime organization parallel to its wartime structure, armed it with excellent artillery (but not so effective an infantry weapon), planned its mobilization in advance, and achieved cohesiveness through a well-organized, professionally competent staff system. Even so, the Prussians nearly frittered these advantages away in 1870 by an ineptly executed concentration of their forces. A badly designed supply convoy system, poorly prepared allies, and rash offensives undertaken by impetuous commanders exposed the Prussians to defeat by a well-mobilized, enterprising opponent. The French, however, could never take advantage of these opportunities because they had never defined their objectives, had evolved no clear war plan, and pursued instead an elusive alliance system with Austria and Italy. The symbol of their strategic unpreparedness was the casual ease with which Napoleon III could insist, shortly before war was declared, that French forces be mobilized and concentrated into a single "Army of the Rhine" under his personal command. With no more rational plan established, the emperor had his way even though his project made no military sense.

It was imperative that the French make optimum use of the trained soldiers available to them by assembling the Army of the Rhine before the Prussians completed their mobilization. The single most notable shortcoming of the French mobilization of 1870 was their utter failure to do so. Similarly the French failed to mobilize the supplies and support services required to maintain the Army of the Rhine. The French army possessed the equipment but lacked the means to have it distributed. The *Intendance* was overburdened and administratively inefficient. Never organized to serve a large European army in wartime, it could neither allocate and dispatch services nor cope with the ensuing shortages once they became manifest.

Set back by the failures of the mobilization the command of the Army of the Rhine was unable to concentrate its forces effectively against the growing Prussian threat. This poorly executed concentration too was the product of insufficient planning.   The defeats at Wissembourg, Froeschwiller, and the Spicheren Heights on 4 and 6 August 1870 thus directly resulted from the faulty French mobilization. Short of soldiers, adequate supplies, and timely support, the 1st and 2nd French Corps were forced by the Germans to abandon strategically important ground, thus leaving France open to invasion. A better executed mobilization and a more intelligently planned concentration combined with the opportunities the Prussians gave the French could have allowed the French army to avoid this consequence.   Once it occurred, however, all the disadvantages accruing to the French compounded in disorderly retreat. Facing dwindling manpower resources, unable to deploy sufficient reinforcements, plagued by increasingly short supplies and chaotically organized services to deliver them, the army was doomed to suffer additional disasters at Vionville, Gravelotte, and Sedan. Probably no commander, no matter how resourceful, intelligent, or resolute, could have extricated the French from the predicament their mobilization and concentration procedures had created. The French army lacked the means to turn the Prussian invasion back. Immobile, incapable of siting its forces to confront the enemy effectively, it sealed itself into inevitable defeat.

The well-known political consequences of the defeat have often been enumerated in the textbooks. The military ones, on the other hand, are less certain. Conventional wisdom maintains that after 1870 nobody could ignore the Prussian-German system and all major powers had to reshape their military institutions in accordance with the German model. This assertion is too glib. Certainly no major European land power with great power pretensions could risk maintaining institutions and practices similar to the ones France kept prior to the Franco-Prussian War. The lessons of 1870 were clear on that matter. On the other hand no power slavishly copied Prussian-German military practices.

France was a case in point. Profoundly shaken by the defeat of 1870, French authorities sought to transform their military institutions to avoid a repetition of the debacle at Sedan and to reverse its result by the reannexation of the "lost provinces" of Alsace and Lorraine. In France, however, no consensus emerged on the means to transform the army, nor have historians since agreed on the extent or the quality of post-1870 military reforms. Some have held that the 1870 defeat initiated a military renaissance that restored France's power and prestige in the ensuing two decades. The 1870s were years of introspection and reassessment, and the considerable thought and debate given over to military topics resulted in significant changes. France adopted the principle of universal military obligation, reorganized its command and staff structure, altered its training methods and tactics, improved the educational level of its officer corps, adopted new and more powerful weapons, and strengthened its frontiers with a strong system of fortifications.[1]   Others question these results.   A recent study has shown that in the post-1870 arms race with Germany, France was doomed to finish second.   France did not really adopt universal conscription until 1889, but by then its rate of population growth had fallen so far behind Germany that France could not really raise an army equal in size to Germany's.   France's improvements in weapons and fortifications ended up being costly, incomplete, and insufficient; the training of cadres of officers and NCOs, especially in the cavalry and artillery, was inadequate; the revamped general staff system was not set up to function, like its German counterpart, as an independent war planning agency, and in any case it was weakened by chronic ministerial instability.   This situation coupled with the continued growth of German military power left France permanently inferior to its rival to the east.[2]

These military shortcomings once again bore bitter fruit on the fields of eastern and northern France in the frightful month of August 1914.   French arms were inadequate to the task of breaking through and defeating Germany in a quick campaign even though this time France had the support of two powerful allies.   France threw away thousands of young men in the disastrous "Battle of the Frontiers," but significantly this time France did not taste defeat.   Through a combination of luck, German mistakes, and timely opportunism, the French army halted the German advance at the Marne in September 1914.   France was saved, but it was also condemned to waging a long, difficult, and debilitating war and winning a deceptive victory.

In one respect the "miracle of the Marne" does represent the result of timely and effective reform.   In August 1914 France's army was badly mauled by the Germans, but efficiently mobilized, assembled, and deployed, it did not shatter.   As a result it could be redeployed at an opportune moment.   Simply put, in mobility it possessed an advantage its 1870 predecessor had so disastrously lacked.   French military reforms of the previous four decades may have fallen short in other respects, but at the beginning of World War I France avoided repeating the errors of July 1870.   Instead its army had the capacity to exploit German blunders.

The shabby mobilization effort of 1870 had been carefully analyzed by French observers.   Whatever other factors they may have attributed to the defeat, and however they proposed to prevent a recurrence of these consequences, they acknowledged the significance of well-prepared mobilization plans.   "Because the principle of big battalions still obtains," wrote Jules-Victor Lemoyne in 1872, "because now as before the greatest chance of success resides in the strategic offensive and accrues to whichever of the two adversaries takes it, because furthermore the adversary more rapidly prepared to begin a campaign is therefore capable of taking the offensive, the whole military organization of a state must be aimed at the prompt and safe mobilization of all its ready forces." A well-conceived and minutely planned mobilization schedule, he added, can allow a nation to organize its armed forces in such fashion that "they can, so to speak, rise out of the earth at the simple dispatch of a telegram."[3]

One of the most observant commentators on French military affairs following the Franco-Prussian War was General Charles-Antoine Thoumas. In a two-volume study published in 1887 he critically examined French military reforms over the decade and a half following the war. General Thoumas devoted a chapter to mobilization and concentration, and in it he described not only the French and German efforts in 1870 but French preparations in earlier wars as well. He concluded that these experiences demonstrated how "a complete transformation in the essential, even capital, part of our military organization was indispensable," and he appended a warning which, by 1914, had become a commonly accepted axiom: "Once it (mobilization) is broached, there is no going back; we can state openly: *Mobilization is war.*" (Italics Thoumas')[4]

Thoumas was pessimistic; he believed France had lost time in the military race with the Germans, and his study details why he though so. Later events--and demographic developments--gave substance to his fears. The campaigns of 1914 and the subsequent conduct of World War I revealed serious defects in French doctrine, training, armaments, and organization. Mobilization and concentration procedures, however, were largely exempt from these conditions. The mobilization of the French army in 1914 was conducted, in Major General Sir Edward Spears' phrase, "without the slightest hitch, an enormous relief in view of the vital importance of keeping to schedule."[5]

General Spears' view may have been too sanguine. He was a lieutenant in the British army recently arrived in France as a liaison officer when he made that observation. But in essence he was correct. In 1914 the French army did avoid a repetition of the confusion, disorder, and helplessness that attended it upon its mobilization and concentration in 1870. Time and effort had yielded advantageous results: their manpower, supplies, and support services were available to them in the amounts expected when they initiated their campaign in 1914. Their plan was inappropriate; so too was the deployment of their available forces. Their objectives were wrecked by German machine guns in the fields of Lorraine during the third week of August 1914. Unlike 1870, however, the French army was physically capable of recovery. They had planned their mobilization--the French General Staff history of World War I points out that all their plans, I through XVII, were mobilization plans--and these supplied the French command with the flexibility and articulation they so desperately needed in 1870.[6] In this respect the "miracle of the Marne" flowed as significantly from the French mobilization of 1914 as it did from other factors. Clearly France had significantly transformed its military institutions in the light of the 1870 experience and shaped them generally in line with Germany's.   In the Franco-Prussian War Sedan proved that General Leboeuf's supply of gaiter-buttons no longer had any significant place in military affairs. In 1914 the Marne showed that the French military had absorbed the lesson.

NOTES

1. See for example Maxime Weygand, *Histoire de l'armée française* (Paris: Flammarion, 1938), pp. 291-298, 301-306, 312-313, 316-317. Other views are more guarded. An old, standard, but useful summary of post-1870 French military reforms may be found in Joseph Revol, *Histoire de l'armée française* (Paris: Larousse, 1929), pp. 203-219 where the author points out shortcomings as well as accomplishments. In English see David B. Ralston, *The Army of the Republic: The Place of the Military in the Political Evolution of France, 1871-1914* (Cambridge, Mass.: The M.I.T. Press, 1967). On p. 372 Ralston writes, "Four decades of constant and unceasing effort had led the army from the shambles of a catastrophic defeat to a point where it could successfully measure itself against the Germans." See also Richard Challener, *The French Theory of the Nation in Arms, 1866-1939* (New York: Columbia University Press, 1952), pp. 32-43, 60-79. On pp. 89-90, however, Challener notes that in the debates over military obligation the French penchant for "historical thinking" and rehashing old arguments "hindered as much as helped their military evolution."   Douglas Porch in *The March to the Marne: The French Army 1871-1914* (Cambridge: Cambridge University Press, 1981) is also cautious but does point out that the reforms of the 1870's and 1880's, accomplished during a time when republican leadership and the military hierarchy co-operated with one another, led to an apparent "golden age" for the army. The reader is left to imply that by 1890 the military thought that the French army had recovered from its defeat. See pp. 41-44.

2. This thesis is maintained by Allan Mitchell in *Victors and Vanquished: The German Influence on Army and Church in France after 1870* (Chapel Hill: University of North Carolina Press, 1984), pp. 29-117. A summary of his views may be found in "'A Situation of Inferiority': French Military Reorganization after the Defeat of 1870," *American Historical Review*, LXXXI, No. 1, (February 1981), pp. 49-62.

3. Jules-Victor Lemoyne, *Notices militaires.   La mobilisation.   Etude sur les institutions militaires de la Prusse* (Paris: Berger-Levrault, 1872), p. 154.

4. Charles-Antoine Thoumas, *Les Transformations de l'armée française*, 2 vols. (Paris: Berger-Levrault, 1887), I, pp. 554-555. His chapter on mobilization and concentration covers pp. 515-568 of the same chapter.

5. Edward Louis Spears, *Liaison 1914, A Narrative of the Great Retreat*, 2nd ed. (New York: Stein and Day, 1968), p. 13.

6. France. Ministere de la Guerre. Etat-Major de l'Armee. Service Historique. *Les Armées françaises dans la Grande Guerre*, Tome I, Vol. I: *Les Préliminaries-La Bataille des frontières* (Paris: Imprimerie Nationale, 1922), pp. 1-17. The mobilization plan of 1914 is summarized on pp. 18-34.

Appendix I

Number of Detachments of Reservists
and Number of Reservists Sent from
Departmental Recruiting Centers to
Depots, 18–28 July 1870

Date	Number of detachments	Number of men
18 July	3	7,889
19 July	10	14,331
20 July	16	25,077
21 July	15	22,597
22 July	23	43,542
23 July	14	22,629
24 July	3	5,471
24-28 July	5	21,484
Total	89	163,020

Source: France, Assemblée Nationale, *Enquête parlementaire sur les actes du Gouvernement de la Défense Nationale: dépositions des témoins*, 5 vols. (Paris: Germer-Baillière, 1872-1875), I, 70-71.

Appendix II

Increase of Manpower in the Army of the Rhine, 27 July–6 August 1870

Date	Number of Men in Army of the Rhine	Increase over previous day
27 July	187,485	
28 July	200,795	13,310
29 July	201,256	461
30 July	231,008	29,752
31 July	240,386	9,378
1 August	251,127	10,741
2 August	255,249	4,122
3 August	260,868	5,619
4 August	267,280	6,412
5 August	269,676	2,396
6 August	272,673	2,977
Total		85,188

Source: Victor Dérrécagaix, *La Guerre moderne*, 2 vols. (Paris: L. Baudoin, 1885), I, 404.

Appendix III

Number of Men Available
to Infantry and Cavalry Units
of the Army of the Rhine
on 1 August 1870

	On Duty with Army of Rhine		On Duty at Regi-mental Depots		Detachments from Depot to Army of Rhine, 1-5 August 1870	
	Officers	Men	Officers	Men	Officers	Men
1st Corps						
1st Div	291	9959	107	3282	---	----
2nd Div	317	9105	112	4445	4	1070
3rd Div	315	8400	135	4805	9	841
4th Div	311	9182	132	4487	1	506
Cav Div	295	3985	105	2011	4	80
Corps Total	1529	40361	591	19030	18	2497
2nd Corps						
1st Div	288	7584	102	4609	4	1288
2nd Div	283	8664	101	4295	3	950
3rd Div	274	8491	116	3695	15	1851
Cav Div	177	2356	57	1281	---	----
Corps Total	1022	27095	376	13880	22	4089

3rd <u>Corps</u>

1st Div	289	8467	114	3442	4	1288
2nd Div	287	7668	104	5055	4	970
3rd Div	290	8735	109	3406	4	1006
4th Div	285	8760	102	3131	---	----
Cav Div	303	4098	112	2028	7	91
Corps Total	1454	37728	541	17062	19	3355

4th <u>Corps</u>

1st Div	287	7583	98	5196	2	750
2nd Div	288	7470	97	4581	3	1100
3rd Div	279	8520	94	4394	3	500
Cav Div	177	2338	60	1087	---	----
Corps Total	1031	25911	349	15258	8	2350

5th <u>Corps</u>

1st Div	336	8119	121	4979	2	550
2nd Div	289	8020	108	4313	5	1516
3rd Div	284	7793	106	4839	8	1106
Cav Div	118	1670	46	950	1	40
Corps Total	1027	25602	381	15081	16	3212

6th <u>Corps</u>

1st Div	288	9010	104	3306	6	1250
2nd Div	257	7753	92	3496	2	700
3rd Div	267	6786	90	4808	2	820
4th Div	215	8105	99	3325	---	----
Cav Div	172	2379	70	1382	---	80
Corps Total	1199	34033	455	16317	10	2850

7th <u>Corps</u>

1st Div	282	7285	99	5071	5	1052
2nd Div	289	8073	100	4401	2	1150
3rd Div	264	7282	92	4134	2	750
Cav Div	219	2819	70	1555	---	85
Corps Total	1054	25459	361	15161	9	3037

<u>Cavalry Reserve</u>

1st Div	163	2471	110	1527	---	----
2nd Div	166	2185	42	863	---	----
3rd Div	162	2080	50	1149	---	----
Res Total	491	6736	202	3539	---	----

Infantry and Cavalry Totals					
1 Aug 1870	8807	222925	3256	115328	102	21390

Figures based on Aristide Martinien, *La Guerre de 1870-71. La Mobilisation de l'armée: mouvements des dépôts (armée active) du 15 juillet au 1 mars, 1871* (Paris: L. Fournier, 1912).

Bibliography

For its length and scope, the Franco-Prussian War of 1870 is perhaps the most written about war in history. Besides the official histories and special studies, there are countless single-author histories of the war as well as specialized campaign studies which usually deal with the strategic lessons to be drawn from the events of 1870. Many of the participants, furthermore, published their war diaries, letters, and recollections. These vary in quality, and French writers were careful not to refer to any personal activities that might point to their own responsibility for the defeat. Still, several of these memoirs are valuable for the profusion of details which lend support to this study. On the other hand there is less in the way of published official documents dealing with military questions. The French general staff history contains several orders, letters, telegrams, and dispatches, located sometimes in footnotes, sometimes in the text, sometimes in special supplementary volumes. Apart from this, the text of the French parliamentary investigation of the republican government which took power on 4 September 1870 yields a few public records as well as much valuable testimony on the troubles the army faced in the first six weeks of the war. Compared to the twenty-nine published volumes of diplomatic correspondence, however, this is not much, and the student who wishes to study army documents must go to the archives.

The most important archival depository for material on the Franco-Prussian War is the *Service historique de l'armée de terre* in Vincennes. Here are the letters, telegrams, orders, circularies, *registres*, instructions, and other documents relating to the War of 1870. From these the scholar can trace the confusing and tortuous history of the mobilization and concentration effort and document details alluded to in other sources. This archive provides the richest source of unpublished material for this study. The Archives Nationales in Paris supplies valuable supplements. Most useful among these are the records of the railroad companies, the series of documents regarding the *Garde Nationale*, and the AB XIX series, which contains copies of every telegram received at and dispatched from the imperial residence at Saint-Cloud in July 1870. Compared with these two repositories the archives of the Ministry of Foreign affairs contain little of direct use in a military study such as this. Even so, one may gain insights into France's putative alliance system from these records, and these highlight the dismal failure in French strategic planning in 1870.

The list of published and unpublished sources which follows contains the works I consulted and judged useful, however slightly, to this monograph. It is not an exhaustive list, but it does cite, I believe, all the major works about the war. Because many of the titles here are general in nature, I believe it is incumbent upon myself to distinguish for the reader those volumes I consider most valuable to my research. This I have done by appending a brief commentary to the listing of those volumes I consider most useful. The list of manuscripts below refers to the series I have consulted in each of these archives.

Manuscripts

Archives nationales, Paris

> AB XIX   Documents isolés et papiers d'érudits, no. 1707-1713
> 13 AQ   Compagnie des Chemins de fer de l'Est
> 48 AQ   Compagnie du Chemin de fer du Nord
> 60 AQ   Compagnie du Chemin de fer Paris à Orleans
> 77 AQ   Compagnie du Chemin de fer de Paris à Lyon et à la Méditerranée
> F^9 Affaires militaires
> F^{14} Travaux publics

Ministère des Affaires Etrangères, Paris

> Correspondance politique, Autriche, 501-503
> Correspondance politique, Bade, 49
> Correspondance politique, Hesse-Darmstadt, 31
> Correspondance politique, Italie, 28-29
> Correspondance politique, Prusse, 378-379
> Papiers Georges Chivot
> Papiers Gramont
> Papiers d'Emile Ollivier
> Papiers Napoléon Ring
> Papiers Stoffel

Service historique de l'armée de terre, Vincennes

La	Guerre de 1870-1871: Divers
Lb	Armée du Rhin
Lc	Armée de Châlons
Lhs	Documents hors série: documents divers
Lm	Historiques des corps de troupe pendant la guerre de 1870-1871
Lo	Mélanges
Lq	Fonds supplémentaire: Versements des états-major de corps d'armée, de division ou de brigades
Lr	Fonds supplémentaire: Versements faits par des officiers généraux ou autres
Ls	Divers
Lv	Successions et dons
Lx	Copies de documents et mémoirs divers
Xm	Garde Nationale
Xp	Les armées françaises de 1791 à 1870
Xs	Organisation générale et administration centrale
1 K 25	Cahier du Général Lebrun
1 K 189	Papiers Ducrot
T 133	Carnets de route de Louis Lebeau

Official Documents and Publications

France. Armée. Etat-major. Service historique. *La Guerre de 1870-71*. 35 vols. Paris: Chapelot, 1901-1913.
> An indispensable, though incomplete, source on the War of 1870. Particularly useful are the supplementary documents which accompany the text.

France. Assemblée Nationale. *Archives parlementaires de 1787 à 1869, recueil complet des débats législatifs et politiques des chambres français imprimé par ordre du Sénat et de la Chambre des Députés*, Series II. 106 vols. Paris: Librairie Administrative Paul Dupont, 1861-1902.
> These volumes are of limited value for this study because the work is unfinished and does not go beyond the 1830's. The reader can, however, consult this for debates on military subjects during the Restoration period.

France.   Assemblée Nationale.   *Enquête parlementaire sur les Actes du Gouvernement de la Défense Nationale: dépositions des témoins*. 5 vols. Paris: Germer-Baillière, 1872-1875.
> Primarily a source on the later stages of the war, it does contain the testimony of some of the leading participants in the events leading up to the defeat at Sedan. Most valuable, and, on the whole, reliable, is the testimony of General Leboeuf, who never published any memoirs.

France. Assemblée Nationale. *Rapport fait au nom de la commission des marchés relatif à l'enquête sur le matériel de guerre par M. Léon Riant.* Année 1873. Versailles: Cerf et fils, 1873.
Very helpful in determining the amount of equipment available to the French army in 1870.

France. Ministère de la Guerre. Etat-major de l'armée. Service historique. *Les Armées françaises dans la Grande Guerre.* Part I: *La Guerre de mouvement (opérations antérieurs au 14 novembre 1914)*, vol. 1: *Les préliminaires- La bataille des frontières.* Paris: Imprimerie Nationale, 1922.

France. Ministère des Affaires Etrangères. *Les Origines diplomatiques de la guerre de 1870-1871, recueil de documents publié par le Ministère des Affaires etrangères.* 29 vols. Paris: Charles-Lavauzelle, 1910-1932.
A major source on the war but of peripheral value to this study.

Germany. Army. Generalstab, Kriegsgeschichtliche Abteilung. *Der deutsch-französische Krieg.* 5 vols. Berlin: Mittler, 1872-81.
This is the official German General Staff history of the War of 1870. Primarily a narrative and written perhaps too hastily, it must be read with care: the Germans tended to cover up their mistakes and ignore some of the major difficulties they encountered.

Germany. Army. Generalstab, Kriegsgeschichtliche Abteilung. *The Franco-German War, 1870-71.* Translated by F.C.H. Clarke, 5 vols. London: Her Majesty's Printing Office, 1874-1884.
The English translation of the official German General Staff history.

Germany. Army. Generalstab, Kriegsgeschichtliche Abteilung. *The Railroad Concentration for the War of 1870-71.* Reprinted in *The Military Historian and Economist*, III, No. 2 (January, 1918).
The only source in English on German military railroad organization in 1870. It is somewhat more frank about German mistakes than most other official German publications.

Journal Officiel de l'Empire Français

Prussia. Army. Generalstab. Kriegsgeschichtliche Abteilung. *The Campaign of 1866 in Germany.* Trs. by Colonel von Wright and Captain Henry Hozier. London: Her Majesty's Stationery Office, 1872.

Newspapers

Le Constitutionnel
Le National
La Presse
Le Temps

Memoirs, Letters, Contemporary Histories

Audiffret-Pasquier, Edmond-Gaston, Duc d'. *Discours prononcés aux séances des 4 et 22 mai 1872 à l'Assemblée Nationale.* Paris: A. Sauton, 1872.

Balland, A. *La Guerre de 1870 et la Commune. Notes d'un jeune Aide-Major.* Bourg: Imprimerie du "Courrier de l'Ain," 1916.

Bapst, Germain (ed.). *Le Maréchal Canrobert: Souvenirs d'un siècle.* 6 vols. Paris: Plon, 1898-1913.
    Excerpts from letters, reports and diaries which were put together by the family of one of the more competent and distinguished French leaders of the war. Especially useful for information on conditions in the army during the mobilization.

Bazaine, François Achille. *Episodes de la guerre de 1870 et le blocus de Metz.* Madrid: Gaspar, éditeurs, 1883.
    Bazaine, the main victim of the war, tried to justify his behavior in this volume of memoirs. It is a less useful source on the mobilization than the memoirs of other important leaders.

Bertrand, C.-E. *Souvenirs de 1870. Notes d'un aide-major auxiliaire.* Paris: J.-B. Baillière, 1900.

Blumenthal, Albrecht von. *Journals of Field-Marshal Count von Blumenthal for 1866 and 1870-71.* Trs. by A. D. Gillespie-Addison. London: Edward Arnold. 1903.

Campagne de 1870. Des causes qui ont amené la capitulation de Sedan. Brussels: J. Rozes, n.d.
    This volume, attributed to Napoleon III, is unusually frank and forthright about serious French shortcomings in preparation for war.

Changarnier, Nicolas. "Un mot sur le projet de réorganisation militaire," *Revue des Deux Mondes*, LXVIII, livre 4 (15 April, 1867), pp. 874-890.

Claretie, Jules. *La France envahie 1870. Forbach et Sedan.* Paris: Georges Barba, 1871.

Cochut, André. "Le problème de l'armée, réorganisation de la force militaire en France," *Revue des Deux Mondes*, LXVII, livre 3 (1 February, 1867), pp. 645-677.

The Daily News Correspondence of the War between Germany and France, 1870-1871. London and New York: MacMillan and Co., 1872.

Devaureix, Général. *Souvenirs et observations sur la campagne de 1870*. Paris: H. Charles-Lavauzelle, n.d.

DuBarail, François-Charles. *Mes souvenirs, 1820-1879*.   3 vols.   Paris: Plon-Nourrit et Cie., 1913.

Ducrot, Auguste-Alexandre. *La Vie militaire du Général Ducrot d'après sa correspondance*. 2 vols. Paris: Plon-Nourrit et Cie., 1895.
      Very helpful letters and memoranda of a keenly observant general who recognized the threat posed by Prussian military institutions and who was disturbed by French unpreparedness for a war he believed would break out.

Failly, René-Louis, de. *Campagne de 1870. Opérations et marches du 5è corps jusqu'au 31 août*. Brussels: A.-N. Lebègue et Cie., 1871.

Fay, Charles. *Journal d'un officier de l'Armée du Rhin*. Brussels: Muquardt, 1871.
      An interesting record of the confusion under which the French labored in July 1870.

Fay, Charles Alexandre. *Projet d'organisation et de mobilisation de l'armée française à propos d'un ordre inédit de mobilisation de l'armée prussienne*. Paris: J. Dumaine, 1872.

Fix, Nathanaël Théodore. *Souvenirs d'un officier d'état-major (1846-1898)*. 2 vols. Paris: Juven, 1898-99.

Friedrich III, German Emperor, 1831-1888. *Diaries of the Emperor Frederick during the Campaigns of 1866 and 1870-71*. ed. by Margarethe von Poschinger. trs. by Francis A. Welby. London: Chapman and Hall, 1902.

Frossard, Charles Auguste. *Rapport sur les opérations du deuxième corps de l'Armée du Rhin dans la campagne de 1870*. Paris: Dumaine, 1872.
      A standard report to the author's military superiors; it incidentally relates the problems of mobilization to actual military operations.

Geschwind, Dr. *Souvenirs d'ambulance: les batailles de Gravelotte et de Saint-Privat*. 11è série, Tome I of *Mémories de l'Academie des Sciences, Inscriptions et Belles-lettres de Toulouse*. Toulouse: Douladour-Privat, 1913.
      Shows, among other things, how unprepared the army medical services were in 1870.

Gluck, Emile.   *Guerre de 1870-1871.   La 4è bataillon de la Mobile du Haut-Rhin.   Journal d'un sous-officer.* Mulhouse: E. Meininger, 1908.

[Grenier, Général].   *Mes Souvenirs de l'Armée du Rhin.* Grenoble: Maisonville et fils et Jourdan, 1871.

Hepp, Edgar.   *Wissembourg au début de l'invasion de 1870.   Récit d'un sous-préfet.* Paris: Berger-Levrault, 1887.

Holstein, Friedrich von.   *The Holstein Papers.* Edited by Norman Rich and M.H. Fisher. 4 vols. Cambridge: Cambridge University Press, 1955-63.

Jarras, Louis.   *Souvenirs du Général Jarras.* Paris: Plon, 1892.
    Jarras, the third ranking staff officer at Imperial headquarters, offers reliable testimony on the confusion that reigned in the high command in the opening days of the war.

Lacretelle, Charles-Nicholas.   *Souvenirs.* Paris: Emile-Paul, 1907.

Laugel, A.   "Les Institutions militaires de la France: Louvois, Carnot, Saint-Cyr," *Revue des Deux Mondes,* LXVIII, livre 1 (1 March, 1867), pp. 5-66.

Lebrun,   Barthélemy   Louis   Joseph.   *Souvenirs   militaires   1866-1870.   Préliminaires de la guerre.   Missions en Belgique et à Vienne.* Paris: E. Dentu, 1895.
    Very valuable memoirs about the negotiations with Austria, the ill-considered "plans" for war against Prussia, and the organization of the high command by the second ranked staff aide to Napoleon III.

Meissas, Alexandre de.   *Journal d'un aumônier militaire.* Paris: C. Duniol, 1872.

Moltke, Helmuth Carl Bernhard von.   *Moltke's Military Correspondence 1870-71* Part I: *The War to the Battle of Sedan.* Oxford: Clarendon, 1923.

_____.   *Moltke's Projects for the Campaign of 1866 against Austria.* London: His Majesty's Stationery Office, 1907.

Montaudon, Jean-Baptiste-Alexandre.   *Souvenirs militaires.* 2 vols. Paris: C. Delagrave, 1898-1900.
    Very helpful observations of a major-general.

Napoleon III, Emperor of the French.   *Oeuvres posthumes et autographes inédits de Napoléon III en exil.* Edited by le comte de La Chapelle. Paris: Lachaud, 1873.
    This collection of letters, sketches, and projects reveals the kinds of minor reform projects that interested the emperor before the outbreak of the War of 1870.

Observations sur l'armée française à propos de la campagne de 1870. Lyon: Charles Méra, 1871.

Ollivier, Emile. *L'Empire libéral; études, récits, souvenirs.* 18 vols. Paris: Garnier, 1895-1918.
    Primarily a political autobiography, this work sheds light on the emperor's failure at reform of the army and the political effects of the Hohenzollern crisis and the defeats of Wissembourg, Froeschwiller, and Spicheren.

Palikao, Charles Cousin-Montauban, Comte de. *Un Ministre de Guerre de vingt-quatre jours, du 10 août au 4 septembre 1870.* Paris: Plon, 1871.
    A helpful work by a well-placed and highly respected officer.

Perroncel, Philippe. *Mémoirs d'un ex-cuirassier de Reischoffen.* Lyons: M. Carruel, 1891.

Pontchalon, Henri de. *Souvenirs de guerre 1870-1871.* Paris: H. Charles-Lavauzelle, 1893.

Quelques vérités sur l'armée française de 1870. Brussels: Combe et van de Weghe, 1871.

Randon, Jacques Louis. *Mémoires du Maréchal Randon.* 2 vols. Paris: Lahure, 1875-77.
    The work of an eloquent, and stubborn, defender of the military institutions France possessed between 1815 and 1866.

Rougemont, F. de. "L'Armée prussienne en 1870," *Revue des Deux Mondes*, LXXXV, livre 1 (1 January, 1870), pp. 5-24.

Ryan, Charles E. *With an Ambulance during the Franco-German War 1870-1871.* London: John Murray, 1896.

Sarrazin, Dr. *Récits sur la guerre de 1870.* Paris: Berger-Levrault, 1887.

Stoffel, Colonel Eugène Georges. *Rapport militaires écrits de Berlin, 1866-1870.* Paris: Garnier, 1871.
    A most important source for any student dealing with either the French or the Prussian armies in 1870 or with the preparations both made for war. An admirable piece of military reporting.

Teller, A. *Esquisses de la vie militaire en France. Souvenirs de Saint-Cyr.* 2 vols. Paris: Charles-Lavauzelle, 1886.

Thoumas, Charles Antoine. *Souvenirs de la guerre 1870-1871.* Paris: Librairie Illustrée, n.d.

_____. *Les Transformations de l'armée française.* 2 vols. Paris: Berger-Levrault, 1887.

Primarily a public report on the reforms adopted by the French army after 1870, these volumes contain large amounts of information on the mobilization and concentration of 1870 by an officer who served in the French army during the Franco-Prussian War.

Thurel, H. *Metz 1870. Les Propos du camp*: *Journal d'un aide-major.* Lons-le-Saunier: C. Verpillat, 1887.

Trochu, Louis Jules. *L'Armée française en 1867*. Paris: Amyot, 1868.
An indispensable source on the habits, practices, and organization of the French army in 1867 by a conservative reformer.

_____. *Oeuvres posthumes.* 2 vols. Tours: A. Mame et fils, 1896.
This work contains a record of the author's experiences in 1870 and some of his observations about French military institutions in 1870.

Veyssière, A. *Impressions et souvenirs 1870-1871. Journal quotidien des événements politiques depuis le 1er juillet 1870 jusqu'à la conclusion de la paix.* Martel: J.B. Valat, n.d.

Bibliographies

Palat, Barthélemy-Edmond. *Bibliographie générale de la guerre de 1870-1871.* Paris: Berger-Levrault, 1896.
This volume is still the only comprehensive bibliography on the Franco-Prussian War. Serious students of the events of 1870 ought to begin their study with this work.

_____. *La Guerre de 1870-1871.* Paris: A Fontemoing, n.d.
A briefer list composed prior to the publication of the *Bibliographie générale.*

Schultz, Albert. *Bibliographie de la guerre franco-allemande et de la Commune de 1871.* Paris: Le Soudier, 1886.
Useful but superseded by Palat's compilation.

General Histories and Studies of Warfare

Addington, Larry H. *The Patterns of War since the Eighteenth Century.* Bloomington: Indiana University Press, 1984.

Baranger, P. *Pages d'histoire militaire. Campagnes modernes traitées dans les conditions fixées par le programme d'admission à l'Ecole Supérieur de Guerre.* II Partie: *Guerre de 1870-71.* Paris: H. Charles-Lavauzelle, 1913.

Bondil, Général "Le Chemin de fer 1871-1914 et guerre 1914-18," *Revue Historique de l'Armée*, No. 1 (Février, 1959), pp. 117-130.

Bonnal, Henri. *Sadowa, étude de stratégie et de tactique générale.* Paris: Chapelot, 1901.

Brackenbury, Henry. *Les Maréchaux de France.* Paris: Lachaud, 1872.

Caemmerer, Rudolf von. *The Development of Strategical Science during the 19th Century.* trs. by Karl von Donat. London: Hugh Rees, 1905.

Colin, Jean. *Les Transformations de la guerre.* Paris: Flammarion, 1911.

Comparato, Frank. *Age of Great Guns.* Harrisburg, Pa.: Stackpole, 1965.

Craig, Gordon A. *The Battle of Königgrätz.* Philadelphia: Lippincott, 1964.

Derrécagaix, Victor. *La Guerre moderne.* 2 vols. Paris: L. Baudoin, 1885.
    A very valuable source of information about the operation of French military institutions by an author keenly aware of the changes in warfare effected by the Prussian victory in 1870.

Ducrot, Auguste-Alexandre. *De l'Etat-major et des différentes armées.* Paris: Plon, 1871.

Dupuy, R. Ernest and Dupuy, Trevor N. *Military Heritage of America.* New York: McGraw-Hill, 1956.
    Although of obviously minor value to this study, this volume nevertheless supplies useful definitions of special military terms.

Earle, Edward M., ed. *Makers of Modern Strategy.* Princeton: Princeton University Press, 1943.

Foch, Ferdinand. *De la conduite de la guerre. La Manoeuvre pour la bataille.* Paris: Berger-Levrault, 1904.

Galtier-Boissière, Jean. *La Grande Guerre, 1914-1918.* Paris: Les Productions de Paris, 1966.

Goltz, Wilhelm von der. *The Nation in Arms: A Treatise on Modern Military Systems and the Conduct of War.* Translated by Philip A. Ashworth. 2d ed. revised. London: Hodder and Stoughton, 1915.
    The author has included a discussion of some of the problems the Prussians encountered during the mobilization and concentration of their army in 1870.

Hanotaux, Gabriel (ed.). *Histoire de la nation française.* 10 vols. Paris: Plon, 1920-1929.

Hittle, James D. *The Military Staff: Its History and Development.* Harrisburg, Penn.: The Stackpole Company, 1961.

Huntington, Samuel P. *The Soldier and the State: The Theory and Politics of Civil-Military Relations.* Cambridge, Mass.: Harvard University Press, 1957.
   An important work, this volume is especially valuable for its consideration of the development of professionalism in modern armies.

Irvine, Dallas D. "The French and Prussian Staff Systems before 1870," *Journal of the American Military History Foundation,* II, No. 4 (Winter, 1938), pp. 192-204.
   A very interesting article describing one of the most important differences between the French and Prussian armies in 1870.

Jouffroy, Louis-Maurice. *L'Ere du rail.* Paris: Librairie Armand Colin, 1953.

Koeltz, Louis. *La Grande Guerre de 1914-1918.* Paris: Sirey, 1966.

Kreideberg, Marvin A. and Merton G. Henry. *History of Military Mobilization in the United States Army, 1775-1945.* Washington: Department of the Army, 1955.

La Gorce, Pierre de. *Histoire du second empire.* 7 vols. Paris: Plon, 1899-1905.
   An old, distinguished, and still valuable work. Vol. V contains an excellent chapter on the Imperial army.

Liddell Hart, Basil Henry. "Armed Forces and the Art of War: Armies," in *The Zenith of European Power, 1830-1870.* Edited by J.P.T. Bury. Vol. X of *The New Cambridge Modern History.* 14 vols. Cambridge: Cambridge University Press, 1957-1970.
   A good summary of military developments in the period indicated by an outstanding twentieth century military historian.

Lincoln, George, *et al. Economics of National Security: Managing America's Resources for Defense.* 2d ed. revised. Englewood Cliffs, N.J.: Prentice-Hall, 1954.
   Of only peripheral value, this volume nonetheless contains a more recent definition of the term mobilization.

Lord, Robert H. *The Origins of the War of 1870.* Cambridge, Mass.: Harvard University Press, 1924.

Luvaas, Jay. *The Military Legacy of the Civil War: The European Inheritance.* Chicago: University of Chicago Press, 1959.

Perré, Jean. *Les Mutations de la guerre moderne.* Paris: Payot, 1962.

Pratt, Edwin A. *Rise of Rail Power in War and Conquest, 1833-1914* Philadelphia: Lippincott, 1916.

An old but valuable and comprehensive discussion of the impact exerted by the railroad upon military science.   It contains interesting information on the problems both the French and the Prussians encountered during the mobilization of their armies in 1870.

Preston, Richard A. and Sydney F. Wise. *Men in Arms: A History of Warfare and its Interrelationships with Western Society.* 4th ed. New York: Holt, Rinehart and Winston, 1979.

Ropp, Theodore. *War in the Modern World.* Durham, N.C.: Duke University Press, 1959.
An outstanding study of the development of warfare since the fifteenth century.

Shaw, G.C. *Supply in Modern War.* London: Faber and Faber, 1938.

Steefel, Lawrence D. *Bismarck, the Hohenzollern Candidacy, and the Origins of the Franco-German War of 1870.* Cambridge, Mass.: Harvard University Press, 1961.

Taylor, Alan John Percival. *The Struggle for Mastery in Europe, 1848-1918.* Oxford: Oxford University Press, 1954.

Van Creveld, Martin. *Supplying War: Logistics from Wallenstein to Patton.* New York: Cambridge University Press, 1977.

Studies of the German Army

Craig, Gordon A. *The Politics of the Prussian Army.* New York: Oxford University Press, 1956.

Frauenholz, Eugen von. *Entwicklungsgeschichte des deutschen Heerwesens.* 5 vols. Munich: Beck, 1941.
Particularly valuable for the texts of important documents on the development of Prussian and German military institutions.

Goerlitz, Walter. *History of the German General Staff: 1657-1945.* Translated by Brian Battershaw. New York: Praeger, 1953.

Jany, Curt. *Geschichte der königlich preussischen Armée.* 4 vols. Berlin: Karl Siegismund, 1928-1937.

Studies of the French Army

Bonnal, Henri. *Le Haut commandement français au début de chacune des guerres de 1859 et de 1870.* Paris: Revue des Idées, 1909.

Bourgue,   Marius.   *Historique du 3è régiment d'infanterie, ex-Piémont, 1569-1891.* Paris: Charles-Lavauzelle, 1894.

Carrias, Eugène. *La Pensée militaire française.* Paris: Presses Universitaires de France, 1960.

Casevitz, Jean. *Une loi manquée: la loi Niel, 1866-1868; l'armée française à la veille de la guerre de 1870.* Paris: Cardot, 1960.
     A solidly researched but little known work accounting for France's failure to adopt Marshal Niel's proposals for a reform in conscription.

Challener, Richard. *The French Theory of the Nation in Arms, 1866-1939.* New York: Columbia University Press, 1952.
     An outstanding work, this volume contains a summary of French opinion on recruitment policy prior to the War of 1870.

Chalmin, Pierre. "Les Ecoles militaires françaises jusqu'en 1914," *Revue historique de l'armée*, X, No. 2 (June, 1954), pp. 129-166.

_____. *L'Officier français de 1815 à 1870.* Paris: Librairie Marcel Rivière et Cie, 1957.
     A pioneering sociological study of the French officer corps in the first half of the nineteenth century.

Coche. "L'Evolution du Train depuis 1807," *Revue historique de l'armée*, No. 1 (Février, 1959), pp. 81-91.

Dagneau, Capitaine. *Historique du 13è régiment d'infanterie.* Paris: H. Charles-Lavauzelle, 1891.

Desmazes, R. *Saint-Cyr, son histoire, ses gloires, ses leçons.* Paris: La Saint-Cyrienne, 1948.

Girard, Louis. *La Garde nationale.* Paris: Plon, 1964.

Girardet, Raoul. *La Société militaire dans la France contemporaine, 1815-1939.* Paris: Plon, 1953.
     A distinguished work which shows that the French army remained essentially apolitical during the period under consideration.

Holmes, Richard. *The Road to Sedan: The French Army 1866-70.* London: Royal Historical Society, 1984.

Kovacs, Arpad F. "French Military Institutions before the Franco-Prussian War," *American Historical Review*, LI (January, 1946).
     A good summary but limited to recruitment laws and policies.

Kuntz, Francois. *L'Officier français dans la nation.* Paris: Charles-Lavauzelle, 1960.

La Chapelle, Comte de. *Les Forces militaires de la France en 1870*. Paris: Amyot, 1872.
>An interesting critique by an admirer of Napoleon III.

Lyet, P. "L'Ecole spéciale militaire, Fontainebleau, Saint-Cyr, Coëtquidan," *Revue historique de l'armée*, X, No. 3-4 (October, 1954), pp. 19-40.

Mitchell, Allan. *The German Influence in France after 1870: The Formation of the French Republic*. Chapel Hill: University of North Carolina Press, 1979.

_____. "'A Situation of Inferiority': French Military Reorganization after the Defeat of 1870," *The American Historical Review*, LXXXVI (February 1981), pp. 49-67.

_____. *Victors and Vanquished: The German Influences on Army and Church in France after 1870*. Chapel Hill: University of North Carolina Press, 1984.

Monteilhet, Joseph. *Les Institutions militaires de la France, 1814-1924* Paris: Alcan, 1932.
>Although generally limited to a discussion of recruitment laws and policies, this is an outstanding work by a writer who believed that a Swiss-style militia would be an ideal form of military organization for France.

Morand, Louis. *De l'Armée selon la charte*. Paris: Baudoin, 1894.

Palat, Barthélemy-Edmond [Pierre Lehautcourt]. "La Réorganisation de l'armée avant 1870," *Revue de Paris*, IV (August, 1901), pp. 525-552.
>A brief, but well-informed, essay on the aborted Niel reforms.

Pech de Cadel. P. *Histoire de l'école spéciale militaire de Saint-Cyr par un ancien Saint-Cyrien*. Paris: Delagrave, 1893.

Pinet, Gaston. *Histoire de l'Ecole Polytechnique*. Paris: Baudry, 1885.

Porch, Douglas. *Army and Revolution: France 1815-1848*. London: Routledge and Kegan Paul, 1974.

_____. *The March to the Marne: The French Army, 1871-1914*. Cambridge: Cambridge University Press, 1981.

Ralston, David B. *The Army of the Republic; The Place of the Military in the Political Evolution of France, 1871-1914*. Cambridge, Mass.: The M.I.T. Press 1967.
>A distinguished work on civil-military relationships in the Third Republic, the author nonetheless takes the later years of the Second Empire into consideration.

Revol, Joseph. *Histoire de l'armée française.* Paris: Larousse, 1929.

Schnapper, Bernard. *Le Remplacement militaire en France; quelques aspects politiques, économiques et sociaux du recrutement au XIXe siècle.* Paris: S.E.V.P.E.N., 1968.

Serman, William. *Les Officiers français dans la nation, 1848-1914.* Paris: Aubier Montaigne, 1982.

_____. *Les Origines des officiers français, 1848-1870.* Paris: Publications de la Sorbonne, 1979.

Simond, Emile. *Le 28è de ligne.* Rouen: Mégard et Cie., 1889.

Titeux, Eugene. *Saint-Cyr et l'Ecole spéciale militaire en France.* Paris: Firmin-Didot, 1898.

Weygand, Maxime. *Histoire de l'armée française.* Paris: Flammarion, 1938.

Accounts of the Franco-Prussian War and its Participants

Ambert, Joachim. *Gaulois et Germains: Récits militaires.* 2 vols. Paris: Bloud et Barral, 1883-1885.

Anderson, J.H. *The Franco-German War. July 15-August 18, 1870.* London: Hugh Rees, Ltd., 1909.

Baratier, Anatole. *L'Intendance militaire pendant la guerre de 1870-1871.* Paris: J. Dumaine, 1871.
    A study of the French commissariat in 1870, with less discussion of supply problems than is in order.

Beaumont, Maurice. *Bazaine, les secrets d'un maréchal (1811-1888).* Paris: Imprimerie nationale, 1978.

Bird, W.D. *Lectures on the Strategy of the Franco-German War 1870 up to the Battle of Sedan.* London: Hugh Rees, Ltd., 1909.

Bibesco, George, Prince. *Campagne de 1870. Belfort, Reims, Sedan. Le 7è corps de l'Armée du Rhin.* Paris: Plon, 1872.

Bonie, Lieutenant Colonel. *Campagne de 1870. La cavalerie française.* Paris: Amyot, 1871.
    This work contains some description of problems facing the French cavalry in 1870, but the author did not think that the cavalry bore any responsibility for these troubles.

Bonnal, Henri. *La Manoeuvre de Saint-Privat, 18 juillet-18 août, 1870*. 2 vols. Paris: Chapelot, 1904.
> Primarily a strategical study written from German sources. Particularly useful for a study of the concentration of the two armies because of the excellent maps attached to vol. I.

Bonnet, Félix. *Guerre franco-allemande. Résumé et commentaires de l'ouvrage du grand état-major prussien*. Paris: L. Baudoin, 1886.

Bourelly, Général. *La Guerre de 1870-1871 et le traité de Francfort d'après les derniers documents*. Paris: Perrin, 1912.

Brunker, H.M.E. *Story of the Franco-German War 1870-71, from 15th July to 18th August 1870*. London: Forster Groom and Co., Ltd., 1908.

Cantal, Michel. *La Guerre de 1870*. Paris: Bordas, 1972.

Chalus, Adhémar de. *Guerre franco-allemande de 1870-71. Wissembourg, Froeschwiller, Retraite sur Châlons*. Becansçon: Marion, Morel, 1882.

Darimon, Alfred. *Histoire d'un jour. La Journée du 12 juillet 1870*. Paris: Dentu, 1888.

_____. *Notes pour servir à l'histoire de la guerre de 1870*. Paris: P. Ollendorff, 1888.

Dauvé, Paul. *L'Ambulance dans la division Abel Douay en 1870*. Paris: H. Charles-Lavauzelle, 1899.
> A standard account of the ambulance services, but of greater interest than most because the author observed the defeat of Douay's division at Wissembourg.

Derrécagaix, Victor. *Guerre de 1870*. Paris: Le Spectateur Militaire, 1871.

Dethan, Georges. "Napoléon III et l'opinion française devant la question romaine (1860-1870)" *Revue d'histoire diplomatique*, LXXII (April-June, 1958), pp. 118-134.

Du Casse, A., Baron. *La Guerre au jour le jour 1870-1871*. Paris: J. Dumaine, 1871.

Duquet, Alfred. *Guerre de 1870-71*. 13 vols. Paris: Bibliothèque Charpentier, 1909.
> A major work that needs to be approached with caution.

Ernouf, Alfred, Baron. *Histoire des chemins de fer français pendant la guerre franco-prussienne*. Paris: Librairie Générale, 1874.
> One of the major works on the operation of the French railroads during the War of 1870. Of less value than the work of Jacqmin cited below.

Euvrard, Xavier. *Guerre de 1870. La Première armée de l'est*. Paris: Charles-Lavauzelle, 1895.

Fabre de Navacelle, Colonel. *Précis de la guerre franco-allemande*. Paris: Plon-Nourrit et Cie., 1890.

Foot, Michael. "The Origins of the Franco-Prussian War and the Remaking of Germany," in *The Zenith of European Power, 1830-1870*. Edited by J.P.T. Bury. Vol. X of *The New Cambridge Modern History*. 14 vols. Cambridge: Cambridge University Press, 1957-1970.

G., A. *L'Armée de Châlons. Son mouvement sur Metz (1870)*. Paris: L. Baudoin et cie., 1885.

Gavoy, Emile-Alexandre, Dr. *Le Service de santé militaire en 1870*. Paris: Charles-Lavauzelle, 1894.
    Particularly good discussion about the shortages of medical equipment and personnel in the Army of the Rhine.

Girard, A. and F. Dumas. *Histoire de la guerre de 1870-71*. Paris: R. Chapelot, 1906.

Guérin, André. *La Folle de guerre de 1870*. Paris: Hachette, 1970.

La Guerre des masses: préparation stratégique des actions décisives. 2 vols. Paris: Baudoin, 1893.

Hooper, George. *The Campaign of Sedan*. London: Bell, 1887.

Howard, Michael. *The Franco-Prussian War*. London: Rupert Hart-Davis, 1961.
    An outstanding work by a distinguished military historian. The preparation of this study would have been more difficult had this volume not been available. Indispensable for all students of the Franco-Prussian War.

Jacqmin, François. *Les Chemins de fer français pendant la guerre de 1870-1871*. Paris: Hatchette, 1872.
    A very reliable report on the military use of railroads in 1870 by an official who helped direct these railway lines during the war.

Lacour-Gayet, G. *La Guerre de 1870*. Paris: Edition du Foyer, 1911.

Lambert, A. *Etude sur l'état moral de l'armée française et de l'armée allemande en 1870*. Paris: H. Charles-Lavauzelle, 1908.

"Leboeuf und die französische Mobilmachung von 1870," *Jahrbücher für die deutsche Armee und Marine*, Band XCVII, No. 289, Heft 1 (October, 1895).

Le Gillou, Louis. *La Campagne d'été de 1870*. Paris: Charles-Lavauzelle, 1938.
A well-prepared but relatively unknown, strategical study which places
considerable emphasis on the military effects of a poorly prepared
mobilization.

Lehmann, Gustav. *Die Mobilmachung von 1870-71*. Berlin: E.S. Mittler, 1905.
The only published monograph on the subject of mobilization during
the war of 1870. Although it is an indispensable source on Prussian
operations, the work is limited to a discussion of the procedure by which
the Prussians recalled their reserve manpower in 1870 and the use made
of each mobilized unit.

Lemoyne, Jules-Victor. *Notices militaires. La mobilisation. Etude sur les
institutions militaires de la Prusse*. Paris: Berger-Levrault, 1872.

Maistre, Paul André. *Spicheren (6 août, 1870)*. Paris: Berger-Levrault, 1908.

Margueritte, Paul et Victor. *Histoire de la guerre de 1870-71*. Paris: G.
Chamerot, 1913.

Martin, Paul. *Guerre de 1870. Batailles sur la Lauter, la Sauer, et la Sarre*.
Paris: Le Spectateur Militaire, 1891.

Martinien, Aristide. *La Guerre de 1870-71. La Mobilisation de l'armée:
mouvements des dépôts (armée active) du 15 juillet au 1er mars, 1871*. Paris:
L. Fournier, 1912.
A collection of tables, regiment by regiment in the French army,
showing the number of men under arms when war broke out, the number
of troops serving in the Army of the Rhine on 1 August, 1870, the number
of men held on their home bases, and the number and size of reserve units
subsequently ordered to northeastern France. The author made no
attempt to explain or analyze his data; nonetheless, this work is one of the
most important sources for this study.

Moritz, Victor. *Froeschwiller, 6 août 1870*. Strasbourg: Presses des Dernières
Nouvelles de Strasbourg, 1970.

Niox, General. *La Guerre de 1870. Simple récit*. Paris: Ch. Delagrave, 1896.

Palat, Barthélemy Edmond [Pierre Lehautcourt]. *Guerre de 1870-71: aperçu et
commentaires*. 2 vols. Paris: Berger-Levrault, 1910.
The condensation of a longer work, these volumes form, in themselves,
an excellent history of the war.

_____. *Histoire de la guerre 1870-1871*. Part I: *La Guerre de 1870*. 6 vols.
Paris: Berger-Levrault, 1903-1908.
All students of the War of 1870 are indebted to this author for his
solid, painstaking research, his lucid account of the war, and his sound
judgment. Although some of his views are outdated, this is still, perhaps,
the best multi-volume history of the war.

Perrossier, Lieutenant Colonel. *De Bitche à Sedan.* Toulouse: Imprimerie E. Privat, 1906.

Picard, Ernest. *1870, la perte de l'Alsace.* Paris: Plon, 1912.

Pratt, Sisson C. *Sarrbrück to Paris, 1870. A Strategical Sketch.* London: Swann Sonnenschein and Co., 1904.

Rocolle, E.R. "Anatomie d'une mobilisation," *Revue Historique des Armées,* No. 2, 1970. pp. 34-69.

Romain, C. *Les Responsabilités de l'artillerie française en 1870.* Paris: Berger-Levrault, 1913.

Rousset, Commandant. *La Seconde campagne de France: histoire générale de la guerre franco-allemande, 1870-71.* 6 vols. Paris: Librairie Illustrée, 1895-96.

Ruby, Edmond and Regnauld, Jean. *Bazaine, coupable ou victime? A la lumière de documents nouveaux.* Paris: J. Peyronnet, 1960.
    This volume which seeks, successfully, to show that Marshal Bazaine did not deserve to be treated as responsible for the French defeat, sheds some light on the problems the French army encountered as a result of their poorly executed mobilization and concentration.

Verdy du Vernois, Julius von. *Studien über den Krieg Auf Grundlage des deutsch-französischen Krieges 1870-1871.* Berlin: E.S. Mittler, 1891.

Wachter, A. *La Guerre franco-allemande de 1870-71.* 2 vols. L. Baudoin, 1895.

Woyde, Charles de. *Causes des succès et des revers dans la guerre de 1870.* 2 vols. Paris: R. Chapelot, 1900.

Index

About the Author

THOMAS J. ADRIANCE is Associate Professor of History at Virginia
Polytechnic Institute and State University.